THE ART OF
AFRICA

THE ART OF THE NEGRO PEOPLES

ELSY LEUZINGER

GREYSTONE PRESS/NEW YORK

Translated by Ann E. Keep, Ph. D.

The author and translator are grateful to Mr. William Fagg, Assistant Keeper of the Department of Ethnography at the British Museum, for reading the text and making many valuable suggestions.

The frontispiece represents a wooden-lidded meat and vegetable bowl of the tribe famous for its carvings, Kwanga (a sub-tribe in Barotseland). A striking feature are the wild ducks, simplified to essentials. Northern Rhodesia. Rietberg Museum, Zurich, Von der Heydt Collection (length 12½ in.).

REVISED EDITION 1967
© HOLLE AND CO. VERLAG, BADEN-BADEN, GERMANY
LIBRARY OF CONGRESS CATALOG CARD NUMBER 60-13819
MANUFACTURED IN THE UNITED STATES OF AMERICA

CONTENTS

List of coloured plates (3) – List of figures with sources (4).

PART I: GENERAL

I. THE APPROACH TO NEGRO ART 9–10

II. COUNTRY AND PEOPLE 11–20
Topography (11). Climate (12). Races (12). Prehistory and history (14). Art and Culture (15).

III. RELIGION 21–29
Conception of the cosmos (21). The medicine-man (23). Art and its function in religion: *ancestor figures, fetishes, animal sculpture, masks, ritual implements* (24).

IV. SOCIOLOGY 30–34
Secret societies and initiation (30). 'Rites de passage' (31). Division of labour (32). The artist (32). Art at the royal courts (34).

V. MATERIALS AND TECHNIQUES 35–52
Wood (36). Calabashes (45). Bone and ivory (45). Stone (46). Clay modelling, (46). pottery and wax (47). Metal: *iron, brass cast, silver, gold* (47). Leather (49). Basket-work (50). Weaving (50). Dyeing technique (51). Colors (52).

VI. FORM 53–80
Sculpture: *content* (53). Form and expression (54). Structure (55). Primitive and 'primary' (57). Naturalistic and abstract style (60). Pole and round sculpture (61). Animal figures (71). Surface and patina (71). Ornamented implements (72). Painting and relief (73). Clothing and ornamentation (75). Architecture: *bee-hive hut, cone-roofed house, gable-roofed house, tembe* (76).

PART II: STYLE REGIONS

I. INTRODUCTION TO THE WESTERN SUDAN AND WEST AFRICA 81–93
Savannah (81). Jungle (84).

94–102   II. WESTERN SUDAN
Bambara (94). Dogon (97). Mossi and Bobo (100). Senufo (100).

103–108   III. THE WESTERN LANDS OF THE ATLANTIC COAST
Djola, Bidyugo, Baga (103). Mende, Kissi, Toma (105). Dan and Kran (107).

119–132   IV. THE EASTERN LANDS OF THE ATLANTIC COAST
Ivory Coast: Baule, Guro, Ebrie, Krinjabo (119). Ghana (123). Togo and Dahomey (125). Early cultures of Nigeria: *Nok, Ife, Benin, etc.* (126). Nigeria during the last century: *Yoruba* (132). Forest tribes of south-eastern Nigeria: *Ijo, Ibo, Ibibio, etc.* (143). Ekoi group (145). Northern Nigeria (146).

148–156   V. CAMEROUN AND WESTERN EQUATORIAL AFRICA
Sao culture of the Chad region (148). Adamawa and Central African Republic (148). The Cameroun grasslands: *Bamum, Tikar, Bamileke* (149). Forest lands of western Cameroun (152). Duala (152). Equatorial forest: *Pangwe, Bakwele, Ogowe style,* Bakota, Kuyu, Babembe, Bateke (153).

166–180   VI. REPUBLIC OF THE CONGO
Introduction (166). Lower Congo: *Bakongo* (167). South-western Congo: *Bayaka, Basuku, Bambala, Bahuana, Bapende* (170). Central Congo: *Bakuba, Bena Lulua, etc.* (173). South-eastern Congo (eastern Kasai, Katanga and Manyema): *Basonge, Bena Kanioka, Bajokwe, Baluba group (incl. Wabembe, etc.)* (178). Northern Congo: *Balega, Bambole, Mangbetu, Azande, Bwaka, Mongala group, etc.* (192).

196–200   VII. EAST AFRICA
General survey (196). South-eastern Sudan (197). Interlacustrine area (198). Kenya, Tanganyika and south-west Ethiopia (198). Swahili coast (199). Rovuma river area: *Makonde group* (199).

201–203   VIII. SOUTH-EAST AFRICA AND MADAGASCAR
Zimbabwe (201). Barotse (201). Madagascar (202).

204–210   IX. FUTURE PROSPECTS

212–217   MAPS

APPENDICES
Table of Cultures (219). Bibliography (222). Glossary (227). Index (230).

LIST OF COLOURED PLATES

1. Leopard, ivory, Benin, Nigeria
2. Head, stone, found in the Welle area, north-eastern Congo
3. Decorated ostrich egg and necklace, Bushman, Namib, Lüderitz Bay, South-West Africa
4. left: *Landa* mask (wood), Toma, Guinea
   right: *Kore* mask (wood), Bambara, Mali
5. *Chi wara,* dance head-dress in form of an antelope (wood), Bambara-Minianka, on Bambara cotton fabric with design
6. *Tellem,* ancestor figure (wood), Dogon, Mali
7. Ancestor figures (wood), Dogon, Mali
8. Dance head-dress in form of an antelope (wood), Kurumba, Upper Volta
9. Antelope mask with female figure (wood), Mossi, Upper Volta
10. Mask (wood), painted blue and white, Bobo-Fing, Upper Volta
11. Buffalo mask (painted wood), Bobo, Upper Volta
12. *Deble,* ritual statue (wood), Senufo, Ivory Coast
13. Antelope mask (wood), Senufo, Ivory Coast
14. left: shoulder mask with girl's head (wood), Baga, Guinea
    right: *nimba* figure (wood), Baga, Guinea
15. *Banda* mask (wood), Baga, Guinea
16. Mask (wood), Dan, Ivory Coast
17. Ointment-pot and ancestor figures (wood), Baule, Ivory Coast
18. Buffalo *(guli)* mask (wood, on *plangi* fabric), Baule, Ivory Coast
19. top and right: masks (wood), Guro; left: mask (wood), Yaure, sub-tribe of Baule, Ivory Coast
20. Gold mask from treasure of King Kofi Kakari, Ashanti, Ghana
21. *Kuduo,* lidded vessel with scene of animals fighting, cast brass, Ghana
22. Verandah posts (wood) with figures of deities, Yoruba style, Dahomey
23. Commemorative head, cast brass, of an Oni (king) of Ife, Nigeria
24. Vessel, bronze, with figure on quartz seat, Ife, Nigeria
25. Head, terracotta, from Ife, Nigeria
26. Commemorative head of a queen mother, bronze, Benin, Nigeria
27. 3 ornaments, ivory encrusted with copper, Benin, Nigeria
28. Mounted figure, bronze, Benin, Nigeria
29. Plaque, bronze: king with musicians, Benin, Nigeria
30. left: Shango staff with female figure (wood), Yoruba, Nigeria
    right: female ancestor figure (wood), Bapende, south-western Congo
31. Hippopotamus mask of a water spirit (wood), Ijo, Nigeria
32. Death mask (wood), painted white, northern Ibo, Nigeria
33. Mask with hinged jaw (wood), Ibibio, Nigeria
34. Ancestor figure, wood, Oron-Ibibio, Nigeria
35. Janus-headed mask, wood covered with skin, Ekoi, Cross River area
36. Gigantic mask (wood), Bacham, Cameroun grasslands
37. Throne of Sultan Njoya, wood studded with beads, Bamum, Cameroun grasslands
38. Carving from a war canoe, painted wood, Duala, Cameroun
39. 3 reliquary figures (wood), Pangwe

40. White mask (wood), southern Pangwe, Gabon
41. Reliquary figure, *mbulu-ngulu,* wood overlaid with copper and brass, Bakota
42. Death mask (wood), Ogowe River area
43. Head (wood) for snake dance, Kuyu, Congo Republic
44. Disc-shaped mask (wood), painted red and white, Bateke, Congo Republic
45. Commemorative figure (wood), Basundi, Lower Congo
46. Looking-glass fetish (wood), Bakongo, Lower Congo
47. Panel, painted bark, Bankanu, south-western Congo
48. left: mask with bird (wood), south-western Congo
    right: mask (wood), twilled plaited work, Bayaka, south-western Congo
49. Hermaphrodite figure (wood), Basuku, south-western Congo
50. Commemorative statue (wood) of King Kata-Mbula, Bakuba, central Congo
51. 3 decorated vessels (wood), Bakuba, central Congo
52. Mask (wood), painted, with beads and cowrie-shells, Bakuba, central Congo
53. Ancestor figure (wood), Dengese, central Congo
54. *Kifwebe* mask (wood), with striated surface, Basonge, central Congo
55. Mask of girl (wood), Bajokwe, southern Congo
56. Corn-pounder and axe (wood), Baluba, south-eastern Congo
57. Neck-rest, ivory, Baluba, south-eastern Congo
58. Mask with horns (wood), Baluba, south-eastern Congo
59. Ancestor figure (wood), long-faced style, Baluba, south-eastern Congo, on plush fabric from Kasai-Sankuru
60. Caryatid stool (wood) of the 'Master of Buli', Baluba, south-eastern Congo
61. Bow-harp, Mangbetu, north-eastern Congo
62. Funerary figures (wood), Gamu-Gofa province, and cotton cloth, Ethiopia
63. Mask (wood), Makonde, East Africa
64. Mask (wood), Balumbo, Gabon

Title-page: lidded bowl with ducks (wood), Barotse-Kwangwa, Northern Rhodesia

LIST OF FIGURES WITH SOURCES

1. Bracelet with buffalo head, cast brass. Bagam, Cameroun grasslands. 4⅞ in. Lindenmuseum, Stuttgart. After GLÜCK, The art of brass casting..., in: Kunstwerkschriften, No. 17.
2. Anklet with fetters, cast brass. North-eastern Liberia. 7¾ in. E.C.,[1] Zurich.
3. Earthenware jug in primary style. Piri, northern Nigeria. National Museum, Copenhagen. After LAGERCRANTZ.[2]
4. Painting from an initiation hut. Wanyamwezi. 15½ in. After CORY, Wall paintings...
5. Paintings on clay dwellings of the Ndebele, near Klipgat, Transvaal. Photo by Schulthess (by courtesy of Conzett and Huber, Zurich).
6. Painting on wall of a house. Eastern Liberia. 5 ft. 7 in. After HOLAS, Mission...
7. Embroidery on a guinea-hen tobe. Hausa, northern Nigeria. 4 ft. 1 in. E.C., Zurich.
8. Cone-roofed dwelling, with painting. Bidyugo. After BERNATZIK, Bidyogo.

9. Sleeping quarters of King Asantehene, Ghana. Impluvium with gabled roof. After T. E. Bowdich, Mission to Ashantee (John Murray, Ltd., London, 1819).
10. Clay fort. Tamberma, northern Togo. Photo by Frobenius. After Germann, Handbuch von Springer.
11. Cupola buildings of clay. Musgu, northern Cameroun. Photo by Mohn. After Germann, Handbuch von Springer.
12. Mosque, built of clay. Mopti, Mali. After Heim, Negro Sahara.
13. Wooden statuette. Bambara. 22½ in. Verité Collection, Paris. After Schmalenbach.
14. Wooden mask. Marka, Mali. J. Müller Collection, Solothurn.
15. *Chi wara*, wooden antelope-shaped dance head-dress. Bambara.
16. Antelope-shaped dance head-dress, Suguni type. Bambara. Wood, 24 in. E.C., Zurich.
17. Antelope-shaped dance head-dress, Suguni type. Bambara. Wood, 23½ in.
18. Wooden antelope-shaped dance head-dress. Bambara. 19½ in. E. Leuzinger Collection.
19. Wooden antelope-shaped dance head-dress, doe with calf. Minianka-Segu type. 36½ in. Rietberg Museum, Zurich.
20. Ritual trough with tellem in relief. Dogon. Wood, 5 ft. 3 in. E. Storrer Collection.
21. Door lock with ancestor figures. Dogon. Wood. After photo by Herdeg.
22. Lidded bowl with horseman, wood. Dogon. 29¼ in. Mettler-Specker Collection, St. Gallen.
23. *Kanaga* mask, wood. Dogon. 44 in. Rietberg Museum, Zurich.
24. Mask of the Dō society, wood. Bobo, Upper Volta. 8 ft. 2½ in. Musée de l'Homme, Paris. After Griaule, Arts...
25. Helmet-mask, wood. Senufo. 36¼ in. Rietberg Museum, Zurich.
26. Wooden statuette. Senufo, Korhogo. 20¾ in. E.C., Zurich.
27. Wooden figure of bird, the emblem of the Senufo. 13¼ in. E.C., Zurich.
28. *Sakrobundu* mask, wood. South-western Senufo. 14 in.
29. Door in relief. Southern Senufo. Wood, 47¼ in. University Museum, Philadephia. After Catalogue, Brooklyn Museum.
30. Plaited mask. Djola, Senegal. 9¼ in. Mus. voor Land- en Volkenkunde, Rotterdam. After Nooteboom, Negerkunst, 1956.
31. Lidded vessel with figures and crocodile, wood. Bidyugo. 12¼ in. After Kjersmeier, Centres...
32. *Anok*, wooden cult implement. Baga, Guinea. 18¾ x 29¾ in. Rietberg Museum, Zurich.
33. Nomori, prehistoric stone figure from Sierra Leone. 5½ in. Ethnological Museum, Basle. After Münsterberger.
34. *Minsereh* figure, wood. Mende, Sierra Leone. 18¾ in. E.C., Zurich.
35. Bundu mask, wood. Mende. 15¾ in. After Sydow, Afrikanische Plastik.
36. Wooden mask with iron bands, cowries and ape's coat. Toma. After photo by E. Storrer.
37. Wooden mask. Dan, Ivory Coast. 8¼ in. E.C., Zurich.
38. Wooden mask with beak-shaped nose. Dan. British Museum. After Christensen.
39. Wooden mask with feathers. Kran, Ivory Coast. 9¼ in. Rietberg Museum, Zurich.
40. Wooden mask. Dan-Kran sub-style. 8½ in. After Musée Vivant, Culture nègre, Paris, 1948.
41. Wooden spoon with head. Kran. 29½ in. E.C., Zurich.
42. Gbekre, the Ape God. Wood. Baule, Ivory Coast. 22¾ in. Ch. Ratton Collection, Paris.
43. Wooden mask. Baule. 13½ in. Ch. Ratton Collection, Paris.

44. Guli, dancer with buffalo mask. Wood; garment of raffia. Baule. 28¾ in. E. Leuzinger Collection.
45. Guli, flat round buffalo mask. Wood. Baule. 15 in. F. Fénéon Collection, Paris. After RADIN and SWEENEY.
46. Wooden door with relief. Baule. 4 ft. 9 in. J. Müller Collection, Solothurn.
47. Gold mask of ram deity. Ivory Coast. After CHRISTENSEN.
48. Pulley-holder on loom. Wood. Guro, Ivory Coast. 4¾ in. Rietberg Museum, Von der Heydt Collection.
49. Zamle mask, wood. Guro. 15¾ in. E.C., Zurich.
50. Wooden figure. Ebrie, southern Ivory Coast. 12¼ in. After RASMUSSEN, Art nègre, Paris.
51. Funerary commemorative figure, clay. Krinjabo, eastern Ivory Coast. 8½ in. E.C., Zurich.
52. Cast brass weight with horseman. Ashanti. 4½ in. Kjersmeier Collection. After KJERSMEIER, Ashanti weights.
53. Cast brass weight with scorpion. Ashanti. 3⅛ in. E. Leuzinger Collection.
54. Cast brass weight with two crocodiles. Ashanti. 1⅝ in. E. Leuzinger Collection.
55. Akua'ba, fertility doll. Ashanti. Wood, 12¼ in. E. C., Zurich.
56. Wooden throne. Ashanti. British Museum. After MEYEROWITZ, Sacred State...
57. Silver ornament: alligator with fish. Northern Togo. 6¾ in. E.C., Zurich.
58. Recado of King Glele. Ceremonial staff with lion. Dahomey. After WATERLOT.
59. Group in brass. Mother and child and pounding-trough. Dahomey. 5¾ in. E.C., Zurich.
60. Wooden figure: consort of Legba deity. Fon, Dahomey. After photo by Herdeg.
61. Terracotta head. Nok culture, circa 400 B.C. Northern Nigeria. 8¾ in. Jos Museum, Nigeria.
62. Stone figure from Esie, Nigeria. In sanctuary in Esie. After DANIEL.
63. Resonator with bird, bronze. Benin. Height of bird 5½ in. E.C., Zurich.
64. Head of snake, bronze. Benin. 17 in. Ethnological Museum, Leipzig. After GERMANN, Handbuch von Springer.
65. Bronze head of King Osemwenede (1816–1849). Benin. 20¾ in. E.C., Zurich.
66. Ibeji, wooden twin figure, Yoruba. 8 in. Rietberg Museum, Zurich.
67. *Gelede* mask, wood. Yoruba. 15¾ in. K.C. Murray Collection.
68. Epa mask with horseman, wood. Yoruba. 39¼ in. British Museum. After UNDERWOOD, Masks...
69. Wooden board for Ifa oracle. Yoruba. 34¼ in. E.C., Zurich.
70. Wooden drum with relief, for Ogboni society. Yoruba. 34¼ in. E.C., Zurich.
71. *Edan*, brass staff, the badge of membership of the Ogboni society. Yoruba. 15 in. British Museum. After catalogue by W. FAGG, The Webster Plass Collection, 1953.
72. Ram's head. Wood. Owo style, Nigeria. 19¼ in. W. Cockin Collection, London. After RADIN and SWEENEY.
73. Knife-shaped mask for yam cult. Ibo. Wood, 13 in. Webster Plass Collection, New York. After PLASS, African tribal sculpture.
74. *Ikenga*, wooden house fetish. Ibo. 26½ in. Carl Kjersmeier Collection. After KJERSMEIER, Centres...
75. Clay group. Kwale-Ibo, south-eastern Nigeria. 11½ in. E.C., Zurich.
76. Crocodile mask of water spirit, wood. Abuan, south-eastern Nigeria. 24¾ in. British Museum. After catalogue by W. FAGG, The Webster Plass Collection, 1953.
77. Animal mask. Ogoni, south-eastern Nigeria. Wood, 17 in. Nigerian Museum, Lagos. After FAGG-ELISOFON.
78. Buffalo mask. Mama, northern Nigeria. Wood, 13¾ in. Charles Ratton Collection, Paris.

79. Dance head-dress with porcupine bristles and horns. Wood. Afo, northern Nigeria. 11½ in. Dr. Jan Ollers Collection, Stockholm. After catalogue 'Negerkonst', National Museum, Stockholm, 1953.
80. Clay figure. Sao culture, Chad region. 7¾ in. Musée de l'Homme, Paris. After PAULME, Les sculptures...
81. Palace of Bandjoun, Cameroun grasslands. After 'Habitat au Cameroun'.
82. Wooden mask, Bamum, Cameroun grasslands. 16 in. E.C., Zurich.
83. Bull mask. Wood Cameroun grasslands. 26¼ in. E.C., Zurich.
84. Elephant mask. Wood. Bali, Cameroun grasslands. 31 in. Lindenmuseum, Stuttgart. After KUTSCHER, Exotische Masken, 1953.
85. Seated ancestor figure with a head as a trophy. Wood, 45¼ in. Batie, Bamileke group, Cameroun. After LECOQ, Bamiléké.
86. Throne with figure. Wood. Bekom, Cameroun grasslands. 6 ft. 1¼ in. Ch. Ratton Collection, Paris.
87. Wooden vessel with supporting figure. Cameroun grasslands. 9 in. E. Leuzinger Collection.
88. Clay pipe with spider motif. Bamum, Cameroun grasslands. 13¼ in. E.C., Zurich.
89. Brass pipe-bowl with head of elephant. Bamum, Cameroun grasslands. 5⅛ x 6¾ in. E.C., Zurich.
90. Double figure. Bafo, Cameroun grasslands. Wood, 4⅛ in. E.C. Zurich.
91. Wooden figure. Pangwe. 20½ in. Gabon. British Museum. After ROY, Arts sauvages, 1957.
92. Decorated nut, a counter used in games. Yaunde, southern Cameroun. 1⅝ in. After PERVÈS.
93. Wooden mask. Bakwele. 9½ in. Tristan Tzara Collection, Paris. After ROY, Arts sauvages.
94. Reliquary figure. Wood overlaid with brass. Bakota style group. 20½ in. W. Münsterberger Collection. After MÜNSTERBERGER.
95. Wooden sculpture. Ambete, Congo Republic. 14¾ in. Rietberg Museum, Zurich.
96. Wooden statuette with bells. Babembe, Congo Republic. 8¾ in. British Museum. After UNDERWOOD, Figures...
97. Wooden figure. Bateke, Congo Republic. 19 in. Ethnological Museum, Berlin. After SYDOW, Afrikanische Plastik.
98. Wooden figure: mother and child. Bakongo. 9¾ in. Rietberg Museum, Zurich.
99. Stone figure from Noqui. Bakongo. 10½ in. Musée de l'Homme, Paris. After PAULME, Sculptures...
100. Nail fetish. Wood. Bakongo. 37½ in. E.C., Zurich.
101. Wooden mask for Bakhimba sect. Bakongo. 11¾ in. Lindenmuseum, Stuttgart. After KUTSCHER, Exotische Masken, Stuttgart, 1953.
102. Small powder jar with animal figure, wood. Bakongo. 5⅞ in. E.C., Zurich.
103. Earthenware pot with group of figures. Bakongo. 18 in. Ethnographical Museum, Antwerp. After OLBRECHTS.
104. Neck-rest with figure, wood. Bayaka. 6 in. E.C., Zurich.
105. *Kakungu* mask, wood. Bayaka. 35¾ in. Tervuren Museum. After ELISOFON-FAGG.
106. Wooden figure: mother and child, with rattle. Bambala. 22 in. E.C., Zurich.
107. Ivory amulet. Bahuana, south-western Congo. Tervuren Museum. After MAESEN, La sculpture décorative, in: Les arts plastiques, 1951.
108. Flat ivory amulet. Bahuana. 2½ in. Rietberg Museum, Zurich.
109. Ivory mask with beard. Bapende. 2¼ in. E.C., Zurich.
110. Wooden mask with horns. Eastern Bapende. American Museum of Natural History, New York. After Jowa Catalogue.
111. *Itombwa* oracle implement; crocodile. Bakuba. Wood, 3½ x 10½ in. Rietberg Museum, Zurich.

112. Wooden mask with cone-shaped eyes. Bakuba. Bakete type. 17¾ in. Ethnological Museum, Berlin. After Sydow, Afrikanische Plastik.
113. Hair-pin, wood. Bawongo, central Congo. 8 in. Rietberg Museum, Zurich.
114. Mother and child, wood. Bena Lulua. 14 in. Brooklyn Museum, New York. After Plass, African tribal sculpture.
115. Mortar with squatting figure, wood. Bena Lulua. 8¾ in. Tervuren Museum. After Schmalenbach.
116. Wooden mask. Bena Lulua. 9 in. Tervuren Museum. After Elisofon-Fagg.
117. Wooden statuette. Bekalebwe, sub-tribe of the Basonge. 6¾ in. E. Leuzinger Collection.
118. Ceremonial axe, handle overlaid with copper. Basonge. 19¼ in. E.C., Zurich.
119. Figure in stocks, wood. Bena Kanioka. 15 in. Rietberg Museum, Zurich.
120. Figure with sceptre, wood. Bajokwe. 11 in. Alain Locke Collection. After Segy.
121. Neck-rest with Earth Mother, wood. Baluba-Hemba. 8 in. E.C., Zurich.
122. *Kaliba*, so-called 'begging figure', wood. Baluba. 17¾ in. E.C., Zurich.
123. Ivory amulet, Baluba-Hemba. 4⅞ in. Rietberg Museum, Zurich.
124. Pestle with head, wood. Southern Baluba. Rietberg Museum, Zurich.
125. Ancestor figure. Wabembe, eastern Congo. Wood, 10¼ in. Tervuren Museum. After Münsterberger.
126. Ivory figure. Balega. 8½ in. Ch. Ratton Collection, Paris. After Roy, Arts sauvages, 1957.
127. Wooden figure. Bambole, north-eastern Congo. 19¼ in. E.C., Zurich.
128. Bark box in human form. Azande. 27¾ in. Rietberg Museum, Zurich.
129. Clay jug with human head. Mangbetu. 11½ in. E.C., Zurich.
130. Wooden mask, painted black and white. Ababua, north-eastern Congo. 11¾ in. Tervuren Museum. After Sydow, Afrikanische Plastik.
131. Wooden mask. Bwaka, north-western Congo. 12 in. Rietberg Museum, Zurich.
132. Masks, wood. Balolo, north-western Congo. 12½ in. Kerels Collection, Brussels.
133. Antelope drum, wood. Yangere, northern Congo. 39¼ in. Musée de l'Homme, Paris. After Griaule, Arts...
134. Wooden figure, primary style. Bari, north-western Nilotes. 18¼ in. Ethnological Museum, Vienna. After Sydow, Afrikanische Plastik.
135. Lidded basket, coiling technique. Barundi, East Africa. E.C., Zurich.
136. 'Vizulu', magical figure with vessel. Washambala, Usambara. Wood, 17¾ in. E.C., Zurich.
137. Throne of Sultan's consort. Wood. Wanyamwezi. 42 in. Ethnological Museum, Berlin. After Sydow, Afrikanische Plastik.
138. Anklet with silver clasp. Wasuaheli, East coast. 4½ in. E.C., Zurich.
139. Helmet-mask, with wax ornamentation. Mavia, Mozambique. Wood, 13 in. British Museum. After Bennet-Clark, in: Man, 1957/117.
140. Stele with bird figure, soapstone. Zimbabwe, Southern Rhodesia. Bird: 13 in.; stele: 47¼ in. Bulawayo Museum. After Sydow, Afrikanische Plastik.
141. Wooden mask with feathers. Masubia-Barotse, South-east Africa. 17¾ in. E.C., Zurich.
142. Neck-rest, wood, with geometrical decoration. Mashonaland. 5⅛ in. E.C., Zurich.
143. Gourd vessel, Manyakaze, Mozambique. 8½ in. E.C., Zurich.
144. *Aloala*. Commemorative funerary post, wood. Antandroy, Madagascar. After Almasi, in: Atlantis, 1939/6.

[1] E.C. = Ethnological Collection (Sammlung für Völkerkunde der Universität Zürich).
[2] For details, cf. Bibliography.

I. THE APPROACH TO NEGRO ART

Negro art attracts and enthrals us by its emotional vigour and clarity of form. Today it has, of course, become a part of world art, holding its own with the art of Europe and the ancient Orient. Its appeal does not lie merely in its exotic character. It has an emotional content which, after prolonged and repeated contact, can awaken in us a profound response. But in order to comprehend fully its singular charm, one must be in the right frame of mind and approach it with due detachment. If interest in negro art had been confined to the ethnologists alone, it would have never emerged from the show-cases of museums. That it has been discovered and made familiar to the general public is the achievement of a number of artists and art collectors who lived and worked at the turn of the century. The European, inhibited by Greek ideals of form in sculpture, could only appreciate the artistic qualities inherent in the African 'idols' to be found in ethnographical museums once he himself had begun to aim at a cubist or expressionist style. Only then did he realize that, long before him, the negro, proceeding from completely different assumptions, had found the most startling forms in which to convey his spiritual visions.

'Discovery of negro art

With his abstract treatment of form, often confined to bare essentials, the negro artist creates completely new, apparently non-real, works of art. Certain forms may appear meaningless to the layman; but to the negro they are the personification of supernatural spirits, the intermediary of vital force, and thus suggest to him a purposeful unity. Attention is generally centred upon the human figure. He accentuates whatever has spiritual significance, without regard for natural proportions. Whatever is unessential is excluded; the form is often compact and concentrated to such an extent as to approach absolute form.

Admittedly, when negro art was first discovered, enthusiasm for it was initially so great, and the impression made by the strange new art treasures was so overwhelming, that no one paused to distinguish between what was good and what was worthless. There was later an inevitable reaction towards a more sober appreciation. But for us today the true qualities of negro art have the same fascination that they had at the turn of the century. Its artistic value is now no longer a subject of controversy, as was the case when everything was contemptuously dismissed as a primitive barbarian curiosity.

Some thirty years ago Eduard von der Heydt, a pioneer in the field of folk art, discovered, half-forgotten in a shop, a negro figure. It so took his fancy that he acquired it, knowing only that it was the visible and tangible expression of a true religious feeling, of a strange ancestor and spirit cult. He needed no further convincing. Today sculpture constitutes the foundation-stone of his noteworthy collection of primitive art in the Rietberg Museum, Zurich. Whoever comes into contact with African plastic art perceives at once that it suggests a sublime spirituality. Static repose and intense energy are co-ordinated in a harmonious whole. Half-closed eyes and forms that have nothing in common with nature attain almost to a higher verity. A breath from the beyond wafts towards us; forces radiate, strike us, and reverberate in perpetual interaction. The more one deals with the interplay of forces, the principles which enabled such harmony and force of expression to be achieved, the more one is struck by the ingenious combinations, audacious ideas, and pleasing proportions one finds in these works. One's interest is aroused, and one asks oneself: Who are the people who created such works? Whence do they obtain their power? What are the spiritual sources of their tremendous creative volition? And finally, what is the message of this art?

These are far-reaching questions, which it is the object of this book to answer. After examining the essence of negro art, chapters will be devoted to man in his environment in past and present, and the function of art within the community, viewed from a religious as well as a sociological aspect. Fundamental problems of form, the various materials and techniques, with their potentialities and limitations, will also be discussed. Finally, an excursion will be made through the individual style regions, in order to obtain some impression of a world so varied that within the compass of a single volume it cannot be examined in full, but only treated in outline.

II COUNTRY AND PEOPLE

From a bird's-eye view the African continent presents a relatively simple picture. Leaving the Mediterranean behind us, we soon recognize the Sahara desert with its oases; to the right rise the Atlas ranges, and to the left lies the Nile valley, skirted by a narrow strip of cultivated land. The waters of the Blue Nile issue from the mountains of Ethiopia; the White Nile takes its source from an extensive swampy area in Bahr el Ghazal, in the southern part of the eastern Sudan. South of the 20th parallel thorn bushes and dwarf shrubs mark the transition from the Sahara to the Sahel which, though sparsely endowed with pasture, is an El Dorado for the hunter. Then a richer green and a red soil indicate the approach of the fertile tropical region: the Sudan forms a broad belt stretching across the continent from the Atlantic to the Red Sea, first as an arid steppe permitting agriculture and a limited amount of cattle-raising, and then, as the rainfall increases, as savannah, with its bushes, open forest, grasslands, cultivated areas and large settlements. The savannah has thrust countless wedges into the primeval forest, which stretches along the Atlantic coast from the Senegal to the Congo, and which in the area of the Equator broadens out into dense jungle.

Towards the east the Sudanese tableland, repeatedly broken by shelves, basins and mountain massifs, rises to form a highland area: the so-called Great Rift valley, formed in the glacial period, when East Africa was split from the Red Sea to the Zambezi by a mighty fissure in the earth's crust. Now, after thousands of years have passed, this landscape presents a magnificent picture, with lakes, waterfalls, volcanoes and snow-capped 20,000-foot mountain peaks, all situated amidst varied vegetation, acacias and baobabs being the most characteristic species of tree. On the far side of the Great Rift a belt of high ground extends southwards from the mountains of Ethiopia.

From the Equator to the Cape we are confronted with the same zones of vegetation in reverse. In the southern Congo primeval jungle again gives way to savannah country stretching from Angola to the Indian Ocean, and in the form of arid steppe down to the

TOPOGRAPHY

MAP. P. 213

Cape. Finally, in the central and western part of South Africa lies the Kalahari desert, a vast salt steppe.

The great rivers — the Nile, Congo, Niger, Zambezi and others — with their innumerable tributaries are of importance in that they provide the means of existence and serve to promote cultural contact. For centuries they have enabled the negro to spread outwards over great stretches of territory. The rivers are treacherous: shortly before reaching the sea, they have still to break through the threshold of the tableland, so that rapids and waterfalls are formed which prevent easy access to the interior from the coast. For this reason maritime navigation has not played an important role in Africa. There were only a few gateways in the north and east that permitted foreign peoples and cultures to penetrate into the continent. In successive waves of migration, they advanced from north to south, or from east to west, or rolled across the steppe land, without meeting any significant obstacle, until their vanguard was lost in the boundless expanse of the jungle.

CLIMATE

Climate and altitude have shaped the physiognomy of Africa, tropical heat being only one of several factors. The degree of atmospheric humidity determines whether the conditions for human existence are to be pleasant and healthy, enervating, or unbearable. Precipitation, again, depends on the season. It matters a great deal in what month the rain-bearing winds blow and where the rain falls. It is also important whether a periodical alternation between wet and dry seasons provides the conditions requisite for agriculture, as in the savannah, or whether the air is saturated by a constant high degree of humidity, promoting the luxuriant vegetation of the evergreen rain forests. Altitude, irrespective of latitude, makes the heat bearable, increasing one's vitality and capacity for work; the nights are cooler, and above 4500 feet there are regions free from malaria.

RACES

ETHIOPIANS: In North Africa and the Sahara, Egypt and East Africa (including Ethiopia), Hamitic culture by and large prevails. Its representatives belong to the Ethiopian race, but often have an admixture of Mediterranean, Cromagnon, Oriental and negroid elements, which account for local variations in characteristics (*e.g.*, the northern branch of the Hamitic people: the Moors, Fulani and Tuareg; the eastern branch: the Beja (or Bisharin), Galla, Somali, Masai, Bahima and Batutsi). Although dark-skinned, these Ethiopians are not negroes. They are tall in stature and slender in build, relaxed in their carriage, of noble appearance, with fine features, without prognathism (projecting jaws), their nose straight and thin, and the form of the head dolichocephalic. They are intelligent pastoral people with a bellicose streak, and lead a nomadic life, wandering across the arid steppes. In more fertile areas they also live together with negroes, in which case the latter attend to the homes and fields, and perform handicrafts — tasks too menial for the proud Hamite.

During the course of history many Hamitic peoples immigrated into the negro lands of the west and south, and by virtue of their special talent for organization became overlords over the native agricultural tribes. Thus the Fulani, for example, are a branch of the Hamites in the western Sudan who, together with their cattle, wander from Fouta Djallon (Guinea) as far as Cameroun, only rarely leaving their children and old folk behind in their villages (cf. Table of Cultures, p. 219).

NEGROES: The negroes, likeable for their guileless candour, inhabit the savannah and forest country. They long ago ceased to be itinerant hunters, and became settled agriculturalists. They are divided into four main races:

a) The heavily-built sturdy negro of the forests, the 'Palaenegrids', with deep-set eyes and projecting jaws, who inhabit clearings in the primeval jungle of the northern Congo, Equatorial Africa and the Guinea coast. They are often to be found living in community with the short-statured pygmies of the dense jungle. The latter are truly primitive creatures, nomadic hunters and food-gatherers, who perform occasional services for the negro, but are never prepared to give up their free way of life.

b) The Sudanese negro (Old Nigritic culture) of the northern savannah, who are tall in stature, and

c) the shorter-statured Bantu negro of the eastern and southern savannah. These two groups are distinguished solely on linguistic grounds, although race and language often need not coincide. The two groups frequently overlap, particularly on the Guinea coast, where they are called semi-Bantu.

d) The Nilote (also Old Nigritic culture) of the eastern and central Sudan. They are of tall, slender stature, with long limbs, and are cattle-breeders and agriculturalists — characteristics pointing to the presence of strong Ethiopian elements.

TABLE OF CULTURES P. 219

BUSHMEN: They were formerly hunters who roamed over much of Africa, and who covered rock faces with mysterious paintings designed to propitiate magic forces in order to obtain their assistance in hunting. They are now to be found in the inhospitable native reserves of the Kalahari steppe in South Africa. Since they have not progressed beyond the food-gatherer stage, they nowadays lead a meagre existence.

These are the major historic races of Africa. Today only the extreme types can be clearly differentiated from one another, for in the course of ceaseless migrations, and conquests of one tribe by another, they have constantly intermingled and interbred.

PREHISTORY AND HISTORY

African man can be traced back to the earliest epochs of the history of mankind. In Africa, as elsewhere, have been found skulls, skeletons, and chipped hand-axes of the Chelles-Acheul culture dating from the Lower Palaeolithic period, human remains of the Pithecanthropus stage, and primitive types of Neanderthal man. Early types of Ethiopians and negroids date back to the Upper Palaeolithic era; Proto-Ethiopian human remains have been found in the Oldoway (Olduvai) ravine and near Lake Elmenteita in East Africa, and Proto-Negroid remains in Asselar, approximately 250 miles north-east of Timbuktu, and elsewhere.

Everywhere in Africa, in the north-east and south, in the Sahara, on the Guinea coast and in the Congo, stone artifacts are to be found: chipped hand-axes dating back to the earliest periods, whose size shows that they must have been wielded by powerfully-built men, as well as microliths, polished stone axes and other artifacts of the mesolithic and neolithic age. In negro Africa the Iron Age began about 400 B.C., there being no intermediary bronze stage. Although the Sahara constituted a tremendous barrier between the cultures of white and black Africa, it was no impediment to the movement of caravans, which have traversed it for centuries, wandering from oasis to oasis in search of water. The Sudanese traded with the advanced peoples of the northern coastal belt: Phoenicians, Greeks, Romans, Byzantines, Moors, Berbers, and through them also with the Sards and Etruscans. Commercial relations with negro Africa brought cultural influences in their train. Indeed, some foreign peoples appeared as conquerors and founded kingdoms, thereby precipitating extensive migrations of population. The first known feudal kingdoms were established by the Berbers and the Fulani in the western Sudan.

The immigrants followed the route from north-east to south-west as well as that from north to south. Time and again there took place influxes of people and ideas from the Nile valley, which opened up the country to influences from the Near East, and even from Persia and India. An important centre for such contact was Napata Meroe, a state with a sacral kingship, as is clearly evidenced by the fact that considerable similarities exist with the kingdoms of Uganda, Kaffa, Monomotapa and Barotseland, as well as those of West Africa and the Congo. Another important route ran through central Sudan to the Chad territory and from the Chad to the regions of the Niger and Congo.

Archaeological finds and the accounts of early travellers show that over the past three thousand years Africa was far from dormant, but on the contrary was pulsating with the throb of dramatic events. However, few artistic records remain to bear witness to the stirring history of the early kingdoms, with their campaigns of conquest and internecine struggles. The history of Africa with its numerous local wars was eventful, and frequently turbulent, but it was not always that these conflicts released forces that stimulated artistic endeavour. This could occur when new kingdoms arose, whose rulers had sufficient foresight to promote, as well as the arts of war, those which could only prosper during prolonged periods of peace.

The real African artist is not the foreign conqueror but the native. The negroes only borrowed from the immigrants as much as was compatible with their own conceptions. Many of them were fanatical champions of their ancient tribal traditions against Islam and, later, Christianity.

African art is diffused unevenly over the various regions. The tourist on African safari who fondly imagines that he will find a precious mask will be doomed to disappointment, unless he is satisfied with some ordinary souvenir. To supply the demand of the Europeans, negroes have shrewdly established a veritable souvenir trade, for which they eagerly carve 'typical' objects. True religious art, where it still exists, remains hidden from the tourist's eyes, since carving is confined to certain specific regions.

Nomads, as is only to be expected, tend to encumber themselves with fewer household effects than settled peoples. The famous rock paintings are as a rule restricted to the former hunting grounds of the Eurafrican hunters of the steppe, such as the Sahara, Fezzan,

ART AND CULTURE

Nubian desert, East and South Africa; in the West they are only found sporadically.

The figure sculpture for which negro Africa has become famous has not attained the same high degree of importance in all parts of the continent. With one people their talents are manifested predominantly in the pictorial ornamentation of their huts, or in pottery, whereas another may be distinguished for its carved masks, or for its brass-casting. Amongst the Old Nigritic tribes in the east sculpture is rarely to be found, but it is highly developed amongst the matriarchal Bantu, and reaches its zenith in the western part of the continent. The western Sudan is famous in this respect, as are the territories stretching from Portuguese Guinea southwards to the mouth of the Congo. Plastic art is of lesser importance in the central Sudan, in the Ubangi-Shari area, and in the northern Congo, but re-emerges with full force in the southern and south-eastern Congo and the adjacent territories. There is also an enclave of sculpture on the plateaux either side of the river Rovuma, between Lake Nyasa and the Indian Ocean.

This clearly shows that African sculpture attains its highest development in the areas of matriarchy, where woman holds a dominant position in society. Equally conspicuous is the artistic wealth to be found in some of the old non-Islamic feudal kingdoms. The existence of strong links between art and culture is undeniable: for culture is the soil from which art derives its purpose and content. Since African cultures show little uniformity, and many other factors are involved in the creation of any particular style, great local differences appear within each cultural group. *With this in mind, I should like to ask readers not to regard the conclusions drawn in this book as generally valid or exclusive. The examples adduced as illustrations of various styles could have been supplemented by dozens of others, so that everywhere one ought to add the words 'et cetera'. In African art exceptions are almost as numerous as rules.*

PLATE 1 — Leopard, emblem of power of certain Benin kings, composed of five large elephant tusks. The inset spots are secured by copper pins and are arranged to form a rhythmic decorative pattern. Benin, Nigeria, 18th century. *British Museum (32¾ in.).*

PLATE 2 — Head of volcanic tuff, isolated find from the Welle river area, evocative of the past. North eastern Congo. *Rietberg Museum, Zurich, Von der Heydt Collection (7¾ in.).*

PLATE 3 — Drinking vessel, decorated with incised design in primary style, made from an ostrich egg-shell, with a necklace of the same material. Used by primitive Bushmen of the Kalahari desert. Lüderitz Bay, South-West-Africa. *Ethnological Collection, Zurich (5⅞ in.).*

a b

PLATE 4a — Landa mask, Toma, the personification of a legendary tribal chief and mighty bush spirit of the Poro society. A powerful effect is evoked in the dance by its rigid cubist form, supplemented by a costume of wild tufts of plumage and fibres. Women are not allowed to see it. Guinea. (22¾ in.).

PLATE 4b — Mask in shape of antelope, Bambara. Distinctly cubist in form. The bulging forehead, overshadowing the deep-set eyes, and the enormous roof of the nose reflect the unrelenting power of the Kore secret society. Mali. *Both in Rietberg Museum, Zurich, Von der Heydt Collection (30¾ in.).*

III. RELIGION

What is the nature of the cosmic conception and the essence of the religion which have imbued the art of negro Africa with such momentum and force? We are today in the fortunate position of having a book on Bantu philosophy, by the Belgian Franciscan Father Placide Tempels, which interprets in a masterly and lucid fashion the thought, evidently most complex, of the Bantu negro. The author has had decades of personal experience of the Bantu, is keenly sensitive to their ways of thought, and documents his work with innumerable native sayings. Herskovits and other scholars corroborate Tempels' findings in regard to other parts of Africa, and my personal knowledge of the region of the Afo in northern Nigeria has led me to endorse his views. What was treated in earlier studies on the subject in an extremely vague and general manner has been systematized by Tempels into a logical and coherent whole. Since his work also touches upon the function of art, I shall take the liberty of outlining his conclusions.

CONCEPTION OF THE COSMOS

Tempels deliberately used the term 'philosophy' in the title of his work because he understood clearly that the Bantu think in abstract terms, and have a system of cognition, metaphysics and ethics, and also a far from inconsiderable ontology which, despite the fact that it is a magic philosophy, the author ventured to compare with that of the West. In the centre of Bantu philosophy stands the conception of a 'vital force', a universal, omnipotent energy around which all thought and action revolve. From this is deduced the imperative: life is to be lived vigorously, for active force is existence, and existence is force. From this conception of a vital force other ideas organically follow. 'Growth of life' means that existence can become either stronger or weaker. The highest aspiration of the Bantu is therefore to acquire and possess great force or power.

'Influence upon life': one force can exert an effect upon another. Illness and death are beyond human control; they affect our lives from a different, more powerful, sphere of influence. 'Gradation of life': forces are graded hierarchically, the higher ones exerting an influence upon the lower. But above all powers stands God,

Magic   Spirit and Creator in one, in whom is all wisdom, and who is his own source of power. It is he who grants existence to the other forces; he animates and conserves them. After him, subordinate in rank, come the ancestral progenitors of the tribe, the first to whom God gave life. As higher spiritual beings, they act as intermediaries between God and man. Next follow other deceased persons. Amongst living beings it is the tribal elders who possess the best part of the vital force. Man, an egocentric being, stands in the centre of creation; but below him animals, plants and minerals also have their share of force. "What we refer to as magic," Tempels remarks, "is to the Bantu mind nothing other than the application of the forces of nature which God places at man's disposal to strengthen his vital force." This dynamic power gives man the great responsibility of co-operating in increasing his vital force, and "choosing freely between the greater and the lesser good, and between good and evil." From this springs the Bantu's strong moral and legal sense. Lying and deceitfulness, theft and sexual abuse, but above all injurious use of magic, are all severely condemned. Ill-will obstructs the exercise of force, disturbs the cosmic order, and must be avenged. For this reason the restoration of order by means of propitiatory sacrifices and cleansing of the life force of the village is of the greatest concern to the Bantu. Tempels even goes so far as to say: "Uncivilized man is still exceedingly conscious of his rights as a human being. The pagan Bantu are closer to Christianity than Christian Europe. They want to be united in love with all living things."

On this rests the whole principle of existence, which remains in being even when man repeatedly succumbs to temptation, and jeopardizes the purity of his *Weltanschauung* by abuses of all kinds.

This cosmic view of the Bantu illuminates, as with a sudden flash of light, many phenomena which have hitherto been obscure and puzzling. It explains the need for ritual acts to strengthen force and to restore order once it has been disrupted. All creatures, including the departed, all beings and things are linked together very closely by the fact that they share in one and the same eternal power. Sculpture, too, which performs a symbolic function, belongs within this world of forces.

Religion constitutes an integral part of this philosophy of existence. Its purpose is to serve an exalted transcendental Creator, the giver of life and preserver of ethical values. Amongst those who live their lives according to religious precepts there are, still today, outstanding personalities prepared to assume responsibility; but, as in every religious community, there also exist men and women who stumble and falter. Among the Afo and the inhabitants of the western Sudan I also have had the opportunity to meet negroes who were men of outstanding character. I have witnessed the genuine devotion with which they invoke their God, and the fervour with which they solicit invisible forces. And in so doing the negro is not so presumptuous as to seek to comprehend the mighty Creator in his totality. He visualizes God in a pantheon consisting of greater and lesser deities: 'sons of God' is the name given them by the Afo. Elements of the vital force are also visible in deified culture heroes, personified forces of nature, and ancestors. The Supreme God animates with his power all matter in the universe (animism). "God lives in every man's body", says the negro. "The heart is Buddha", says the Indian. All the qualities which are of use to man are drawn upon to strengthen one's vital force, and are represented symbolically.

Religious acts are supervised by a priest, or medicine-man. He is chosen by the council of elders, or a secret society, to perform this responsible function on account of his extraordinary abilities, such as clairvoyance, sensibility and intelligence. His installation, however, does not take place until he has undergone a long period of training, and his restraint and courage have been tested, by an experienced teacher, who initiates him into the study of healing methods and the efficacy of plants and minerals for this purpose.

THE MEDICINE-MAN

The master also imparts to his pupil his knowledge and experience acquired through association with supernatural forces. The smith, whose contact with fire evokes magic ideas, often performs the function of priest as well. The good medicine-man uses his strength and wisdom for the benefit of the whole community; the bad one may in certain circumstances abuse his tremendous power. A clever medicine-man, for instance, can send his soul by night into the realm of the dead, see the gods and hear their voices, and interpret the meaning of visions and dreams. According to Tempels' theory, he can perceive, influence and control the operation of forces; he can act as a medium through which they can be transmitted, and can determine by consulting the oracles when the time has come to take certain action. He is consulted by all who are hard pressed, and holds all the strings in his hands. He warns and cautions against possible dangers, upholds order, and determines the future. His familiarity with village problems, his empathy, and his knowledge of medicine, together with his power of hypnotic suggestion, all contribute to ensure his success. He protects, heals, and exorcizes evil spirits. To transgress his commands would be presumptuous. The sense of responsibility which he shows in his actions gives his charges confidence in him. After the ritual has been carried out, they return home in a relieved state of mind, and their joyous demeanour indicates that they have re-established a pure and untainted relationship with the 'sons of God'. Not every negro village is constantly threatened by evil spirits, as so many missionaries maintain. The medicine-man is the equal of the demons, and knows what counter-measures to take against them. Being a shrewd psychologist, he equips himself for his ritual performances with a spectacular costume and trimmings, to enhance his dignity and to surround himself with an aura of mystery.

The negro draws a clear distinction between white and black magic. He distinguishes between the magic exercised by the medicine-man and the obscure practices of evil sorcerers and witches — demons who, in the guise of panthers and snakes, cause trouble and harm by night, devouring the souls of their victims. These he fears; and many masks are used to ward them off.

ART AND ITS RELIGIOUS FUNCTION

Art, which for the negro is the visible expression of the invisible and transcendental, is particularly well suited to play its part in various religious rites.

The most important works of sculpture are fashioned by the medicine-man, the smith, or by an independent artist, who must be inspired by the exalted religious function of his work. Aware that he is creating a temporary abode for the spirit, an emanation of God, he sets about his task with great devotion and concentration. He is inspired by a vision. He proceeds from ideas treasured by the community and handed down from generation to generation. Many are the rules which he has to observe in order to give his work the proper effectiveness.

Ancestor figure

The negro makes no images of the great God of Creation, but the sons of God, and particularly the progenitors of the tribe, are afforded a worthy habitat in the form of works of sculpture. These men, who were the first mortals, the negro imagines in a state of sublime repose, their arms resting upon the torso, knees or chest, the body stretched out or squatting, roughly in the way in which the dead are buried. But they are always given the shape of non-real beings; the head, the seat of intellectual powers, is often accentuated, or else the navel, the centre of life and the link between mother and child. The figure is decorated with various *coiffures,* tattoo markings and emblems, enabling the ancestor to recognize his figure and to take up his abode there joyfully. Narrow slits are left for the eyes, since the ancestor is considered still to be able to see and act. It is rare that such figures are fashioned in such a way as to excite terror, for the ancestor is a good friend who gives protection and blessing. The figure is no fetish, but a symbol, an effigy; it is the seat of supernatural power. Although dead, the ancestor places his power at the disposal of the living.

The priest knows what measures to take in order to invoke the spirit. With rattles, bells and chants he is invited to take up his abode in his image. If he favours the figure with his presence, it becomes imbued with his power, which is also automatically transmitted to those present at the ceremony. In order to persuade the spirit to stay inside it, the sculpture has to be as beautiful as possible — or 'good', as the negro says, for to him 'beautiful' and 'good' are more or less synonymous. At festivals he adorns the figure with beads, anoints it with *tukula,* sprinkles it with chewed coco-nut, and endeavours to entertain it with all manner of dances. Sacrifices of various kinds enhance its vitality; the souls of the departed sip the sacrificial blood poured over the figure, and thus establish themselves inside it. The first fruits of the harvest, a share of the game caught when hunting, and even some of the beer that has been freshly brewed, are all offered to the ancestor figure.

It is the medium through which the negro converses with the ancestral spirit, and solicits him with the most varied requests. In reply the Pomdo figure of the Kissi makes a bow, the figure of the Ijo trembles, and, in a case of perjury, the figure of the Bakundu spirit rocks.[1]

To the ancestral figure, the abode of the progenitors of the clan, solicitations for fertility are addressed. The mother of all things becomes the symbol of conjugal bliss, and later of fecundity in general — for richly-provided fields are the desire of all agricultural peoples. Its assistance is invoked in all stages of the agricultural cycle. Women desiring a child tie one of these figures upon their backs; young girls are given one to ensure fertility; and childless women procure one, in order to have the opportunity of living on inside it (figures of twins, pp. 141, 192). The large statues, the communal property of the village, are usually looked after by the priest, kept in a shrine, and brought out when needed for ceremonies. They are often placed upon graves, where people go to take counsel with them. Statuettes occupy pride of place in the home as personal protective figures. They are regarded as private property, and are often buried together with their owners. During ceremonies they are taken out of the house, in order to be charged afresh with the force of life.

Other cult figures Besides the tribal progenitors, other great figures of the past are also deified, such as mythological heroes and founders of states and dynasties, who are credited with outstanding deeds for the benefit of the tribe, and who are endowed with special attributes (*e.g.,* Odudua and Shango, or the legendary kings of the Bakuba).

Fetish The dividing-line between the regularly consecrated, small personal ancestor figure and the fetish is an indistinct one. The fetish is an object endowed with magical powers for certain specific purposes, and employed either in a defensive or offensive capacity. It gives protection against illness, on journeys, in childbirth, or during wars and hunting expeditions. Wherever there is danger, and there lurk evil sorcerers who cannot be dealt with by material means, the fetish is brought into play.

Amongst the millions of strange, often revolting, fetishes to be found in Africa, there are only a few that can claim to possess any artistic value. They have no exalted religious function to fulfil. They are usually produced by the medicine-man, for an artist would rarely waste his time on such objects. If a fetish proves to be ineffectual and powerless, it is scourged, broken into pieces, destroyed, or given to the children as a toy. But if it is to be sold to a foreigner, it has first to be deprived of its power.

Animal sculpture Bearing in mind that, in the negro view, animals, although creatures endowed with vital force, rank far below man in the hierarchy of forces, it is not surprising that animal figures are less common than those of human beings. They exist, but perform subsidiary functions, such as tutelary spirits and guardians, or as personifications or symbols of certain powers (for example, the ram representing a God of Heaven, and the animal-headed gods and heroes, of the Ivory Coast and Dahomey). Animals also appear in masked costumes; they act, speak, invoke spirits, and intimidate the onlooker. It is usually specific qualities of an animal which are represented, because of their association with certain abstract ideas. Thus strength is symbolized by buffaloes, crocodiles, elephants, hippopotamuses, lions, panthers and boars, fighting spirit by horse-antelopes, and swiftness of movement by snakes and lizards, whilst the tortoise suggests advanced age. In Africa, too, the belief in were-animals fosters the idea that evil sorcerers turn into ravenous beasts of prey by night. The ape often represents a deceased person; or alternatively the accent is laid upon its playful qualities. But for the Baule an ape god, Gbekre, passes judgement upon the souls of the departed. Birds, as creatures of the heavens, are seen as intermediaries between this world and the next.

Several animals (such as the spider and the chameleon; for the latter, cf. p. 96) are connected with certain myths. The motif of an animal that affords man some help and protection in many cases originates in an ancient myth, according to which animals rescued the founders of the tribe, or created some important object of cultural value. It is more probable that the rendering of animals in Africa arose from a need for power and protection than from sheer totemism. Recollections of former hunting expeditions may also be involved here (cf. p. 99).

Attempts are hardly ever made to represent an animal as such. This would be too trivial a theme. Instead, the negro endeavours to invoke the power of the entire species by symbolizing its characteristic features. Often, to obtain greater potency, various animal symbols are combined, human characteristics being introduced as well. Thus the Banda mask of the Baga is a combination of human being, crocodile and antelope. The *anok*, originally a bird, is suddenly given teeth in its beak and becomes a crocodile, although its face is that of a human being. The Bambara add to their antelopes various animal motifs, such as, for example, the tail of a chameleon.

Numerous looking-glass and nail fetishes used by the Bakongo, as well as the divination implements employed by the Bakuba, are represented as animals. Animal motifs appear in reliefs, in paintings on walls and doors of houses, on neck-rests, loom pulley-holders, sacrificial vessels, drums, pipes and lids. In case of illness the Bahuana substitute for their customary plaited door a wooden one bearing the symbol of life, a lizard.

Masks   Whereas in the case of the ancestor figure we were dealing with a static principle, the mask represents the active, or dynamic, aspect. Whenever man feels himself threatened by demons against whom he can do nothing with his natural resources, he solicits the active intervention of the good spirits by sacrifice and invocation. In order to get the spirit to manifest itself through a mask, a great deal of effort and much careful staging are required on the part of the dancer who wears it: the ritual takes place by night; he dons a grotesque costume; and the atmosphere is raised to fever pitch by the use of sacrificial blood and the rhythmic beating of drums. Spellbound by the intensity of his belief, the bearer of the mask feels himself permeated and transformed by its power. After some time he falls into a state of ecstasy and begins to act the part of the spirit he is invoking. He speaks with a change in his voice, announces in an esoteric tongue the message received during his trance, and performs with strange steps the movements by which the demon is exorcized. At that moment he is master: no request may be denied him — this is the exacting law required by the masks.

Among the Basonge it was formerly thought necessary to sacrifice a human being to invoke divine power (Plate 54), and in north-eastern Liberia ritual required that a mask which had proved a failure in battle should be given new vigour by human sacrifice. Later on, however, the expedient was resorted to of substituting a cow smeared with a few drops of blood from a man's forehead.[2] In Nigeria the masked dancers undergo special ablutions and make sacrifices before they don their masks. They believe they would die if they were to conduct themselves improperly whilst wearing the masked costume. Among the Mende the woman representing the Bundu devil carefully covers up her body, hands and feet, in order not to come into contact at any point with the spirit, which she imagines as possessing a fearful all-consuming power.

These powerful masks are employed in important ritual acts, particularly in the death rite, in order to exorcize Nyama, a force of revenge which sometimes signifies a threat, and which is envisaged as part of the soul, half material and half immaterial.[3] But they also play the more peaceful role of transformed deceased persons, who wish to converse once more with the living; for now, speaking from the next world, their statements carry weight. The spirits are invoked at harvest time, generally in order to give them thanks.

Their aid is also solicited before the sowing of crops, to ensure fecundity, to send rain in times of severe drought, or to pass divine judgement during judicial hearings. Masks with breasts portrayed on the forehead or cheeks (Gio, Bafum) denote fertility. In southern Nigeria members of the secret societies perform dramas, in which masked dancers take the part of souls from the realm of the dead. In the case of the Pangwe the departed spirits are represented by dancing marionettes. But in many places these sacred rites, once strictly observed, have now been turned into comic performances; the masks are used in farce, or serve as bugbears to frighten children, whilst the puppets are employed in comedies (by the Ibo, Ibibio and Bambara). But even though everyone guesses the identity of the person wearing the disguise, though women are allowed to watch from close quarters, and the masked men frolic about and cut capers for the amusement of the audience, nevertheless a vestige of the demonic power formerly attributed to the masks still remains.

These figurative representations are an integral part of the equipment used by medicine-men, members of secret societies and mask-bearers. For generally, irrespective of their size, they are regarded as symbols of vitality which give the various implements the importance essential for them to perform their proper function.

Ritual implements

A few examples of such implements may be given here: a staff for invoking deities (Shango), rattles, drums and bells for attracting their attention, fans for describing the magic circle, goblets and vessels for sacrificial offerings and libations, and divination implements. The Bambara dancer rides a hobby-horse which can occasionally take the form of a bird. Horns, sacrificial axes, ritual knives, ladles and wands — all these objects, whenever they serve a ceremonial purpose, are especially elaborately decorated with symbols of power.

Lit.: [1] Sydow-Kutscher; [2] Harley; [3] Baumann, Nyama...

IV. SOCIOLOGY

Religion is the true mother of all negro art. But the manners and customs of the community, as well as the everyday life of the village, also play their part, and have inspired the negro to create great works of art for functional purposes.

Art is the most natural means of expression for a people that has not yet learned to write. It is the language everyone understands. It tells the story of the tribe, the myths and legends of the glorious past. It bestows the necessary dignity upon sacral rites and emphasizes the seriousness of court proceedings. When the judge dons the sacred mask, he is deemed to be an embodiment of divine power; in his presence no one would dare to tell a lie, and all dispute is stilled. The masks compel submission, not without a trace of fear as well: women do as they are told, debtors pay their due, and matrimonial loyalties are preserved. The police make use of the mystery with which masks are imbued to command respect. Amongst the Mende, when judgement is pronounced, the *minsereh* figure shakes, and the verdict automatically falls upon the guilty party (pp. 108, 169).

Secret societies In most districts where carvings are produced, the structure of communal life is maintained by societies, consisting of men, and in exceptional cases also women, who have been tested as to their fitness for membership. Among some tribes these societies are strictly exclusive, and membership can only be acquired after undergoing difficult ordeals and making offerings. Among other tribes they embrace all able-bodied males, distinguishing between them according to age and other degrees of merit. All societies derive their authority from the power entrusted to them by mighty spirits. They are guided by a spirit who on important occasions appears in masked costume or takes up abode in the ancestor figure. He ensures that tradition is scrupulously observed and order maintained — that order which alone can guarantee the tribe's happiness and prosperity.

Initiation In this way the elders of the tribe exert an influence upon successive generations. They transmit their experience to the young men through initiation, by the good example which they set, and in particular through the bush school, run by the priest-magician, a place where every young member of the tribe is instructed in its duties, laws and customs. Sculptures, wall-paintings, proverbs and songs are used in teaching. In the north-east of Liberia initiates are confronted with masks and challenged to battle before being allowed to learn their secrets and don the masked costume. Wherever masks and secret societies prevail, a symbolic ceremony is always held when the initiates complete their training, which at the same time denotes their admission into adult society. This is an event celebrated with magnificent masked dances and songs, which sometimes reach a climax in wild orgies. Now that they have attained the age of puberty, and are marriageable, the moment has arrived to show the young men the tasks before them: to become independent of their mothers and to ensure the continued existence of the tribe. An act of such significance must, in the negro mind, take a ceremonial form.

The orders given by the secret societies to the initiates, and the ordeals to which they are subjected, are strict. Absolute secrecy is imperative, for the force they wield is that of the supreme spirit, whose weapon is poison. The elders, who are nearest to the ancestors and possess most insight into things, know from experience how to win the young men's respect and obedience, and how to persuade them to perform any desired service. Care of the aged is thus no problem in these districts.

These societies serve primarily to foster education and to maintain order and morality. Their influence upon the character and standing of a tribe is immeasurable. Even the chief must subordinate himself to the secret society, so that his power is not absolute, in contrast to lands with a sacral theocratic form of government, where the role of secret societies is played by the nobility and court officials. Certain masks indicate the rank and status of the members of the society (Ekoi, Balega).

Masks and sculptures, as a visible expression of a supernatural vital force, accompany the negro throughout his life, in which conception, puberty and death are the most important moments. Fertility increases a woman's standing; hence at sacrificial festivals the mother-and-child statue is invoked to endow women with additional power. The *chi wara* antelopes dance in pairs across the fields, for it is one and the same force that enables men, plants and animals to grow and flourish. In school, at initiation, at work, in

'Rites de passage'
(stages of life)

justice or in war: these sculptures are always tangibly present. They satisfy a social need, by giving purpose and order to the group (pp. 117, 190), controlling the negro's relationship with supernatural forces, ridding him of feelings of guilt and fear, and relieving tension through burlesque games.

Division of labour A sharp dividing-line is drawn between the work of men and that of women. It would be regarded as discreditable to perform tasks appropriate to the opposite sex. In the same way the arts and crafts are also the function of either one sex or the other. In most regions men are responsible for building houses, forging metals, carving and plaiting. Women work as potters, spinners and dyers, particularly in the west. In the Sudan it is the men who weave, whereas in parts of West Africa and the Congo this task generally falls to the womenfolk. In their capacity as potters the women also mould the clay reliefs on the walls of houses, but the men seldom allow them to participate in work on clay religious sculptures.

The artist The artist generally enjoys a high reputation within his tribe. He meets a social need for enhanced vitality, and transmits prestige, beauty and joy. His status is, however, not everywhere the same. In the case of some agricultural tribes arts and crafts are no more than a side-line. During the dry season, when the fields lie fallow, and the farmer has no other occupation, he gladly takes to carving, bartering his work for other goods. If he is particularly talented, this, together with the prospect of material gain, quickly leads him to become a specialist. In such cases the community is prepared to relieve him of his economic cares, so that he may devote himself to his art during the rainy season as well. In the course of time there develop veritable family enterprises, in which professional secrets are handed down from father to son, but concealed from outsiders. Finally, where there is sufficient demand, there are entire villages or castes that specialize in one particular branch of art (the Bena Mpassa, for example, supply the Basonge with masks). People think nothing of undertaking a long journey in order to visit a famous artist.

The artist's social status depends on the particular cultural group to which he belongs. Of especial interest is the position of the smith, to whom, owing to his contact with fire, magic powers are ascribed. He often has the additional function of medicine-man, chief, or maker of magic figures, in which case his wife engages in pottery. The smith is highly respected amongst the negroes of West

Africa and the Bantu south of the Equator, but held in low esteem by the Hamitic peoples of East Africa; indeed, smiths there form an isolated caste, taking wives only from other families engaged in the same craft (cf. p. 94).

At court the wood-carver acquired the highest rank of nobility. As an emblem of the honour bestowed upon him, the Baluba sculptor was allowed to carry an adze decorated with a head; normally, an axe of this type was carried by no one other than the king himself. Amongst the Bayaka carvers had honorary titles conferred upon them.

If a young man shows a certain talent as a carver, he serves an apprenticeship with a well-known sculptor, paying him with gifts. Practice and imitation form the basis of his training. Once he has become independent, he is obliged to set aside part of his earnings for his teacher over a period of several years. Whilst working he has to observe certain rules; the work should not be primarily the expression of his personal imagination, but should follow the principles required by the traditions and conceptions of the community. Only then will it possess power benefiting the whole tribe. Despite these limitations the sculptor manages to find ways and means of instilling subtlety into his work, adding a personal note of his own, and producing an arresting effect upon the beholder. Carving is no trifling matter. A good carver will not take his work light-heartedly; for him the creation of a cult object is a supremely sacred act. Before commencing his work he will undergo some form of ritual cleansing, refrain from all pleasure, and then withdraw into the seclusion of the bush, undisturbed by anyone, so that he may devote himself to his work with complete concentration. Time and again one may hear an artist say that he has to think hard, that his work is laborious, or that he would prefer to be working with his friends in the fields. But then he is captivated by some vision, inspired by some dream, and feels within himself the will to create.

A true vocation, coupled with real devotion to the work in hand, is essential for quality and success. There is always a lurking danger that love and care may yield to routine, and that the chance of rapid financial gain may lead to decadence and weakness, particularly where traditional ways of belief have been exposed to alien influence.

The names of prominent artists are remembered for many years, and the reputation of a work often reflects upon its creator. Thus William Fagg, in his studies of the Yoruba, was not only successful in identifying the style of individual villages, but even in discovering the artists' names. Bamgboye, for example, the carver of magnificent compositions in the manner of Epa masks, was first an Ifa priest, and was later appointed as a teacher at a native art school, whereupon he unfortunately lost much of his original freshness and vitality.

Art at the royal courts   In the areas where the king sits, god-like, upon a throne, surrounding himself with all power and worldly pomp, art ceases to be based on religion. It is no longer sacral, but decorative; instead of fulfilling a higher spiritual purpose, it serves practical needs. The monarch monopolizes it to glorify his own person and deeds (Benin, Dahomey, Bakuba); he orders the erection of imposing halls, and surrounds himself with insignia of his authority: thrones, drums, crowns, sceptres, axes (Plate 56) and tobacco pipes (p. 151). The ruler also assumes complete control of entire branches of art, such as the polishing of beads and the casting of precious metals. The artist lives solely from court patronage, and his ideas and talents have to conform to the wishes of the monarch. Competition develops between guilds of craftsmen, the more talented artists being honoured by the king with the highest decorations. For artistic achievements are highly rated at those courts where the appreciation of beauty develops with refinement of manners, and where the king is able to differentiate between inferior mass products and real works of art characterized by elaborate execution, wealth of ideas and measured rhythm.

V. MATERIALS AND TECHNIQUES

When one considers the laborious and complicated methods which the negro artist is obliged to emploi, his achievements seem all the more admirable. Everything is done patiently by hand, with utter dedication, elaborate craftsmanship and love. He uses the materials at his disposal with consummate skill. Technical exigencies are overcome and turned to decorative effect; difficulties of combination are elegantly bridged. Nothing gives a forced impression, even where motifs applicable to one particular technique have to be adapted to some other material (*e.g.*, plaiting motifs to wood, brass-casting, etc.). The negro appreciates the decorative value of such simple materials as he can find locally, and employs them for trimming and ornamentation. In the forest areas and in the rainy savannah he utilizes vegetable fibres, grains, seeds and ivory, whilst pastoralists have an aptitude for working leather. The negro also constantly uses objects which he obtains from foreign countries by barter, e.g. cowrie-shells from the Indian Ocean, a symbol of fertility and wealth, metals of all kinds, or bright beads, such as have been sold to Africa since ancient times.

Some of the materials employed are evidence of extremely interesting cultural ties, such as the building of clay or mud in the Sudan and the highly developed art of bronze casting at the royal courts, the vertical loom in West Africa and the horizontal man-operated treadle-loom in the Sudan, or the various plaiting techniques of the Hamites and negroes. The arts received a tremendous impulse from the desire of rulers for majestic splendour; the training of entire guilds of craftsmen can be attributed to their patronage. Extensive commercial contact with other lands, by means of the caravan trade across the Sahara and the Sudan, led to the introduction of hitherto unknown techniques and gave a stimulus to fresh impulses.

The choice of particular materials and their diffusion often depend upon traditional religious conceptions, upon the mystic relationship between man and nature. The teeth and horns of strong animals convey power, as does the wood of trees in which spirits reside. The fear of forces unleashed by working the material necessitates compliance with certain rules before commencement of the operation. Abstinence and fasting, sacrifice and prayer — these, more often than not, are the laws that govern the negro's mode of work. When dyeing, he makes an offering, and has his implement blessed by the priest, before each new phase in the work.

WOOD Wood is by far the most popular of the materials which the negro uses. To him it is not dead matter, but remains a living thing throughout the entire process; cutting and chopping cause it pain, and for this the spirit in the tree is begged for forgiveness. This is why we come across so many different rites in connection with the carving of wood. The kind of wood used determines the method of working: in the Sudan carvers work with hardwood to obtain a fairly rough angular surface; the Baule, on the other hand, have a predilection for various kinds of soft wood, which they smoothe and polish with affectionate care. The most frequently used kinds of wood are that from the bombax tree, as well as some similar to ebony and mahogany.

Tools The carver works without using a vice. The tool he employs is an adze, a small axe with an arched blade at right angles to the handle. He holds it by the blade and wields it like a knife with great sleight of hand, bringing out even the finest details. The finishing touches are added by means of a knife, graving tool and chisel. For boring holes, he uses a piece of red-hot iron. The grooved surface of the carving bears signs of heavy blows from the adze; but if the rough edges and incisions are to be smoothed over, the surface is planed and polished with splinters of stone, abrasive leaves, or a sort of primitive plane. Then follow the techniques necessary to protect the green wood from weathering and from the ravages of termites. Many artists polish the carvings with a mixture of soot and grease, or put them for a few days into a mud-bath. Others treat the wood with sap from roots and leaves, or with fine camwood powder. The object is then blackened with the smoke and dust from the hut. It is worn down by handling, and a libation of beer and sacrificial blood serves to bring about the inimitable bronze-coloured patina which gives the old carvings their particular charm. The sculptures are in most cases monoxylous, made out of a single piece of wood, so that the form of the tree remains tangible and recognizable. This requires great artistry. Only in exceptional cases is a large forked branch or something of that kind used to render striding or sitting figures, or figures with expressive gestures. It is rare for movable limbs, lower jaws or ears to be

PLATE 5 — *Chi wara,* once sent out by the Creator to instruct the Bambara in the cultivation of corn; their dance, performed in pairs in the fields, ensures fecundity and power for all. Despite its extremely decorative structure, this buck, of the Minianka-Segu type, suggests the mythical combative antelope. But its proportions can only be properly appreciated if one imagines the carving towering above the head of the dancer, in his fibre costume and red face-mask. *(31½ in.).*
The cotton fabric patterned with fine river mud is a painted symbol of the cosmos (pp. 45, 79). **Mali.** *E. Leuzinger Collection.*

PLATE 6 — Female ancestor, with lip-plug, soliciting rain. The open hand invokes the rain; the other one stops it. The ancient *tellem,* the origin of which is no longer known, are enshrouded in mystery. The Dogon keep them in granaries and place sacrificial vessels before them. Mali. *Rietberg Museum, Zurich (38½ in.).*

PLATE 7 — Ancestor figures, Dogon, highly abstract. That of the couple has ingeniously balanced volumes and intermediary spaces. The force of the vertical line is counter-balanced by the man's arm around the woman's neck, producing a fine relationship between the two figures. The woman replies with a gentle inclination of her head; this barely perceptible asymmetry gives the composition great charm.
As tribal progenitors they possess particular generative power. In their honour an annual festival of the dead is held, with sacrifices and requests for health, fecundity and a rich harvest. If one of the dignitaries of the society dies, his body is left for some time in the grotto sanctuary next to the statues. Mali. *Rietberg Museum, Zurich, Von der Heydt Collection (24¾ and 26¼ in.).*

PLATE 8 — An antelope-like being, non-real, full of grace and elegance, with inlaid seeds glittering against a light blue ground. The Kurumba dancer of the Aribinda region fastens the carving to his head by means of plaiting, particularly at the end of the mourning period, to drive away the souls of the departed from the village. Upper Volta. *Musée de l'Homme, Paris* (27½ in.).

PLATE 9 — Koba antelope, emblem of the Mossi of the Yatenga region. The mask symbolizes an earth and bush spirit, and is employed by the Wango society at funerals and to protect fruit. There is a strange discrepancy between the abstract non-real face of the mask and the superimposed vital Earth Goddess, with her lively button eyes. Upper Volta. *Rietberg Museum, Zurich (42½ in.).*

PLATE 10 — Rare plastic helmet-mask of the *Dō* guardian spirit, Bobo-Fing. The spirit manifest in the masked Dō dancer is held in high esteem; should the mime break the mask, he must make atonement as for a murder, and the mask is ceremonially buried. Upper Volta. *Rietberg Museum, Zurich (15¼ in.).*

PLATE 11 — Buffalo, tribal animal of the Bobo, suggesting power by its eyes, enhanced by concentric rings, by planes bearing lines of tattooing, and by the grandiose curve of the horns. Upper Volta. *Rietberg Museum, Zurich (29½ in.).*

43

PLATE 12 — *Deble*, ritual figure of the Lŏ society, Senufo (Cercle de Korhogo). At initiation, to induce fertility, novices strike the ground, in a slow vibrating rhythm, with this figure, which originally stood upon a pedestal. Everything is designed to promote concentration: the compact monumental form of the Mother Goddess, with her heavy breasts, and the composure and seriousness of her tranquil countenance. Northern Ivory Coast. *Rietberg Museum, Zurich (37½ in.).*

represented, or for a carving to be made from more than one piece. Nails and adhesives, if used at all, serve the purpose of decoration. Painting is found more frequently on masks than on figures. Although monochrome generally prevails, (a white ghost-like colour, for example, indicating the world beyond), gaily adorned masks and figures are no rarity. Decoration is afforded by tattooing in symbolic colours, natural hair, inlaid eyes, skin covering (Ekoi), animal tusks, horns with magical properties, garments made of material and feathers, necklaces and buckles: all these are drawn upon to honour and delight the figures as though they were living beings. Amongst the Yoruba and certain tribes of the Cameroun grasslands figures, masks, thrones and even calabashes are covered with brightly coloured beads. The guardian figures found amongst the Bakota, and the masks of the Bakuba and Marka, are copper- or brass-covered. When the Baule and Ashanti seek a particularly elaborate effect, they affix thin plates of gold to the wood by means of fine gold pins; elsewhere plates of silver of tinfoil are used. As far as the diffusion of wood carvings is concerned, certain differences can be observed, in that the art of the settled negroes of West Africa and the Congo has almost an excess of figure motifs, whereas the pastoral and semi-nomadic peoples of East and South-east Africa, and many negroes of the Old Nigritic culture, adopt simpler and austerer pattern-work in decorating their implements. Gourds, owing to their softness, are worked into vessels of all kinds. In order to obtain a cup-like shape, they are often tied off whilst still growing. The negro incises, scratches or burns various designs into the rind, adapting his motifs (figures and geometric drawings) to harmonize with the form. Particularly famous are the calabashes of Dahomey, with their illustrations of proverbs, as well as the milk containers of certain pastoral tribes (Masai, Fulani, etc.). Precious ivory, initially highly valued as a symbol of power and as a hunting trophy, is elaborately worked by several tribes, despite the primitive tools at their disposal and the extraordinary hardness of the material. Ancient Benin produced real masterpieces: double bangles in open-work, impressive ivory panthers, magnificent masks, and elephant tusks worked in relief. Even recently jewellery, bells, hair-pins, trumpets, handles of fly-whisks, etc., made of ivory have been produced in West Africa. The masks of the Bapende and the Balega, and also the charms of the Bahuana, have a note of distinction about them. The Baluba make pretty mascot figures

CALABASHES

BONE AND IVORY

of ivory or hippopotamus tusk, deftly taking advantage of the slight curve of the tusk. In the Lower Congo even the large molars of the elephant are utilized in this way. Many of these mascots have obtained a warm reddish-brown hue through contact with the skin and their having been rubbed with *tukula* and oil. The ivory objects manufactured for export and adapted to European tastes are very far removed from these old masterpieces of ivory work.

STONE Stone is not commonly used in negro Africa. It is rare both in figure sculpture and in architecture (except for Zimbabwe, Kilwa, and a few girdle walls and foundations of store-houses). But the few relics that remain cast much light upon the past history of Africa. The magnificent find by the river Welle stands out as unique (Plate 2); and the splendid stone finds of Ife may be regarded as solitary witnesses to the existence of the ancient kingdoms. The stone figures of Esie in Nigeria and of the Lower Congo, as well as the megaliths of southern Ethiopia, are likewise isolated phenomena. Soft steatite (soapstone), which can be worked more easily, was used to make the eagles and stone bowls of Zimbabwe and the figures of the Mende and Kissi country.

CLAY MODELLING Clay modelling would provide a rewarding theme for study. It has inspired spontaneous creative activity amongst negroes from almost all parts of the continent, and runs through the whole history of African art from the earliest stages (Fig. 3) up to the evolution of the most mature classical style. But as the clay was only inadequately baked, African clay sculptures are very delicate, and are rarely to be found in museums — and then usually in fragments. The finds that have survived include those of Nok, the Sao in the Chad area, Mopti in the bend of the Niger, Luzira in Uganda, Kaffa, Leopoldville, and others, but above all the magnificent terracotta heads of Ife. Today we also find numerous reliefs in clay on walls of houses, mud reliefs (Yao), figures of animals, roof-top ornaments, fetishes, pipes, and whole groups of figures in clay; they are, however, generally of no artistic value. The only ones at all remarkable are the sepulchral figures of the Krinjabo and Ashanti kingdoms, the tobacco pipes from the Cameroun grasslands, the figure-shaped vessels of the Bakongo, Mangbetu and Kaluena, and the figures made by the Ibo and Ekoi. The Ashanti clay pipes are decorated with proverb subjects.

Modelling in clay, like pottery in general, is in the hands of the womenfolk, with the wife of the smith often acting as a potter.

The pipes from the Cameroun grasslands may be regarded as coming within the sphere of carving, because here the men cut the figures out of the clay while it is still damp. Throughout Africa children are in the habit of modelling toy figures in clay.

Earthenware vessels are moulded freely by hand, without recourse to the potter's wheel. Although the rotary disc has long been known in Egypt and North Africa, it has never been adopted by the negroes, except by the Hausa and Bakongo. The device used by the negro potter as a base is the broken-off neck of a vessel. She moulds the vessel either by scooping out a lump of clay or by rhythmically building up coils of clay, which are then made smooth. The primitive coiling technique is still to be met with today: a piece of rope is rolled down the damp clay, leaving a regular pattern. Some women potters press a plaited roulette on to the clay, and cut in linear patterns with pointed sticks, completing the vessel by adding handles, hooks and knobs. The pots are then put into the shade for several days in order to dry, and finally placed on a layer of wood, covered with grass, and baked for a short time. The storage-pots used by the Baya, Bechuana, Hausa and those living on the Benue are painted red and black. On the Lower Congo the menfolk act as potters. Beeswax is used comparatively rarely for modelling dolls and ornamenting masks (western Sudan, East Africa, Bajokwe).

POTTERY

Wax

In contrast to most primitive peoples of the South Seas, who never advanced beyond the Stone Age, Africans have been familiar with metals since ancient times; indeed, iron was known before bronze. In approximately 400 B.C. iron appears to have been introduced to West Africa from the kingdom of Napata, situated along the central reaches of the Nile; for iron has been found in the Nok culture in northern Nigeria. In the course of time it superseded blades of polished stone. Lances are made of iron, and are furnished with barbs, torsades, and open-work patterns, as are also ceremonial axes and throwing-knives (Fig. 117). As far as figures are concerned, mention must be made of the monumental statuary of Dahomey, the statuettes of the Bakuba, and certain animal figures in East Africa. Woto, the mythical king of the Bakuba, is said, according to Torday's information, to have introduced iron into his kingdom about the 6th century A.D.

METAL

Iron

Almost everywhere in Africa iron was smelted before the Arabs, Indians and others embarked upon the practice of importing it

Cast brass

on a large scale from Europe and the Orient. (On the status of smiths, cf. p. 32).

African bronze, and all other alloys including brass, which attained great importance in the kingdoms of the Guinea coast, contain little tin, but more zinc and lead; for this reason it is best to call them 'cast brass'.

The two most important techniques are solid casting, a process in which a hollow, scooped out of the clayey or sandy soil, serves as the mould, and the process of melting out the wax, the *cire-perdue*, or 'waste mould', process. The most famous cast brass works are those made by the cire-perdue process. First of all the figure is moulded in wax, or sometimes, in the case of large objects, around a core of clay. Ornamentation is then applied, in the form of dots and lines of wax, and carefully moulded. Upon this wax model a coating of clay is applied; it is then heated, so that the wax melts and runs out (cire-perdue), and the molten metal is poured into the place where the wax had previously been. Finally, the core of clay is broken up (*i.e.*, 'lost form'), so that every cast remains in a single piece. Further finish is obtained by polishing, engraving, filing and punching (cf. p.129). Other techniques are: embossing and hammering, inlaying metal into other materials, tin tarsia (on the Suaheli coast), the art of damascening copper and brass, and finally the braiding of handles and whole implements with copper and brass wires (South-east Africa). The complicated waste mould technique reached negro Africa by at least two routes: straight across the Sahara (with motifs of the Sards, Etruscans, and others), and across the Sudan from the Nile valley. In the ancient kingdom of Ghana brass casting was known already at an early date: bronze figures from the Gundam area are described by al-Bakrî, writing in the 11th century. His account is corroborated by finds in tumuli of the legendary Killi, as well as in the ruins of Lobi, dating from a period between the 9th and 11th centuries.

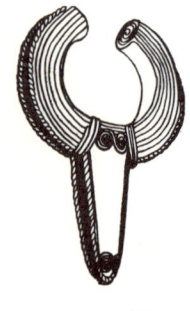

The cultural stream from the ancient Orient flowed through the Sudan as far as the Chad area, watered the kingdoms of Yoruba and Benin, and later those of Sao, Jukun and Nupe, finally reaching the courts of the sultans of Tikar, Bamum and Bagam in the Cameroun grasslands (Fig. 1). The embossed and punched metal work of the Nupe bears ornamentation of plant motifs in a florid and markedly Byzantine-Oriental style. The masterpieces of brass casting will be examined in detail in the chapters on Nigeria and Ashanti (Fig. 2, a Kran shackle-like anklet).

Silver Silver is mainly worked into jewellery, particularly in Mohammedan countries, where gold had been prohibited by the Prophet, and in those areas subject to Arab influence. In those parts we find hinged silver anklets (Fig. 138) and fine objects in Lamu work (gold-foil, rosettes, dotted lines and tendrils, inlaid in silver). As material the silversmiths simply used melted-down coins, such as the Maria Theresa thaler, hammered out and drawn out into a wire. The alligator's head worn as a chest decoration by chiefs of the Togo hinterland has a curious foreign appearance (Fig. 57).

Gold Little has survived of the fabulous gold riches once possessed by the ancient kingdoms of Ghana, Melli and Darfur, or of the gold ornaments of the king of Ashanti and the kingdom of Monomotapa. Since gold was only appreciated for its material value, and little attention was paid to its artistic worth, gold objects were melted down again. For this reason the magnificent Ashanti gold mask, one of the treasures of King Kofi Kakari (Plate 20), is almost the sole surviving evidence of a splendour and ostentation that vanished long ago. On festive occasions the ruler of Ashanti wore large embossed and hammered gold breast-plates; his garments, and the hilts and sheaths of the ceremonial weapons he carried, were ornamented with gold; and his throne was decorated with golden bosses, rosettes and stars. Many of these splendid ornaments were merely covered with gold-foil hammered fine, rather in the manner employed today by the Baule to cover their ceremonial implements. Until recent times the Ashanti and Anyi still used the cire-perdue technique for casting small gold figures and masks.

The filigree technique — motifs in Spanish-Moorish style from North and North-west Africa — did not, of course, penetrate far beyond the Sahara — perhaps as far as Senegal, the western Sudan and the Ivory Coast. In general objects in gold are only to be found within the range of the highly developed neo-Sudanese cultures. The negroes preferred copper, iron and brass to gold.

LEATHER Leather is the material of pastoralists and hunters. Tanning is in general a simple process: the hide is merely treated with a little fat to retain its suppleness. Tanning with vegetable matter was only introduced in highly developed cultures. The eastern Hamites joined together pieces of hide and leather in mosaic form. The Masai paint harmoniously proportioned abstract symbols on their leather shields, whilst their womenfolk wear magnificent leather coats adorned with fringes, beads and cowrie-shells.

Leather-working has become a highly skilled art in the western Sudan (Mandingo, Hausa, Fulani), where the lavish ornamentation can be traced back to Berber and Islamic influence. Their great rivals in this kind of work are the Tuareg of the Sahara.

Of the various ways of ornamenting leather, the following may be mentioned: painting, incising, punching, pressing and plaiting, etching, embroidering and *appliqué* work. The dyes are obtained from seeds, roots, and ferric oxide, and give the leather a warm red or reddish-brown hue; green, the colour associated with Mohammedan ritual, is sometimes added. The Hausa and Mandingo travel through all parts of the Sudan and the Guinea states, trading in leather bags, cushions, harness, swords, ornamental daggers, powder-horns, quivers, hats and shoes.

BASKET-WORK Over extensive areas of Africa men spend their spare time plaiting. Especially during the dry season, when work in the fields ceases, young and old can be found sitting together in the village marketplace, passing the time in this way. They use knives and combs, and their teeth and toes as well.

The material for plaiting is obtained in the steppe, in the form of fibres of leaves, stalks of banana plants, date and raffia palms and papyrus, as well as sorghum and other grasses. In forest areas pandanus and lianas are more generally used.

In West Africa twilling prevails, whilst the coiling technique is probably of Hamitic origin. Both of them offer a variety of forms and patterns, used in baskets, bowls, sieves, lids, winnowing shovels, bags, shields and quivers. In addition to these objects one finds plaited mats hung from walls, benches to rest on, and even cushions and ornaments. As far as the patterns are concerned, the craftsman is generally content to use alternately first black and then uncoloured material, thereby producing a geometric design (Fig. 135).

WEAVING Weaving, which developed out of the more intricate methods of plaiting mats, is performed on a simple hand-loom. In West Africa the womenfolk weave on a vertical loom; but in the neo-Sudanese region it is the men who attend to the looms, which are horizontal man-operated treadle looms for weaving narrow bands, the materials woven being chiefly cotton and wool. Similarly, it is the men who join together the narrow lengths of fabric to form large pieces of cloth, sew the tobes and tunics, and

even add the embroidery. The tobes of Bornu in the Chad region, for example, are cut like shirts and lavishly decorated with silk embroidery (cf. p. 76). The Ashanti used to unravel Dutch silk fabrics and re-weave them according to patterns of their own.
Dahomey is well-known for its superb *appliqué* work, which was reserved exclusively for the king. Ingenious designs in open-work were formerly produced in West Africa, and the Yoruba wove fabrics with a plush effect, rather similar to those made by weavers in the Kasai-Sankuru area of the Congo, in the early Napata kingdom, and in Egypt. On the Guinea coast and in the Ekoi area fabrics were produced of cotton and raffia.

If the pattern is not woven in, the whole length of material is dyed. The negro is familiar with several methods of dyeing:

Dyeing technique

1. The direct method: fabric and bark cloth are painted or stamped (Ashanti, Baganda, Mangbetu).
2. The corroding method: the Bambara, for example, dye their cotton fabrics yellow with sap obtained from roots. On this yellow ground they paint ornaments and arabesques with mud, coating them with a highly corrosive soap. The fabric is then treated once more with mud, and, when the corrosive has taken sufficient effect, soaked in water several times, so that the light-coloured ornamentation stands out distinctly against the darker ground (Fig. 5).
3. The 'resist' method ("stopping out" process): this comprises the *tritik* and *plangi* processes. The material has to be folded or tied up in small flaps and bunches; alternatively, small stones and seeds are sewn, or small pieces of cane or stencils placed, on to the material. When this has been done, it is dyed, generally with indigo, and spread out to dry. It is only then that the knots are untied, and the small stones and pieces of cane removed, revealing most attractive patterns (Baule [Plate 18], the Cameroun grasslands, southern Nigeria). More rarely we find other kinds of 'resist' techniques being employed, such as the *ikat* and *batik* techniques (Soninke, Yoruba); in the latter case the material is covered with various sorts of paste.

Unfortunately, cheap imported cotton prints offer fierce competition to the locally-dyed fabrics, particularly since the manufacturers of the imported fabrics often succeed in making deceptively close imitations of local designs, in order to attract native buyers. Today native fabrics are chiefly found at traditional tribal ceremonies.

Colours It is clear why the negro nearly always relies on red, white and black dyes. These are colours of mineral, animal and vegetable origin which are easily accessible to him. Moreover, they evoke definite associations in his mind, since black, white and red are symbolic colours. The formulas for obtaining the dyes are often secret, known only to certain families. White, obtained from lime and plant ash, suggests supernatural forces, danger and death. It is therefore the colour used to daub children at the age when they are attending the bush school, sick people, and masks which represent ghosts. In western Sudan and amongst the Yoruba white is symbolic of purity and divinity.

Black, obtained from soot, coal, etc., often symbolizes the earth. Red implies energy, vitality and joy; it appears in the fire of the smithy and has magical properties. Red colouring-matter obtained from camwood is used by tribes in the Congo and elsewhere to paint themselves at festivals of rejoicing; and red is used to paint young men when they undergo initiation, to show that they are entering into the adult world. Statues are treated with camwood powder, *tukula,* for camwood is a protection against termites.

Indigo blue, as well as green and yellow, are characteristic of highly developed cultures.

Painting the face with colour, in rings, dabs and streaks, is in many places a substitute for wooden masks, and perhaps even antedates their use.

VI. FORM

Sculpture is undoubtedly the finest manifestation of negro art. This is not simply a happy coincidence, but the climax and consummation of a meaningful trend of development. Most negroes would find it impossible to envisage a world without sculpture. For it not only mirrors their spiritual outlook, their relationship to their gods, but is also indispensable for their social life.

Sculpture includes ancestor figures, masks, fetishes and ritual implements, as well as secular figures, animal carvings and utensils. The significance of these has already been discussed in the chapters on religion and sociology. As regards the materials employed, it is sufficient to recall that the negro chiefly uses wood, then clay, ivory and metal, but only rarely stone; for masks he also employs plaited materials, bark, leather and gourds, as the occasion arises. This predilection for wood has led to the deplorable fact that it is rare to find sculptures that are more than a hundred years old; for wood, even if it is very hard, cannot stand up for any length of time to atmospheric changes or to the ravages of termites. According to the accounts of early Arab travellers, ancestor figures existed already in the ancient kingdom of Ghana.

Let us now turn to the question of form, which leads us to our central theme. It is important to bear in mind from the start that, so far as sacral sculpture is concerned, the negro artist experiences an impulse and desire to give concrete form to an abstract idea. To his mind art serves to make the invisible visible. What prompts and inspires him is a vision which cannot be expressed purely in the naturalistic forms familiar to him from his environment. In order to give this vision form, he co-ordinates both naturalistic and abstract, cubist and expressionist elements into an entirely new unity. It must be emphasized once again that for the negro art serves first and foremost a religious purpose; he feels it would be presumptuous for him to fashion a sculpture in human form. It is only in the field of secular art, when rendering heroes and god-like kings, that he grapples with a subject in an effort to reproduce its natural elements and proportions in a manner true to life.

Margin notes: SCULPTURE; *Content*

Form and expression

The question now arises: how does the negro succeed in rendering artistically such abstract ideas as divine power and majesty, sublimity, repose or death?

Power is suggested by large heads, sparkling eyes, swollen abdomens and voluminous breasts. It is implied by the horns of buffaloes, rams and antelopes and the snouts of crocodiles. In order to express the idea of power, the artist utilizes all these elements, enhancing their effect by the form: by rigid contours, and by the dynamism of clearly broken-up planes and cubes with a rhythm all their own. Power is also symbolized by angular limbs, crowns pressing down heavily upon the head of the wearer, sturdy legs, a pronounced depression under a bulging forehead, and a heavily accentuated navel.

Idea of the transcendental

The idea of the transcendental, of supernatural majesty manifested in noble dignity, tranquillity and composure, can be expressed by static poise, symmetry and frontality: principles which negro art adheres to with consummate skill. The impression of repose is conveyed by the balanced harmony of all elements. The central axis sustains and focusses attention. A tranquil posture, a tangible concentration, subtle transitions between different parts of the body, restrained gestures and the dark bronze tone of the patina — all these are designed to give an impression of solemnity which evokes a feeling of awe in the beholder. From the ancestor's countenance there radiates an aura of serenity, yet in his narrow eye-slits there is a flash of his living presence, seen also in the formation of the cheeks, the shape of the nostrils and the fulness of the lips. The light from his eyes glides over clearly-defined curves, loses itself in the adze marks on the surface, and is reflected in the brown tone of the skin. The silence of death, the bridge to the world beyond, is rendered by forms derived from the human skull, and is represented with rigid austerity by the hollow eyes, sunken cheeks and pointed chin. In some cases inlaid eyes evoke an otherworldly impression of restrained vitality.

The consummate skill with which the negro sets about his work shows that he reacts as intensely as we do to the capacity of various forms to express emotional qualities. In appreciating negro art, we must be prepared to forget for a moment the Greek ideal, and try to understand an entirely different means of expression that is utterly divorced from naturalism. However sympathetic and unprejudiced we may be, it will always be difficult for us to interpret.

But it must be observed in this connection that the great 20th-century European artists have notably facilitated our approach to the world of negro art. By their rendering of abstract ideas Maillol and Henry Moore, the Fauvists and Cubists, Kandinsky, Klee and Picasso (the last-named himself greatly inspired by negro art) have opened up new vistas before us. If we try to see things through their eyes, it will be easier for us to understand the spirit of negro art.

Structure

It would be inaccurate to assert that the negro perceives forms only from the standpoint of their capacity as mediums of expression. It must be added that he systematically fuses them and relates them to one another as cubist elements. As he cuts the trunk of the tree, he sees in his mind's eye the dynamic effect of his figure as a whole. He does not work so spontaneously as is generally assumed. His successful correlation of curves, planes and cubes, of depressions and elevations, is not simply a matter of chance. Whilst he is working, the artist turns his block of wood round and round, examining it from all angles with an eye to true three-dimensional form. He knows that a bold curve calls for some contrary effect and that duplications and concentric circles produce definite focal points. He has long been aware of the importance of shadow, and plays off delicately designed portions against smooth and voluminous planes. Where ornamental cicatrices occur, he treats them in such a manner that their aesthetic and symbolic effects coincide. He feels that much of the charm of the work will depend on the nature of the material and the manner in which he plies his tool; he is also aware that, for all his keen observation of nature, he must exclude a certain amount in order to intensify the effect he is seeking. If African sculpture gives such a monumental impression, despite the fact that statues are seldom more than three feet high, this is undoubtedly due to the artist's skill in economizing and simplifying detail, which leads to greater concentration of form.

It is the negro's pronounced sense of rhythm, so evident in his dances and music, that gives his sculpture life, dynamic force and tension.

It would be wrong to think that the repose and harmony of negro sculpture derive from the fact that it is carved out of a solid block of wood. The wealth of materials at the artist's disposal affords him plenty of scope for work along different lines, as is shown by his group compositions in clay and cast brass. To obtain a highly differentiated form from a solid block of wood can under certain circumstances be more difficult than carving a figure with detached arms (Dahomey, Ekoi) or equipping a mask with hinges (Ibibio, Kran). Group compositions that are monoxylous (*i.e.*, made in one piece) are chiefly to be found in southern Nigeria, the Cameroun grasslands and the southern Congo. Often they represent mounted men; the mother-and-child motif probably appears most commonly amongst the Yoruba, Afo, Bakongo and Bena Lulua, of all the tribes in Africa. Asymmetrical arrangement is also to be found sporadically over the entire continent.

In negro art figures are rendered seated upon a stool or throne less frequently than they are rendered standing. The seated figures are portrayed with their legs crossed, squatting, or resting their elbows upon their knees. Kneeling expresses the reposed posture of women, or can occasionally denote reverence and devotion. The compact form is often broken by arms and hands, making offerings or stretching out towards the heavens with expressive gestures. They support the heavy head, are clasped under the chin, or touch the beard.

Proportion When modelling a figure, the negro is guided by the particular importance possessed by the various parts of the body, whether the proportion corresponds to anatomical truth or not. We have already seen why, in his sculpture, he accentuates the head, eyes, genitals and navel: these are parts of the body associated with certain supernatural forces. We are thus dealing with eccentric proportions, which one could call 'proportions of significance'. This ensures that all the essential elements are placed in correct relationship to one another. Everything that incorporates an idea, everything that serves an aesthetic function and makes for balance, is accentuated and treated especially elaborately. With his need for symmetry and order, the negro prefers to follow the vertical median axis, which he intersects at certain intervals with horizontal ones. His sense of harmony often leads him to seek the golden mean.

In order to intensify the effect of a figure, or to enhance the power of expression of a mask, the artist utilizes most ingenious forms. The two-faced Janus head is to be found in nearly all lands of the Guinea coast and the Congo; masks with four, or even six, faces (Mende, Yoruba, Pangwe, Ekoi, Baluba) and two noses (Picasso!) appear less often. Whether the trunk-shaped, *retroussé* nose of the Bayaka figure has some spiritual association, or is merely prompted by a playful whim on the artist's part, we unfortunately do not know.

The negro's good taste is shown by experiments conducted with some men of the Dan and Balega tribes. When a number of different masks were put before them for their opinion, they selected without hesitation those that seemed to European eyes the most beautiful and perfect specimens.

Is negro art primitive? No — if the word 'primitive' is understood to mean something crude, barbaric and contemptible. Yes — if by 'primitive' we mean something honorable, as the term is applied, for instance, to the Fauvists in European painting.

Primitive and 'primary'

Anyone who watches a negro artist at work, sees his concentration, methodical approach and sure sense of style; anyone who perceives his striving for beauty and expression, and his talent for grasping essentials, will never dare to apply the term 'primitive' in the sense of backward, unskilled or crude. Just as little can negro art be considered naïve; for no one is naïve who starts by thinking out his work in such a deliberate and masterly fashion.[1] All that we can say is that it is primitive as regards level of technique. But how great have been the achievements of the African with his 'backward' media! His costly works in cast brass and gold bear no trace of the difficulties involved in the cire-perdue process. His achievements in pottery are so outstanding that it is easy to forget that he works without a potter's wheel. A simple adze is no impediment to success in expressing his ideas in sculptural form. Primitive? What an inadequate label for an artist who not only overcomes adverse circumstances, but makes use of them to enhance his artistic potentialities.

However, the cognate term 'primary' (*primär*), coined by Felix Speiser with regard to Melanesian art, can be accepted without hesitation as applicable to the early stages of all art, including that of Africa — to the earliest arrangement of confused scribblings (Plate 3) and crude, fumbling attempts to express an abstract idea in lapidary form without giving it specific features. The primary style, homogeneous and as yet little differentiated, is the style adopted by all peoples in their first stages of artistic development. An artist who had not yet advanced beyond the primary style, and who tried his hand at sculpture, was content to suggest face, limbs and bodily posture in a rudimentary and clumsy manner. But these earliest examples of man's creative volition are so spontaneous that they often have great charm (Fig. 3, Piri earthenware jug, northern Nigeria, and Fig. 134).

Style Certain tribes, and even whole groups of peoples, have developed unmistakable styles of their own: a product of their concept of the world and their personality, fostered by impulses from without and inspired by the vision of the individual artist. But the artist's range of ideas is limited by his environment, and by tribal myths which are not exclusive to him alone, but belong to the whole community. Once a sculptural form has been evolved, and has become established in the community as a power-charged work, it can hold its own for centuries. Naturally, it will be repeatedly modified, simplified and diversified, without forfeiting any of its essential characteristics. The sculpture now becomes inseparable from a certain style. As long as his concept of the world remains intact, the negro always remains deeply attached to his symbols, regarding them as infallible, never failing to exert their due effect. The pair of small *ibeji* figures of the Yoruba, which found their way into the British Museum in 1854, can hardly be distinguished from the innumerable versions made of them in our own day. And yet William Fagg has succeeded in establishing the individual variant form of each region in the Yoruba lands. The Dogon use in their ceremonies some eighty different types of mask for each of forty dance-steps: eighty different masks, all in the same style (for variations on a single theme, cf. also Figs. 15—19, antelope superstructures on dance costumes worn by the Bambara).

Each style is, of course, the product of long-standing tradition and continuous practice, and is firmly established; yet to some extent it is subject to the action of time, engendered by extraneous influences, and to the artist's own inner development.

Some ethnologists were tempted, whenever they came across some African style characterized by particular clarity and consistency, to trace the cultural impulses concerned — for, they reasoned, this might well reveal extremely interesting parallels. The inference is that all major areas of African sculpture at some time came into contact with the highly-developed cultures of the Mediterranean and the ancient Orient, in particular that of the Nile valley. But the style that eventually crystallized out of the clash between old and new, between native and alien influences, acquiring unity in the hands of some individual artist, reached its climax in the development of a style unique to one particular community —

FIG. 3

often, indeed, in a form of expression quite distinct from neighbouring styles, which from our own vantage-point it is difficult to assess.

All attempts to explain the diffusion of negro art by reference to some ingenious scheme of classification based on pairs of concepts, such as concave and convex, naturalistic and abstract, classical and pre-classical, pole sculpture and round sculpture, break down in the light of the actual situation prevailing in Africa today. A land which has developed about one thousand different styles cannot be compressed so easily within the rigid framework of a catalogue. Whoever takes upon himself the task of tracing back specific cultures and drawing parallels between them will soon discover that he is on the wrong track, for he may chance to find in the very next village a style which completely contradicts his earlier observations.

African sculpture is in general statically and symmetrically posed. The contours of the tree-trunk are always perceptible, and serve to underline the compactness and austerity of the figure. Both types, pole sculpture and round sculpture, are to be found in a vast number of variants.

The chief centres of pole sculpture and of cubist style are in the western Sudan, amongst the Dogon, Bambara and Bobo; on the Guinea coast, amongst the Baga, Kran and Toma, Ijo, Oron-Ibibio and Mama; in Cameroun, amongst the Yabassi; in Gabon and the Congo Republic, amongst the Bakwele, Bakota and Bateke; in the Congo, amongst the Basonge, Balega and Ababua. Pole sculpture is also to be found in areas of East and South-east Africa, with the variants general throughout the continent (Map p. 216).

Round sculpture, on the contrary, is more naturalistic, gentle and organic, and gives the impression of flesh over the bone structure. It is to be found especially in Sierra Leone and on the Ivory and Gold Coasts; in Dahomey, Ife and Benin, amongst most Yoruba, Ibibio, Ekoi, in the Cameroun grasslands, and almost everywhere in the western and southern Congo, particularly amongst the Bakongo, Bajokwe and Baluba, and — quite unexpectedly — among the Makonde in the east.

Pole sculpture and round sculpture are found together among the Bidyugo, Senufo, Dan, Pangwe, eastern Baluba and Makonde, where they fuse and form a new unity.

Naturalistic and abstract

How is it to be explained that there is such a wide swing of the pendulum between these two poles, 'abstract' and 'naturalistic', in the various style regions of Africa, and that naturalistic and abstract forms frequently blend with one another? This cannot be accounted for either by racial or environmental factors, and still less by extraneous influence; otherwise it would not be possible for a single tribe to treat statues in a naturalistic as well as in an abstract manner — both styles, indeed, sometimes being present in the same figure.

Hermann Baumann points to the connection between the matriarchal Bantu and round sculpture, and between the partriarchal Old Nigritians and pole sculpture. William Fagg suggests that Islam tends to promote the abstract. But as we know that one tribe can employ both styles, the question arises whether the degree of abstraction does not depend to a considerable extent upon the function, in which case, however, the factors mentioned also come into the picture.

Abstract ideas and spiritual beings are rendered in the purest and most convincing manner in the cubist form, obtained by anonymous means, which is all spirit. The naturalistic form is more earth-bound, more anatomical, more personal. It is thus truly fascinating to observe, in the case of naturalistic figures, how completely they fulfil their purpose, to portray a human being. This is seen most impressively in the commemorative heads of Ife; for instance, in the magnificent, anatomically correct, but sublime portrayal of the almighty priest-king, symbolic of the glorification of a sacrosanct ruler. Such sculpture is also to be found in Benin, in Cameroun and amongst the Bakuba; and the Ashanti gold mask (Plate 20) is likewise an image of a particular individual, probably of a conquered enemy.

In the Lower Congo it is the custom to erect individual sepulchral monuments, the naturalism of which may be due to European influence. It is easy to understand that in matriarchal districts, where female fertility is closely associated with the prosperity of family and fields, an attempt should be made to render the Earth Mother in a realistic manner. The same factor could account for the realism of the Senufo ritual figure (Plate 12), found in a region where art is usually treated in a strictly abstract manner. The Baule also produce portraits as well as ancestor figures, and for this reason have a certain tendency towards realism. Fetishes,

PLATE 13 — 'Fire-spitter', a Senufo mask, worn horizontally at a slant. In the Gbon cult, when all those not initiated have disappeared into their huts, it appears to drive away witches and devourers of souls, followed by the priest, disguised in a mask and a raffia costume, and carrying a whip; to the noise of horns, imitating the bellowing of a bull, he performs mighty leaps and acrobatic feats; with the aid of a burning tinder, sparks of fire are emitted by the dancer through the jaws of the mask. Northern Ivory Coast. *Rietberg Museum Zurich (32¾ in.).*

PLATE 14a — Baga shoulder mask, typifying a young girl. The lower part should be covered by a raffia garment. When this spirit roams through the bush, the tiny head with its shiny copper eyes towering high above all human beings, it gives a fascinating and weird impression. Guinea. *Rietberg Museum, Zurich* (25¼ in.).

PLATE 14b — A *nimba* statue, representing fertility. The guardian of Baga villages, it stands at cross-roads in a hut concealed under large trees; it gives special protection to pregnant women. Characteristic is the highly abstract head with crooked nose, representing the supernatural power of fertility. Guinea. *Rietberg Museum, Zurich* (24 in.).

PLATE 15 — Banda mask, Baga, representing a high rank in the Simo secret society, and feared accordingly. It is worn on the head, horizontally and at a slant. At its approach all those not initiated flee horror-struck into their huts for protection. Abstract human facial features, crocodile teeth, antelope horns and ears, decorative spirals and other motifs are combined to form an impressive and imaginative work. Guinea. *Rietberg Museum, Zurich (4 ft. 8 in.).*

PLATE 16 — Mother mask, Dan. Its general appearance, on stilts and in a flowing garment of cloth, is one of majesty. It settles strife and protects the newly-born. The beauty of the mask lies in its naturalistic form, sensitively perceived but greatly simplified. With its distinct symmetry and dark colouring, it radiates an aura of calm. Ivory Coast. *Ethnological Collection, Zurich (9¾ in.).*

PLATE 17 — Two Baule ancestor figures with decorative *coiffure* and tattooing; arms carved on to the body, clearly indicated. The character of the dignitary portrayed is rendered in a comprehensive manner. The well-proportioned ointment-pot is said to be the work of a long-deceased artist of high repute; the Baule were loath to part with it. Ingenuity is shown in the gradual upward movement and the way in which the smooth intermediate part enhances the significance of the head. Ivory Coast. *Rietberg Museum, Zurich, E. Leuzinger Collection.* Figure on right 13¾ in.; figure in centre 15¾ in., and ointment-pot 9¾ in.

PLATE 18 — The *guli* (buffalo) is transformed by the Baule into a non-real being by highly abstract treatment. It is *Kakagye,* the spirit of the dead, who resides in the huge mask, worn diagonally on the crown of the head (cf. Fig. 44). At night, to the weird sound of horns, it devours witches and demons; it also gives protection against bullets. The sight of one is fatal to a woman. Ivory Coast. *E. Leuzinger Collection (28¾ in.).*
The indigo-dyed cotton fabrics can frequently still be seen in isolated Baule villages (cf. p. 51). *Ethnological Collection, Zurich (3 ft. 8½ in. × 5 ft. 3 in.).*

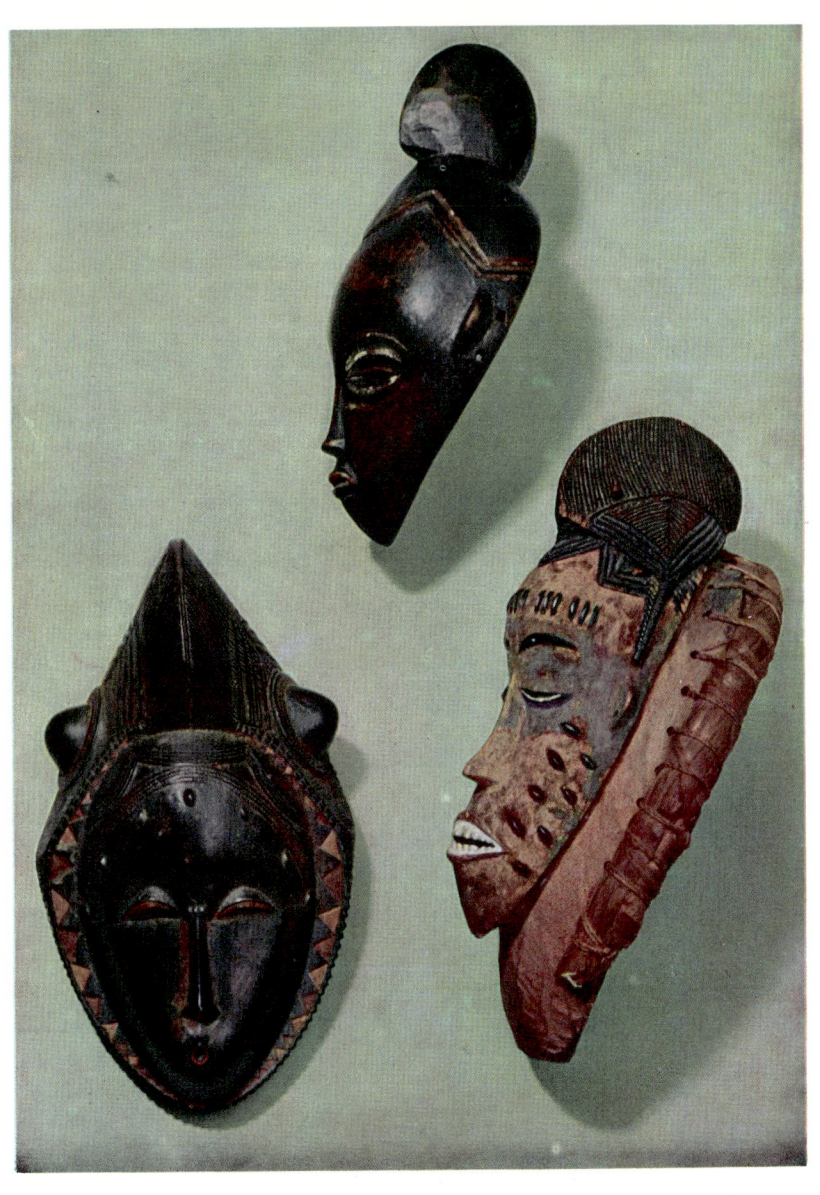

PLATE 19 — Guro and Baule masks, used for magical practices and at funerals of members of the secret societies. The actual facial features of the negro are refined to such an extent that they seem otherworldly. Elegance is combined with harmony. Both Guro masks (top, right) have a zigzag hair-fringe, the high forehead and the delicate ridge of the slightly upturned nose forming a fine continuous curve. The somewhat flatter mask (left) with its decorative serrated border is characteristic of the Yaure, a sub-tribe of the Baule; it resembles the Guro masks in many ways. The Baule say that emotion is expressed solely by the mouth: a pout conveys sadness; conversely, when the teeth are visible, this conveys cheerfulness. Ivory Coast. *All in the Rietberg Museum, Zurich, the two last-mentioned in the Von der Heydt Collection (Top: 12¼ in.; left, Yaure: 12½ in.; right: 13¾ in.).*

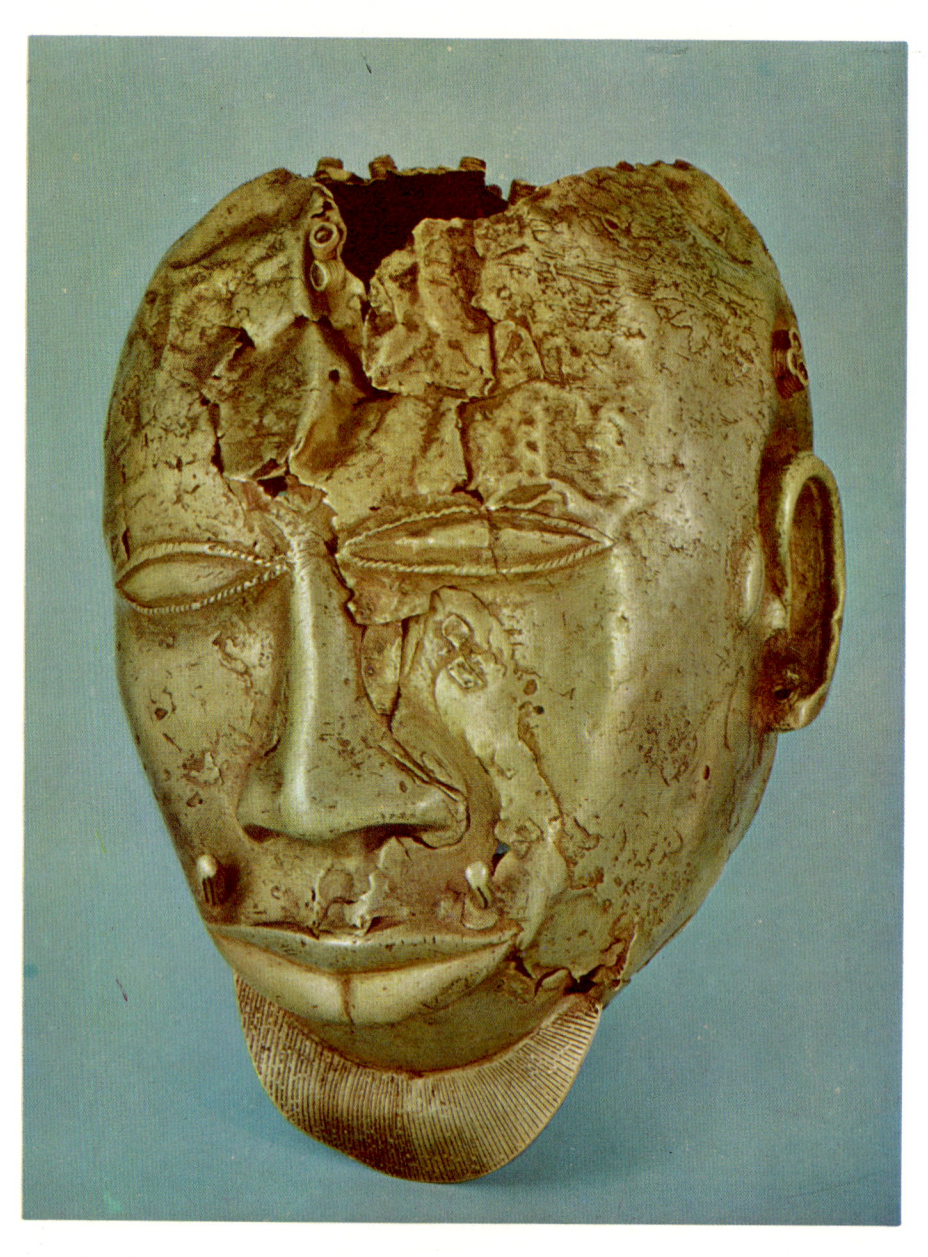

PLATE 20 — Magnificent mask, cast in pure gold, weighing 3 lb. 5 oz., two thirds life-size, from the treasure of the Ashanti king Kofi Kakari: the expressive countenance of a strong-willed ruler. A portrait-like naturalism is always sought in the rendering of earthly personages. The ring below the beard suggests that it may be a trophy mask of a vanquished enemy, fastened by the victor to his throne. Ghana. *Wallace Collection, London (6⅞ in.).*

which the negro envisages as actively working, are often realistic in form, with threatening gestures and eyes wide open.

In numerous sculptures we are struck by the contrast between head and torso, in that the head, the seat of spiritual force, is elaborately fashioned and realistic, whereas the torso remains in a crude primitive form; it is almost as though artistic tension had slackened off after the head had been carved. But in reality this is simply a matter of the torso having a different function to fulfil: it complies with the laws of statics, and bears an abundance of distinguishing marks.

The most striking characteristic of a cubist figure is probably the strongly accentuated bulging forehead, topped either by striated hair or by a hat-like superstructure. This is the abode of the spirit. The forehead overshadows the eye-sockets, which are inset very deeply, in order to direct attention inwards. The eyes themselves are sharply defined and shaped like coffee-beans, or as half-ovals, squares, cones, tubes or slits, depending on the function they fulfil.

Pole sculpture

It is remarkable how, in different districts often situated far apart from one another, abstract treatment of the face led to a heart-shaped form (Figs. 25, 93), with high-arched eyebrows, joined at the bridge of the nose, sweeping outward across the temples and cheeks, and meeting at the mouth. In addition to this, the part of the cheeks thus encompassed is often painted white, concentrating attention upon the eyes, as the essential feature. Unlike their sculptures, negroes in actual fact possess prominent cheek-bones and rather protruding eyes; the deep-set eyes which distinguish many of their sculptures therefore serve the purely formal function of enhancing the introversion of the work.

The nose, as a rhythm-giving element, is represented as a line, arrow, triangle or sharp curve, and the mouth as a slit, square, tube or disc, or else is indicated by being given a different colour. With some sculptures the chin juts forward boldly to the point of prognathism; but with others the profile line is either straight or truncated horizontally below the mouth; the beard is cube-shaped. The eyes are rendered as solid blocks, rings or half-ovals, or else are circular or crescent-shaped; at times, however, they are left out altogether. The neck, a straight or slightly inclined column, occasionally with a sharp jagged protuberance to suggest the Adam's apple, or with rings, is joined on naturally to the jutting shoulder-line. The breasts are spherical or cone-shaped. The sharply protruding abdomen, with its accentuated navel, is continued in the elegant curve of the loins and back (negro lordosis).

Their zigzag rhythm gives the limbs an expression of restrained movement. The arms are often fashioned as if in relief, not detached from the body; the legs have the appearance of thick-set, sturdy stumps; the feet are enlarged, if the artist wishes to emphasize that they bear the weight of the body. The hands and feet are roughly indicated, but with sharply set-off contours. The feet and the pedestal often form one piece. Sometimes the head appears to be exceptionally small in proportion to the elongated body and limbs, so that the general impression left by the figure is one of subtle ingenuity (East Africa and the western Sudan, Plate 14a).

Round sculpture — Here we are confronted with a completely different, though equally uniform, aspect of the African's artistic sense. In round sculpture account is taken of anatomical form, which is transmitted to the work. But at the same time nature is not simply copied photographically: it is translated, elevated and idealized; the significance of the limbs is preserved, and, where action is represented, the sense of movement exaggerated. The head receives most considered treatment; it is often a quarter the size of the whole figure, and is generally lavishly decorated. In the massive headdress knots, combs, coils and cues may be seen. The figures at Esie and Benin, as well as those of the Kwale Ibo and Bakongo, have hat-like superstructures, and the figures of dignitaries and gods at the courts of Nigeria, Cameroun and the Congo wear striking caps and crowns. The initiation masks of the Bayaka, the Gelede and Epa masks of the Yoruba, the *ikenga* figures of the Ibo and the masks found in the western Sudan are embellished with crests of carved or real plumes, and even with superstructures consisting of whole figure groups. The forehead and face are tattooed. Here, too, the semi-closed eyes with their heavy lids suggest death and the world beyond; wide-open eyes, on the other hand, attest to vigilance and vitality. They are frequently inlaid with glass, pieces of mirror, metal nails, beads or cowrie-shells, and often a still more realistic note is struck by pupils, eyebrows and lashes, executed in fine hatching (Nigeria, Cameroun, Mende).

The cheeks are round, and delicately curved; the ear is represented in its organic complexity or only slightly simplified; the nose is broad, sometimes *retroussé*, sometimes with distended nostrils. In round sculpture it is in particular the mouth which conveys the expression — a role for which it is naturally equipped by the negro's full lips. The most beautiful examples are the heads of Ife, the ivory mask of Benin, the gold mask of Ashanti, or the figure of Buli. In many figures even tongues and teeth, complete with their deformities, are to be seen; teeth made of iron or bone, and even real teeth, are often inserted. By an open tooth-filled mouth the Baule sought to give the impression of cheerfulness; whereas a mouth suggested by a small disc, on the other hand, was designed to give the face a sad expression (Plate 19). The female figures of the Makonde have a lip-plug, as do some of those of the Dogon and Yoruba. The ancestor is often given decorative whiskers or a beard. The neck is tattooed and adorned with rings. The bronze heads of Benin seem almost about to drown in their splendour of jasper and carnelian beads.

The body is frequently covered with cicatrices, which have a symbolic significance as well as a decorative purpose. The voluminous, generally pendulous breasts, and the other parts of the body are true to nature, though monumental, and are subordinate to the figure as a whole. The knee is often represented as a circular disc, and the fingers and toes provided with joints and nails.

The Dan mask (Plate 16) is a perfect example of the poise achieved by a blending of realistic and abstract forms.

Despite the predominance given to the human figure, the characteristics of animals are also sharply observed and accurately rendered. The texture of the plumage of birds, for example, is treated by the Bini in a masterly fashion. All possible elements are used to enhance the decorative effect: the horns of antelopes and rams, the spotted coats of leopards, the scales of fish, snakes, lizards and scorpions, the shells of tortoises and the menacing teeth of crocodiles. Like the human figures, those of animals also bear tattoo marks and wear rings.

Animal figures

The dark bronze tone produced by the mud-bath, smoke, blackening and greasing is so suited to negro sculpture that figures are rarely painted, and if so, never in a naturalistic manner, but mostly in the symbolic colours red, black and white. Paint is applied more profusely by the Yoruba, Duala and Kuyu. Only the superstructures and masks made with an eye to spectacular effect are more colourful. Many figures and thrones glitter with beads and cowrie ornaments, metal covering, metal pins and gold-foil. In prep-

Surface and patina

aration for great festivals the negro bedecks his figures with a kilt, jewellery, natural hair steeped in ochre, and plumed crowns. In more recent times we find works of sculpture attired in articles of clothing, such as jackets, shoes or even trousers. But in the environment of the ancient courts of Benin and Ife robes and armour formed part of the costume of the ruler and his notables.

ORNAMENTED IMPLEMENTS

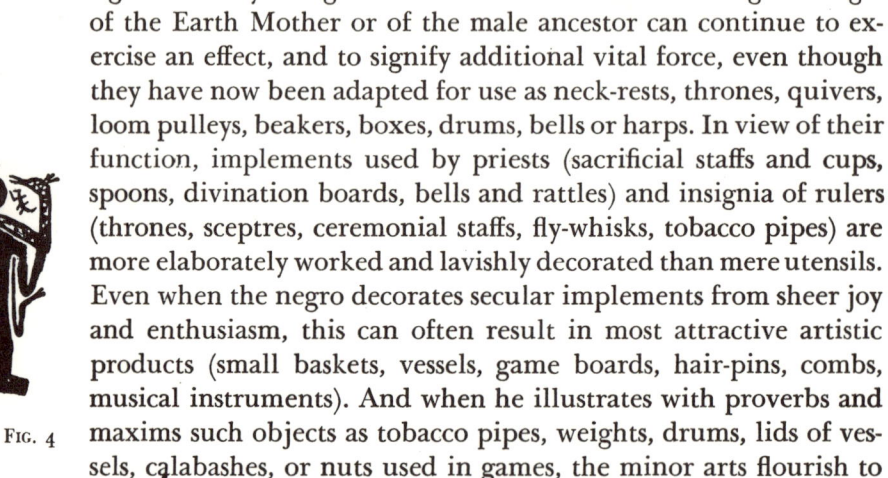

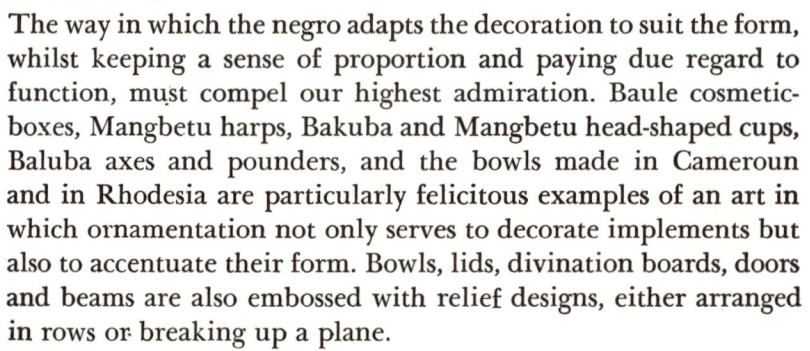

In the areas where carving is highly developed, figured decoration is not restricted to ceremonial ritual objects, but is also applied to ordinary implements and objects in everyday use. In this way it can often occur that a secular implement can acquire enhanced significance by being decorated with motifs of ritual origin. Images of the Earth Mother or of the male ancestor can continue to exercise an effect, and to signify additional vital force, even though they have now been adapted for use as neck-rests, thrones, quivers, loom pulleys, beakers, boxes, drums, bells or harps. In view of their function, implements used by priests (sacrificial staffs and cups, spoons, divination boards, bells and rattles) and insignia of rulers (thrones, sceptres, ceremonial staffs, fly-whisks, tobacco pipes) are more elaborately worked and lavishly decorated than mere utensils. Even when the negro decorates secular implements from sheer joy and enthusiasm, this can often result in most attractive artistic products (small baskets, vessels, game boards, hair-pins, combs, musical instruments). And when he illustrates with proverbs and maxims such objects as tobacco pipes, weights, drums, lids of vessels, calabashes, or nuts used in games, the minor arts flourish to exuberance. But they soon degenerate into cheap shoddy articles when the hope of financial gain leads to mass production and rapid careless work.

FIG. 4

The way in which the negro adapts the decoration to suit the form, whilst keeping a sense of proportion and paying due regard to function, must compel our highest admiration. Baule cosmetic-boxes, Mangbetu harps, Bakuba and Mangbetu head-shaped cups, Baluba axes and pounders, and the bowls made in Cameroun and in Rhodesia are particularly felicitous examples of an art in which ornamentation not only serves to decorate implements but also to accentuate their form. Bowls, lids, divination boards, doors and beams are also embossed with relief designs, either arranged in rows or breaking up a plane.

The tribes of East and South-east Africa emulate those of West Africa in the perfection of their purely ornamental geometric-abstract decoration. They produce fine vessels, baskets, spoons, head-rests and painted shields, as well as elegant lances, the decoration on which is well-harmonized and serves to elaborate the form.

Graphic ornamentation may take the form of painting, notching, engraving or poker-work, and be impressed or incrusted with nails, pins, beads and snail-shells. Many of the motifs employed are borrowed from plaiting (Bakuba beakers). They are often given a name and have symbolic significance ascribed to them: thus a zigzag line can suggest lightning, a snake, water, fire or the mane of an antelope (Bambara); a circled dot may refer to the sun as a source of great vitality (Ashanti) or to the eye. The dot-and-circle motif was already used by the ancient Egyptians, and was later particularly cultivated by the Arabs, as is shown by the facts of its territorial diffusion. In general, it is the blank walls of houses which invite ornamentation and lavish decoration. The African generally does not make a preliminary sketch of the motifs, but works free-hand, spontaneously following his creative inspiration, or mere routine, as his talent allows, and thus succeeds in obtaining ever new variants within the given motifs.

FIG. 5

PAINTING

African painting derives its origin from rock paintings. Since the materials used as a ground are generally not durable (*e.g.*, clay, bark or sand), the paintings are exposed to the threat of rapid decay. Painted symbols serve as a medium of communication, and are used by illiterate teachers in the bush schools as a means of instruction (Plate 47, Fig. 4, p. 198). Painting is seen as increasing vitality, and is applied to the cult objects of families, secret societies and totem clans. Finally, it also serves rulers as a means of satisfying their desire for ostentation (Bamileke).

Negro artists find their most rewarding field of activity in painting

the inner and outer walls of royal palaces, small storage-huts and temples, parapets and furniture (beds) (Figs. 5, 9). They cut out the damp plaster and fill in the depressions with colour, often adding supplementary decoration in the form of incrusted cowrie-shells and beads. The bead trimming on implements also produces an effect close to that of painting.

FIG. 6

Wherever old customs still prevail, negro painters prefer geometric designs: zigzag lines, triangles and squares, circles and semi-circles, dots, stripes and chequer motifs. When human beings and animals are represented in paintings, which is rare, they are shown free-standing, without perspective or horizon (Fig. 6, Liberia). The most common colours are again red, white and black. If use is made of blue, green or yellow, or if tendrils, spirals, stars, moons or crosses are incorporated into the design, this indicates Islamic or other extraneous influence. Loud gay colours and figured scenes, found mainly in the coastal regions, betray European influence. Negro artists do not use a brush, but feazed sticks, feathers or simply their fingers.

The areas where painting is to be found do not necessarily correspond to those of wood-carving.[2] With the exception of ritual paintings for secret societies exclusive to men, the work is generally done by women. The art of painting is practised by the Bidyugo in the west, in the Sudan, in the Guinea hinterlands, and right across to the Cameroun grasslands and the Ubangi Shari area; it is particularly intensively cultivated in Fouta Djallon (Guinea), in northern Cameroun, and by the Ibo for their Mbari festival. Paintings are also to be found in the south-western region of the Congo and among the Bangba on the river Welle, where, in the village of Ekibondo, every house is painted,[3] as well as in East Africa (Wanyamwezi)[4] and in South-east Africa (Ndebele,[5] Angoni, Basuto, Bechuana), where still today women use the most varied motifs and colours to form rich gaily-coloured decorations (Fig. 5).

RELIEF

Wall sculpture is an art form which by and large runs parallel to that of painting. The superb designs and figures, modelled out of the clay of the wall, are often painted as well, in order to enhance their effect (cf. p. 125). The figures are usually of animals and human beings with a symbolic character. They are to be found on the interior and exterior walls of places of worship, and serve to ensure fertility and power. The granaries of the Dogon, Gurunsi,

Senufo and Bobo are decorated in relief and are particularly attractive. The Hausa engrave their clay façades with texts from the Koran, reduced to monogrammatic form. Of singular beauty are the doors, lavishly decorated with reliefs, found among the Yoruba, Baule and Senufo (Figs. 29, 46), and, in Benin, the elephant tusks and bronze plaques, also worked in relief.

CLOTHING AND ORNAMENTATION

A detailed separate chapter would really be necessary to deal properly with negro clothing and ornamentation.[6] The latter is not merely a matter of chance and accident, but stands in some meaningful relationship to the wearer. It expresses a ruler's dignity, a priest's rank, the status of a married woman; it denotes the charm of a young girl, the standing of a wealthy man, the success of a hunter or warrior. It is most pronounced at the courts, where prestige and position are important matters. Those who adorn their bodies with decorative cicatrices bear the self-imposed pain without complaint; they do not shrink from putting tight spiral bands around their neck or arms, or heavy rings on their ankles (Figs. 2, 138).

The designs on these brass-cast rings result from the technique employed: the cire-perdue process lends itself to the fashioning of twisting spirals and herring-bone motifs, which constitute an attractive feature of many decorative rings from the Guinea coast (Figs. 1, 2). The use of copper and iron, and later of brass, and the African's exuberant delight in gaily-coloured beads, give their

FIG. 7

jewellery its distinctive *cachet*, which lies not only in the materials employed but also in the way in which they are worked and combined. The ornamentation rarely ventures away from the cus-

75

tomary geometric motifs, and it is only the development of brass casting that gives rise to attractive new designs. (For precious metals, cf. p. 49). The Mangbetu have made their small seat-mats into decorative objects of unusual beauty.

As the practice of wearing full clothing gains ground, so the use of jewellery decreases proportionately, particularly in Islamic areas. Its place is taken by lavish embroidery on bags, collars and strips on the front and back of the wide flowing garments worn there. The embroidered tobe of the Hausa, for instance, has become festive attire over extensive areas of the Sudan (Cameroun, Nigeria, the western Sudan, and among the Tuareg of the Sahara). The design of this embroidery incorporates local symbols and varies from one place to another. Motifs drawn from the rich treasury of Oriental, and in particular Byzantine and Arab, patterns are related quite arbitrarily to local traditions by their wearers: to the Nupe the long wedges shown in Fig. 7 suggest knives, [7] to the Bambara the ritual posts of the royal palace; the roundel is interpreted by the former as the sacred royal drum, by the latter as the sun snake. [8]

The patterns dyed or painted on clothing fabrics mainly serve a decorative purpose (cf. p. 51). The East African pastoralists have fine leather coats studded with beads and cowrie-shells, and the chiefs of the Baganda have splendid tobes made of painted bark.

ARCHITECTURE African architecture, a subject that can only be treated in outline here, is by and large suited to the locality and the economic requirements of the people who live there. The numerous shifts of population have, however, repeatedly interrupted continuity of style, but have thereby led to a great variety of types of dwelling.

The building materials used by the negro depend upon his natural environment. In the forest areas he has recourse to wooden beams, veins of palm-frond midribs and bamboo; for roofing purposes he makes use of leaves, grasses, plaited mats and tree bark. In the steppe country clay and hard termite earth are utilized. Branches and stakes are plastered with clay, and tied bast takes the place of nails and pegs. Stone is rarely used (cf. p. 46).

Bee-hive huts TYPES OF DWELLING: The most primitive form of African dwelling is without doubt the cupola or bee-hive hut. Its archetype is the wind-shelter built by the pygmies: stakes are placed in a circle, their lower ends being buried in the earth, and the top thirds being bent inwards and tied together in the centre; the dome-like roof thus formed is covered with *phrygia* leaves. The bee-hive hut has spread over extensive areas of East and South-east Africa (Herero, Angoni, Basuto, and partially to the Fulani nomads in the west). Development took place by adding plaited mats, skins and plaster of clay, internal supports, doors and barrel-shaped porches. It is easy to see why such a simple structure, which could easily be transported from place to place, was popular amongst nomadic peoples. The slant of the roof, which may be either gentle and almost flat or steep like a tent, presents many aesthetic potentialities. The most splendid cupolas are to be found in the capitals of the Baganda and Banyoro in the region of the East African lakes. A type of dwelling with a cone-shaped roof and a cylindrical base, constructed separately, is to be found over wide areas of the steppe (Fig. 8). The cone-shaped roof huts of East and South-east Africa and of the Nilotes are similar in shape, but built on different principles. In the latter case the roof does not rest upon the base, but upon supports placed around the dwelling in the form of a circle.

The wall is frequently made of lattice-work plastered with clay, or, in the Hausa states of Nigeria, of lumps of clay moulded to form

FIG. 8

Cone-roofed house

FIG. 9

a smooth surface. In many Nilotic and central Sudanese dwellings the walls are lined with patterned mats. (In the palace of one king of the Barotse such mats line the interior walls). The space between the wall and the ring of poles supporting the roof forms a sort of shady verandah.

The general appearance of the dwelling depends upon the shape of the roof, which may be either sloping, or onion- or bell-shaped (Nuer), or may sometimes tower up like the steeple of a church (Bena Lulua, Azande). The tying together of the ribs of the roof, necessary for structural reasons, is turned to good effect, and forms an attractive decorative element. The Bapende even decorate their roofs with wood carvings, whilst the inhabitants of Togo, Ethiopia and elsewhere use pottery superstructures for this purpose. Roof and base are pleasantly combined in certain granaries and ritual huts amongst the Krej, Nilotes and Azande, as well as in the hinterland of the Guinea coast. They are divided by a floor of beams into sleeping quarters and a store-room. Occasionally the dwellings are divided into several small rooms by walls.

Gable-roofed dwelling

The rectangular gable-roofed house, generally constructed of vegetable materials, is confined to relatively limited areas in the forest regions of West Africa and the western and northern Congo. It is built in one of two ways: either on stakes, in which case the roof is supported by a framework of rafters resting on the stakes, the spaces between the stakes being filled up with material and plaited mats, resulting in a compact structure; alternatively, it can be built of six panels of vegetable material, without a firm foundation in the ground. Owing to their pliability, these panels have the great advantage of standing up to the wind and being easily transportable.

FIG. 10

Tortoise-shaped roof

The tortoise-shaped roof is formed when the ridge is bent downwards on both sides by the weight of the roof covering. The roof often protrudes outwards on one gable side, and is supported by wooden posts, thus forming a shady and convenient verandah. The gable-roofed dwelling was particularly common in the areas that formed part of the early kingdoms. The palace of King Munsa of the Mangbetu was a large airy hall measuring about 150 feet by 75, and 50 feet high. In the residences of the Guinea coast and in Cameroun four rectangular houses are built around a courtyard, the *impluvium*, the original form of which was introduced from the Mediterranean (Fig. 9, p. 129).

With its relatively extensive mural surfaces, the gable-roofed dwelling affords ample opportunity for artistic decoration (ornamented wattle, painted bark, etc.).

A fusion of these types has produced the magnificent cupola construction of the Cameroun grasslands (Fig. 81).

Tembe

The *tembe* is a flat square dwelling built of branches and clay, almost completely sunk into the ground as a protection against the weather and enemy attack. It is confined to a limited area of East Africa between Lake Victoria and Mount Kilimanjaro. Tembe dwellings were built close together in groups, leading to the formation of labyrinth-like settlements with passage-ways and courtyards which, seen from the outside, gave the appearance of a single compact unit. The multi-chambered subterranean buildings of the western Sudan (occasionally also found in East Africa) were likewise sunk into the earth. Similar structures are to be found in the western Sahara and the Mediterranean area. Western Sudanese architecture has also been influenced by the building of clay or mud *(Lehmkomplex)*, fostered by ancient Mediterranean, Oriental, and later also by Islamic influences. Palaces, forts and mosques, and, indeed, even whole settlements of flat box-

FIG. 11

like dwellings (Zinder) are built of clay — either simply of lumps of clay or of rectangular air-dried bricks (Bambara and Bobo). The supporting beams are set off against the walls, forming one of the decorative features characteristic of the mosque style, which is of Moorish origin, with its hedgehog-like towers, merlons, and clay walls in relief (Fig. 12). The interior walls of the palaces, the sleeping quarters, and the storage urns are also made of clay.

In the hinterland of Ghana, Togo and Dahomey we even come across forts which are clear examples of the principle of clans living as self-contained units, on the defensive against the outside world

79

(Fig. 10). Their tower-like cone-roofed huts are enclosed by a massive wall. The inner courtyard is covered over by a terrace on which the family lives during the daytime. The upper floors are reached by means of ladders.

The peak of achievement in African clay architecture is to be found in the bold cupola structures of the Musgu, who live on the Logone south of Lake Chad (Fig. 11). The exterior walls are covered with decorative designs, effectively set off by the plain doorway. The building is divided into several small rooms and is pleasantly and refreshingly cool.

Lit.: [1] Gerbrands, Art.....; [2] Haselberger; [3] Scohy; [4] Cory; [5] Meiring; [6] Leuzinger; [7] Baumann, Kunstgewerbe; [8] Pâques.

PART TWO

STYLE REGIONS

I. INTRODUCTION TO THE WESTERN SUDAN
AND WEST AFRICA

Although the name Sudan means 'land of the blacks', it is a wide SAVANNAH
open country, and, with its red soil, light green bushes and forests,
rolling fields and gay bustling markets, anything but gloomy and
black. The only thing that is black is the colour of the skin of its
inhabitants, the sturdy Sudanese. Sudan is an accepted term used
to denote the grassy savannah country extending from the thorn-
bush-covered steppe to the primeval forest of the Guinea coast and
the Congo. The climate is tropical, with a clearly-marked rainy
season in summer, and a dry season in winter.
In this tour through the various regional styles we shall restrict
our attention to the only area to have produced sculpture of any
note, i.e., the territory lying to the west of the Niger bend and
stretching as far as the edge of the jungle. Its tall, proud inhabitants
are diligent agriculturalists. They grow mainly millet and maize,
working with a hoe, and have developed a firmly-established tribal
organization, a religion of their own and a noteworthy culture.
Their myths and legends tell of a glorious past.
The Sudanese negro has some Ethiopian blood in his veins, for
his Old Nigritic culture was exposed to many diverse Hamitic,
Mediterranean and Oriental influences (cf. p. 19). It is nowadays
quite clear that the dynamic nature of the immigrants stimulated
the latent talents of the negroes and led to cultural achievements
of a magnitude that can now only be conjectured. The Sudanese
had particularly close contact with northern peoples such as the
Berbers, Moors, Tuareg and Arabs. At the time when civilization
flourished in Carthage, Cyrene and Rome, the Sudan was export-
ing gold, ivory and slaves, and importing fabrics, copper and beads,
by way of the caravan routes across the Sahara. The Sudanese bar-

Early kingdoms

tered their gold for salt, brass and textiles until recent times. Around the markets where these goods were exchanged large towns grew up. The strangers from the north brought with them not only copper and beads, but also new ideas and techniques. These fresh impulses fostered and strengthened the negroes' self-assurance and helped them to appreciate their own talents. They learnt better methods of organization, and founded in the Sudan several kingdoms with brilliant courts. In the accounts of al-Bakrî (11th century) Yâkut al-Rûmi (13th century), Ibn Batûta and Ibn Khaldun (14th century) there are enthusiastic descriptions of the splendour and riches to be found in the negro capitals. Ghana, for example, was a kingdom founded by the Berbers, which between the 4th and 13th centuries extended its authority over the area between Senegal and the Upper Niger. The negro kingdom of Melli or Mali (Mande tribe), proclaimed in the 11th century, reached its climax under Mansa Musa, who was a Moslem and undertook a great pilgrimage to Mecca (1324—6); here he engaged teachers and architects, who built mosques and palaces and brought culture and refinement to his court. A mighty rival to the kingdom of Melli appeared in the neighbouring state of Songhai, which reached the zenith of its power under Askia in the 16th century. On the ruins of Melli the Bambara founded in 1660 their kingdoms of Segu and Kaarta, which in 1850 succumbed in turn to the onslaught of

Fig. 12

El-Hadj-Omar, the conqueror of Tukulor. In the Upper Volta there arose in the 11th century the kingdom of Mossi-Dagomba. The influence of the highly-developed cultures also reached the Guinea lands and fostered the establishment of states in this region as well: Ashanti, Dahomey, Ife and Benin were brilliant courts, whose existence would have been unthinkable without the influences from the Mediterranean and the Orient. The Chad region was the most important gateway for the caravans that streamed in by way of Kordofan-Darfur from the Nile valley and Ethiopia, bringing new impulses into the Benue and Niger valleys, the grasslands of Cameroun, and the Congo. As a result Nigeria in particular could soon boast important kingdoms: Yoruba, Benin, Nupe, Jukun, Bornu, and the states of the Fulani and Hausa.

Advanced cultures

Although in the course of time these states either collapsed or degenerated into cruel despotisms, they nevertheless gave a fillip to cultural development in the Sudan, both in the intellectual and in the material sphere. To the round huts of the indigenous Old Nigritic peoples were now added flat-roofed dwellings and granaries, fort-like structures and great palaces with inner courtyards, all of them made of unbaked clay.

To understand the complex cultural scene in the Sudan, where old and new overlap, one must first draw a distinction between the 'Old Sudanese' or Old Nigritic peasant culture and the 'neo-Sudanese' culture of the immigrant peoples.

Old Sudanese society was based upon the large patriarchal family, living in an enclosed homestead. Power was exercised by an elected council of elders, and especially by the chief, the upholder of tradition. An important function was fulfilled by the 'lord of the soil', who administered the property of the community.

Old Sudanese

The neo-Sudanese developed the system of chiefs to its extreme by establishing a powerful sacrosanct monarchy. Under pressure from the Fulani, Moors, Arabs and others, they allowed Islam to penetrate into the country. Thus one finds, chiefly in the towns, the cactus-like minaret of the mosque (whence the muezzin daily summons the faithful to prayer; cf. Fig. 12). But Islam failed to oust the deeply-rooted ancestor and spirit cult of the isolated rural population. The peasants did not forget the devastating Muslim invasions, and showed no inclination to accept the religion of these alien warriors. Christianity meets with similar resistance. The negro recognizes the dangers of materialism which, despite its

Neo-Sudanese

religion, European civilization brings in its train; he is also aware of the threat which it presents to his ancient time-tested order, and defends this with all his might. For this reason even nowadays in certain areas stout resistance is offered to the penetration of Christianity and Islam, and the indigenous religion, in which art is deeply rooted, still provides the stimulus for works of sculpture, as it did in former times. Autochthonous art still flourishes over wide areas of the western Sudan and the Guinea lands.

Arts and crafts The pomp and splendour of the courts encouraged the neo-Sudanese to develop applied arts and crafts and to practise ingenious techniques (brass casting by the waste form method, filigree, embossing, etc.). The adoption of full clothing promoted the art of weaving: the women span the cotton thread, whilst the men wove it into fabrics on their treadle-looms (for dyeing techniques, cf. p. 51). Woollen blankets with geometric designs are a speciality of the area near the bend of the Niger.

The Hausa and Mandingo are famed for their fine work in leather, decorated by the most varied methods. As ornamentation they favour bands of plaiting, braids, crossed loops, rosettes, curls, crosses and swastikas, and near-squares with loops at the corners and curved edges. In the larger towns the artisans formed closed corporations; they married only women from within their own guild.

Wave after wave of the peoples that surged across the Sudan were swallowed up by the primeval forest. This jungle covers with luxuriant growth a comparatively narrow strip of coast from Senegal southwards to northern Angola, spreading out over a large area in the equatorial zone of Gabon, the Congo Republic and the northern part of the Republic of the Congo. In Liberia and eastern Nigeria the coastal forest is particularly dense, but it is interspersed with numerous wedges of savannah in the part of the Ivory Coast inhabited by the Baule, in the eastern part of the Gold Coast, in Togo, Dahomey, and western Nigeria.

JUNGLE

In Equatorial Africa there are no dry seasons. Rain falls throughout the year, but is particularly heavy in spring and autumn. Sowing and harvesting of crops take place all the time, and when the land is exhausted the villagers move on and bring new areas under cultivation. Although the climate makes for exuberant fertility, man has many enemies: the constant heat and humidity by night as well as during the day, the tsetse fly and other insect pests; the fever-ridden swamps and depressions make it almost impossible for

PLATE 21 — *Kuduo*, Ashanti vessel for souls, cast brass, cire-perdue technique. On the lid animals fighting (leopard clawing an antelope); the body of the vessel encircled by rosettes and plaited bands. These *kuduo* were formerly used in cleansing ceremonies, and thought to give power throughout the owner's life; they were placed in his grave, filled with gold dust and other treasures. Today they serve secular purposes. Ghana. *Ethnological Collection, Zurich (12½ in.).*

PLATE 22 — Verandah posts on the residence of the king of Savé, south coast of Dahomey. The gods Odudua, represented as a woman, and Obatala, represented as a horseman, between plaited bands denote the style of the southern Yoruba. Dahomey. *Musée de l'Homme, Paris (4 ft. 5¼ in. and 4 ft. 4 in.)*

PLATE 23 — Cast brass head portraying an *Oni* (king) of Ife, from the golden age of the 13th century. Particularly elaborate are the organically rendered facial features, the scarification, and the crown, lavishly decorated with beads. In the small orifices ritual bead pendants may have been inserted. Nigeria. *British Museum (13¾ in.).*

PLATE 24 — Cast brass ritual figure, recently found in Ife, the sacred town of the Yoruba, also assigned to the 13th century. The figure of the queen is ingeniously combined with the ritual vessel, a stool in the shape of a fine quartz seat with a handle, and with the small stool, forming a united whole. Nigeria. *In the possession of the Oni of Ife (4½ in.).*

PLATE 25 — Commemorative head from Ife, terracotta. The male artists who made these clay casts in moulds showed consummate skill. The firing took place in a heap of ashes heated to about 300° C. Nigeria. 13th century. *In the possession of the Oni of Ife.*

90

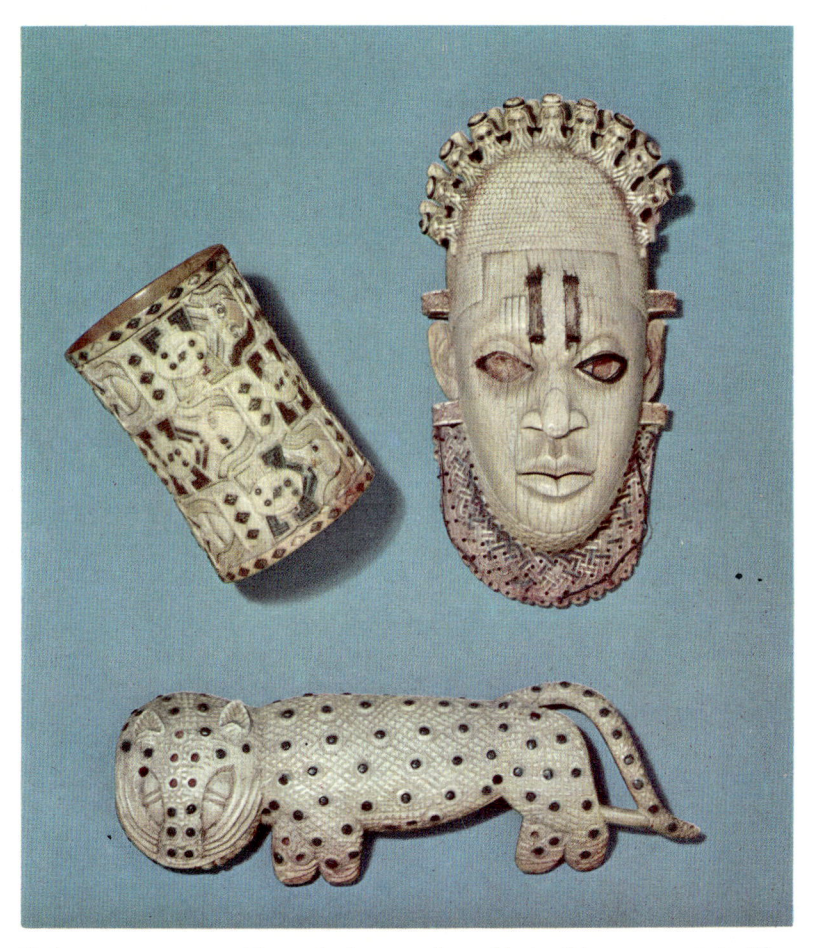

PLATE 27 — Mask, arm ornament and leopard; three precious objects of ivory encrusted with copper, from Ancient Benin. The magnificent mask, with its organically-shaped ears, crown of bearded heads of Portuguese, and beaded ornaments, was worn as decoration on the chest, and symbolized the sacrosanct kingdom of Benin at the height of its power in the 16th century *(9½ in.)*.
Heads of Portuguese also appear as a motif on the arm ornament *(6 in.)*. The small leopard is also a symbol of authority *(9½ in.)*. 18th century. All from Nigeria. *British Museum.*

◀ PLATE 26 — Commemorative head, bronze, from the altar of the Queen Mother of Benín. According to tradition it is said to have been placed there by Oba Esigie, one of the most brilliant kings, in honour of his mother Idia. The sensitive rendering, the thinness of the cast (only ⅛ in.) and the tight collar of beads indicate the early Benin period (beginning of the 16th century). The lattice-work pattern covering the typically female hair-dress corresponds to the jasper, coral and carnelian beads worn by rulers as emblems of their authority. Nigeria. *British Museum (15¾ in.)*.

PLATE 28 — Bronze horseman, dating from the middle period of Benin. From the costume it can be inferred that the warrior, with his plumed crown, came from the northern states of Nigeria. 17th century. *The torso is in the Ethnological Collection, Zurich, and the head in the British Museum.*

the negro to survive at a level consonant with human dignity. And yet he has succeeded in prevailing over the primeval forest where it is not too dense! By burning clearings he has wrung from the hostile jungle patches of cultivated land, which he works with primitive implements (hoe, planting-stick), planting yam, taro, manioc — and, under Sudanese influence, also rice.

The jungle makes communication with the outside world a difficult matter, and the tribes there live an isolated existence in small family groups. Their settlements take the form of long straggling villages with gable-roofed huts. Tribes with a highly-developed culture live side by side with others less advanced. Benin, an island of culture in the midst of the jungle, testifies to the manner in which man's creative impulses can triumph over the most arduous natural conditions. Extensive areas of the jungle are dominated by secret societies, whose masks are of an astonishingly high artistic quality.

II. WESTERN SUDAN

BAMBARA

The Bambara are one of the foremost tribes of the western Sudan, and are about one million strong. By race they belong to the great Mandingo group, but linguistically to the Mande-tan complex. As a result of a marked Ethiopian streak they are taller and lighter-skinned than other Sudanese negroes. They are an intelligent dignified people, proud of their warlike past. Nowadays they are peaceful agriculturalists, who strongly uphold their ancient tribal customs against Islam and Christianity.

The influence of the Bambara extends far beyond the areas which they themselves inhabit. Bambara style includes the art of tribes living near or amongst them, such as the Khassonke, Malinke, Marka and Minianka. The different variants of style cannot easily be identified from the evidence of collected pieces. One may think one has identified, say, a Khassonke figure by its curved nose, only to discover to one's surprise a similar nose on a pure Bambara work. Their sculpture was in the hands of the Nuni. The Nuni are a caste of ancient stock, feared and despised by the Bambara; they are spread over an extensive area of the Sudan, act in the capacity of smiths, and concern themselves with masks and magic as well as carving.

STYLISTIC CHARACTERISTICS (cf. p. 16): architectonic force and rigid, angular forms; transverse hair-dress (similar to the pert sideways-projecting plaits still made today by Bambara women); concave face with straight profile and angular mouth (Fig. 13). Segu figures have an aquiline nose which, continuing the line of the head and forehead, forms a bold curve; the body is slender and columnar; the breasts semi-spherical and often placed low down; the arms hang freely, occasionally having large paw-like hands and open palms.

The statues of the Malinke are somewhat more vigorous, with a frog-like projecting mouth and an elaborate *coiffure*.

The Bambara rarely apply colour to their statues, but furnish them with ornaments and metal nails, insert cowrie-shells and beads to form eyes, and attach dainty brass rings to the nose and ears.

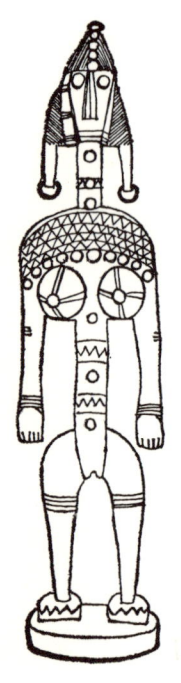

FIG. 13

Masks One evening when I was driving across the savannah not far from

Bamako, I came across a group of dancers wearing masks of lions, hyenas, antelopes and abstract spirits, making their way down to the river with wild leaps and bounds and abrupt whirlings and twirlings. They were about to offer sacrifice to Kore, the mighty water spirit, because for a long time no rain had fallen. In this way I found very striking evidence of the fact that even today Bambara masks are used in rites that are still extant. I discovered that they are treated like human beings, presented with sacrificial gifts, and buried with funerary rites once they have served their purpose. They are a requisite of the religious societies, an embodiment of the manifold emanation of Faro, creator and ruler of the Universe, who gave man conscience and introduced order and sense of responsibility, and who watches over labour and the administration of justice.[1] A simple angular mask serves to represent his determined countenance, and endows its bearer with unlimited power. The Kore society, responsible for the fertility of the fields, employs masks of lions, hyenas and antelopes (Plate 4b). The member who represents the mighty Kore himself rides a pole with an abstract horse's or bird's head, which is a masterpiece of stylized art. N'tomo, the tutelary spirit of boys before they enter adult society, is a special type of mask, also fashioned in a simple cubist style and adorned with a large number of cowrie-shells. His function is to inculcate in them a sense of discipline and solidarity. The mask of the Marka, in the Cercle de San, is of slender form with a tapering chin; the decorative element is enhanced by painting or a covering of sheet-metal. The Marka dress their masks in gaily-coloured costumes made of cloth; they always appear in pairs, to represent man's courting of woman (Fig. 14).

The animal masks have led to ingenious abstractions. The Bambara call them *boli,* a collective term for all figures in which the mighty earth spirits reside: they place them in the fields to ward off demons (elephants, earth-hogs, etc.).

The Bambara also add decoration in the form of slender figures and faces to stools, locks on storage-huts, sacred sistrums, flutes and other objects used by the secret society. In the Mopti and San district there are carved and costumed marionettes used in performances of burlesques and comedies.

The objects which have won Bambara art international fame are the *chi wara:* superstructures on masks in the shape of antelopes — the antelope being the emblem of the Bambara tribe (Plate 5). It

FIG. 14

Antelope superstructures

is fascinating to trace how this basic motif has been repeatedly modified by being combined with figures and other animals. This is proof of the fact that the Bambara do not adhere slavishly to their models, but give free rein to their imagination, and, indeed, end by giving their visions a strictly abstract form.

On the Upper Niger, in the area within the influence of Bamako, the horizontal type of antelope mask is the one chiefly found. The horns curve upwards and outwards; the mouth is often wide open, as though the beast were whinnying with joy; the back has a delicate curvature; the surface is covered with fine notches to suggest the coat, and is often also treated proportionally and smoothly. The tail is sometimes curled up like that of a chameleon — for the chameleon was believed to give man immortality; as it moved so slowly, and was overtaken by other animals, this brought its immortality into question. The legs are indicated by a sharp zigzag line; the horns are often multiplied and embellished with small figures of women and birds (Fig. 15).

In the villages lying in the direction of Buguni the horizontal form of antelope mask is superseded by the vertical Suguni type (Figs. 16, 17). The Bambara say that this is the older form, and is an attribute of a wild antelope dance. In this case it is the mane that is stylized in chevron form; the body of the antelope stands upon a mount which combines arbitrarily a number of animal elements (chameleon, horse, duiker), and is often crowned by a female figure. The profile line of the sculpture is treated with particular consideration. Of the specimens to be seen in European museums there is not one that resembles another. The naturalistic form gives place to ever more abstract and surrealist forms, until one important characteristic — the horn or the mane — stands out clearly and geometrically, to direct attention upon the power of the spirit (Fig. 18). The Bambara are also in the habit of adding these meaningful motifs to implements in daily use. When I once asked what the design of the fabric shown in Plate 5 signified, I received the reply: *"c'est l'antilope!"*

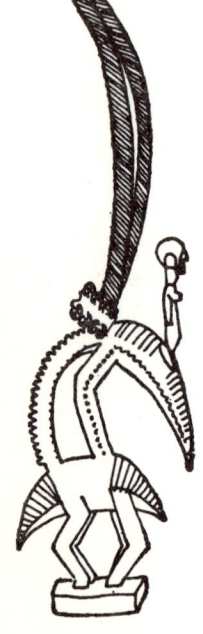

Magnificent chi wara antelopes (Plate 5) also stem from the area between Segu, San, and Kutiala (and partly even in Minianka territory), which is generally assigned to the Segu style. They are vertically accentuated; on the buck the pierced design of the mane forms a link between the small, short body and the curved horns; the doe, on the other hand, has straight horns and no mane; on its back stands the calf with its short legs (Fig. 19). One of the many marvels of black Africa is the veritable artistry with which antelopes are combined with other creatures, and variously portrayed, now in an organic-naturalistic, now in an abstract form, depending upon the region and the artistic sense of each people. The exuberant and ingenious interplay of forms, the clarity of line, the imaginative rendering of curves and manes, the rhythmic balance — of all this the plates in the present volume can give only a suggestion.

The ceremonial chi wara dance is performed on all important occasions: when invoking the gods to send rain or to make the fields fertile, before hunting, at funerals and at initiation festivals. It is executed by the young men, and watched by the young maidens, who appear lavishly adorned with cowrie-shells and who clap their hands in accompaniment.

DOGON

The Dogon, as they call themselves, or *Habbe* (unbelievers), as they are referred to by the Fulani, migrated from the south several hundred years ago and settled on the inaccessible rocky plateau of the Niger bend, south of Timbuktu, between Bandiagara and Hombori. Several Dogon tribes have barricaded themselves in this natural fortress, which can only be reached by means of rope ladders, to protect themselves from enemy attack and to safeguard their tribal culture from Mohammedan fanatics. The sparse cultivated land on the rocky terraces and cliff edges can be irrigated only with difficulty; millet and vegetables are the chief crops.

Dogon art is as stubbornly individualistic as the tribe itself, and for this very reason constitutes one of the finest landmarks in African art. The oldest group of sculptures, perhaps carved more than two hundred years ago, is the so-called *tellem* (Plate 6).

CHARACTERISTICS: hard wood resembling stone, with an ash-grey or red fine-cracked patina; expressive dynamic poses, sometimes with gestures evocative of pathos — for example, with arms raised, or hands placed on the ear-lobe as if to catch a sound; the mouth open as though calling out; the chin exactly rendered; many figures arranged in pairs on a pedestal, or represented as hermaphrodites, with the face framed by a beard and the breasts pointed; the navel prominent; the back curved; the line of the hips plastic, and sharply broken up; often kneeling on enlarged feet, wearing jewellery, or carrying an axe or a child. Made from the same hard wood are the *bazu:* expressionist, highly stylized animal figures with

FIG. 17

wide open jaws, who are guardians of fields and trees, and are used to afford protection against thieves.

Tellem with raised arms, often combined with animals, are also to be found on ritual implements, stools and troughs (Fig. 20). These troughs are still in use today to test the strength of young initiates into the secret society.

A more modern phase of Dogon sculpture is highly static and geometric, which enhances still further the aura of solemnity, serenity and majesty (Plate 7).

CHARACTERISTICS: sharply defined volumes; angular forms, rarely broken by curves; body and limbs faceted; the navel pyramid-shaped; the head, with its straight profile continuing the line of the median hair-crest, often describing a graceful semi-circle, truncated horizontally at the chin; eyes and mouth triangular or square; ears semi-circular tabs; the nose straight as an arrow; often wearing beards and lip-plugs.

FIG. 18 The same motifs, but treated more simply and rigidly, are repeated in the reliefs on door-leaves and shutters. Door-locks (Fig. 21), perch seats, butter-dishes, and other objects can all provide a habitat for the mythical ancestral pair.

Since the Dogon are keen horsemen and organize dances performed on horseback, their figures also include stylized horses and riders, as, for example, on their ritual vessels (Fig. 22). Rumour has it that at important ceremonies the priests and dignitaries of the tribe used to eat human flesh out of these vessels. [2]

As well as being schematic and rigidly conventional, Dogon masks can also take a daring abstract form. How eerie is the effect of the magnificent ape mask from the Musée de l'Homme, so familiar from reproductions!

CHARACTERISTICS: slender, occasionally rectangular, tapering contours; sunken cheeks, the vertical hollows so formed being separated by the bridge of the nose; the latter board-shaped, or alternatively broken by a chevron line, producing a decorative profile; the mouth treated in an abstract manner, or projecting forward as a cone; human faces intermingled with elements of mythical animals, such as antelopes, hyenas, buffaloes, apes, birds and serpents.

The human masks personify high-ranking dignitaries, priests, hunters, medicine-men, or even Fulani maidens.[3] The multi-
FIG. 19 tiered mask consists of a face with a plank in open-work, about 15

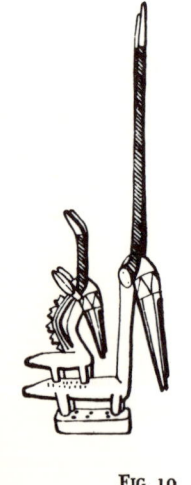

98

feet high, a form derived from the Dogon cosmogony and conception of the world.

The *kanaga*, a mask topped by a kind of Lorraine cross (Fig. 23), is of great ideological significance. On the very top we once more see the ancestral couple. The curious phenomenon of the Lorraine cross has been the subject of the most varied interpretation. Most authorities agree in regarding it as the hunting symbol of the bird in flight. Kjersmeier holds that it suggests the crocodile in Dogon mythology, according to which the first settlers rode through the river on the backs of crocodiles. According to Griaule the cross is a symbol of equilibrium between heaven and earth, of divine order in the cosmos. [4]

Polychrome masks are supplemented by a fibre costume dyed red, cowrie-shells and plaiting. Each of the different kinds of mask, of which there are about eighty, has its special dance-step; of these the kanaga dance is said to be particularly wild. Even the multi-tiered mask, despite its size, is brought out to perform acrobatic dances. The masks, requisites of the Naba rite, appear at all important events in the village; at the funeral of prominent members of the society, they dance on the roof terrace of the house of the deceased. Animal masks serve to comfort, with their dances of mimicry, the souls of the game killed in hunting, and are called upon to protect the fields against pilferers. All these masks derive from the enormous mother mask, often about thirty feet long, which is naturally too large to be carried about. In a prominent position over its angular face there is an open-work panel, with a geometrical design arranged in a step-like pattern, which joins on to the great wide-open jaws; for this reason it has been interpreted by some scholars as a crocodile. The mother mask, venerated as a most sacred object, is kept in a holy of holies, where sacrificial offerings are brought to it for its gratification. It is the abode of the primeval human soul, nyama, the immortal force of life.

A mother mask is generally made once every sixty years for the

FIG. 20

MOSSI

great Sigi festival. Since Dogon masks are made of the light wood of the bombax tree, they break easily and have to be continually replaced; thus they rarely survive to great age. The motifs of these masks are also found depicted on the rock walls of the sanctuaries, reduced to simple symbolic form and painted red, white and black.

The Mossi, to the south-east of the Dogon, were an active people who founded stable states; their towns were centres of Islamic culture. It is thus all the more surprising that Old Nigritic manners and customs should have been able to survive in rural areas. But little remains in the way of carved figures.

CHARACTERISTICS: oval white face, treated in an abstract manner, without mouth or ears; triangular cavities for the eyes; the midrib serving as a nose; almost perpendicular horns and ears; the male masks furnished with an open-work crest six feet high, the female ones bearing a female figure with cylindrical body structure and pointed breasts; the limbs provided with joints; painted black, white and red (Plate 9).

BOBO

Among the various groups of Bobo peasants native to **Mali** and the Upper Volta, a special place is held by the Bobo-Fing (black Bobo), in the area of Bobo Djulasso. Sculptured masks such as that shown in Plate 10 are rare. One that is familiar is the personification of the village tutelary spirit, Dō (Fig. 24), a mask adorned with heraldic symbols, which clears the district of demons at funeral rites and at the beginning of the agricultural season.

CHARACTERISTICS: masks in vertical or horizontal form; red and white geometric designs, and numerous chequered, chevron, triangular and circular motifs; round eyes; square or lozenge-shaped protruding mouth; representations of creatures such as butterflies, birds and buffaloes, which have some esoteric significance (Pl. 11). The high slender geometrically-designed antelope masks show affinity with those of the Duala. The neo-Sudanese tribe of Lobi carve protective figures and pounding-benches with two or four supporting figures.

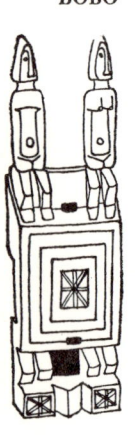

FIG. 21

SENUFO

The Senufo, or Siena, as they call themselves, who today number more than a million, inhabit vast areas in the north of the Ivory Coast, certain districts of the Upper Volta and of Mali. In contrast to their neighbours, these peaceful conservative agriculturalists have not experienced statehood, and for this reason have maintained intact the beliefs and customs of their ancestors. The Minianka, a northern branch of the Senufo, are under the artistic influence of the Bambara. Senufo wood-carving is centred in the area around Korhogo, in the hinterland of the Ivory Coast, in the midst of the fertile rainy savannah.

The arts are in the charge of certain castes, amongst which the wood-carvers, smiths and bronze casters enjoy high esteem.

The finest carved objects are inspired by the cult, centering upon the great Mother Goddess, of the Poro secret society. The choicest masterpieces were preserved in their sacred grove, where entrance was forbidden to all strangers on pain of death. They were brought to public notice only a few years ago, when the prophet Massa introduced a new fetish cult, causing these ancient sanctuaries to be abandoned. It is to him alone that we are indebted for our knowledge of the great artistic achievements of the Senufo.

CHARACTERISTICS: 1: *deble* type: elongated, cylindrically-shaped torso and limbs, mounted on a narrow pedestal; the head, which is sometimes small, supported by a long neck (Plate 12). 2: the *degele* (Fig. 25), used by members of the society in their nocturnal death rites, is different in type: it is a helmet-mask, topped with figures, treated in a very abstract manner, and in this case without arms. By accentuating the 'heart line', the serious composed faces gain in concentration. The smooth and proportionate treatment of the genitals contrasts with the ribbed body, thus creating acute artistic tension. 3: amongst the small statuettes there are also masterpieces, full of vitality, with boldly simplified forms; the angular lines, projecting forwards, are rhythmically related; the hair-crest has a flap over the forehead; the mouth and chin protrude; the breasts taper to a point; the abdomen bulges forwards at the level of the navel; the arms are long, and the hands and feet often exaggerated and given the shape of paws; the rearward incline of the shoulders and curvature of the back giving the figure equilibrium (Fig. 26).

These figures — standing, seated or mounted — decorate the lidded vessels placed in the village market-place at funerals to hold sacrificial offerings. Girls carry them to obtain fertility; they serve in oracles, and, where they appear in pairs, in the cult of twins; they enhance the importance of dignitaries' staffs and decorate such everyday objects as chairs and butter-dishes. When the young peasants compete to show their skill in husbandry, these figures are placed in the fields. The winner of the contest is greatly honoured,

FIG. 22

and rewarded by having the best marriage prospects.⁵

The bird, as the tribal emblem of the Senufo, plays a part in their ritual; it is represented in much-simplified form, often with outspread wings, and also appears as ornamentation on masks and pulley-holders on looms (Fig. 27).

The Senufo artist displays his vitality to fullest extent in the socalled 'fire-spitters', which play a part in the Gbon cult (Plate 13). In the centre, around the eyes and nose, are grouped elements of various animals: boars, hyenas, buffaloes, antelopes, crocodiles, apes, storks, vultures or chameleons; their jaws with gnashing teeth are sometimes shown in duplicate.

After these impressive helmet-masks the small face-masks of the south-western branch of the Senufo evoke a rather feeble and lifeless impression, particularly as they have recently been degraded to the level of souvenirs, and are bought and sold commercially (Fig. 28).

CHARACTERISTICS: stylized hair-dress, with combs, a small cue, and appendages like little legs; tattooing; on the figure of the ancestral mother of the tribe, horns and other animal motifs above the delicately formed face. These masks used to appear at funerals in the sakrobundu cult of the Lō society.

On the door of the clan sanctuary shown in Fig. 29 there is a rich relief, comprising several typical Senufo symbols (a sakrobundu mask, a ritual riding scene, shackles, tortoises, crocodiles and birds).

FIG. 23

FIG. 24

The decorative type of mask with its characteristic appendages was later copied in brass castings. There are pretty little amulet figures and finger-rings with bulls' heads — the emblem of the medicine-men, who grip the ring tightly between their teeth during the healing ceremony.

Lit.: ¹Dieterlen; ²Kjersmeier, Centres I; ³Griaule, Masques Dogon; ⁴L'art nègre, prés. afr.; ⁵Kjersmeier, Centres I.

III. THE WESTERN LANDS OF THE ATLANTIC COAST

The next stage in our tour of regional styles takes us to the lands on the western coast of Africa. Although Senegal is certainly negro country, it has been so greatly influenced by Islam and neighbouring Mauritania that no figure sculpture worthy of mention could develop there. The finds in pre-Islamic graves of the Serer, with their ornaments in gold and copper, also point to the influence of the north. Thus we are left only with the plaited helmet-masks of the *Djola* the Gambia, and of the Banyun on the Kasamanka. These masks are comic objects with protruding tubular-shaped eyes, topped with horns of oxen and antelopes, and trimmed with red abrus beans. They are worn by young men at circumcision ceremonies, and when begging in the surrounding villages (Fig. 30). It is not really until we reach the Bissagos Islands of Portuguese Guinea that we come to an important centre of carving, with round sculptures in both abstract and naturalistic style. According to Bernatzik, it is the abstract figures of the departed that are of greater antiquity. In more recent times great distress and catastrophes have inhibited the development of carving. Massive ungainly heads of cattle with natural horns give their war-canoes a menacing appearance. Hippopotamuses and other masks are worn in religious rites and for entertainment.

The matriarchal customs of the *Bidyugo* have undoubtedly fostered their great love of ornamentation and frequent use of the fertility-evoking motif of the female figure. Young maidens indicate their maturity by placing upon their backs large much-simplified figures with long bodies and straddled legs. Smaller sculptures are used as dolls.

CHARACTERISTICS: rounded forms; the head flattened horizontally; low forehead, cap-like hair-dress, cut in the page-boy style; a fibre kilt carved on the figure; the legs as bulbous stumps. The motifs are varied: human beings standing, striding out, or carrying vessels. Where they occur on spoons they are elegantly adapted to the curve of the handle. Animal sculptures are found on objects of all kinds (Fig. 31, a food-bowl). The *Baga* group, which in-

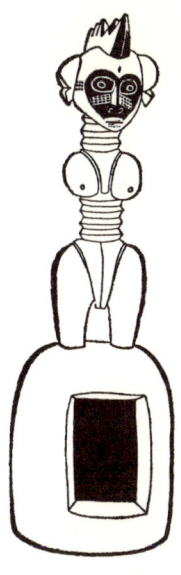

FIG. 25

FIG. 26

103

cludes, as well as the Baga themselves, also the Nalu, Landuman and related tribes, still belongs racially and culturally to the West Mandingo group of the Sudan. The Baga say that they immigrated into Guinea some time ago from the area near the source of the Niger. The tribes which were the last to arrive have only been converted to Islam in individual instances, and have thus preserved their vigorous style of carving, which is related to that of the Bambara.

CHARACTERISTICS of the most common type: highly abstract treatment; massive heads with bold aquiline noses; the head thrust forward, supported by raised arms (without hands) thus, preserving the equilibrium; the body heavy and barrel-shaped; the legs short and sturdy (Plate 14b). Figures of both sexes constitute the base of the large drums of the Simo secret society, which regulates and controls the social and religious life of the Baga. The various ranks within the society have their corresponding masks, which are brought out after the harvest, when threshing rice, or at the funerary rites for members of the society. The shoulder mask known as *nimba*, which is often reproduced, is of enormous size: an approximate idea of its appearance may be gained by taking the head in Plate 14b and magnifying it several times; the bust rests upon four supports on the bearer's shoulders, concealed by a wide dress of raffia. The smooth skin areas contrast with others engraved with hatching, herring-bone patterns, and other designs, accentuated by a covering of copper nails, making for balanced harmony. The *coiffure* is bordered by diadem-like pointed arches; the eye-lids are heavily accentuated half-ovals. To ensure fecundity the members of the society dance around the mask, which weighs about 150 lbs.; pregnant women enjoy its special protection. A different, more delicate type of this shoulder mask is shown in Plate 14a; Plate 15 reproduces a coloured 6-foot high Banda mask, representing one of the higher ranks of the Simo society. The subtle artistic talents of the Baga and Nalu are also shown by the *anok*, a massive head, reduced to essentials. The short colum-

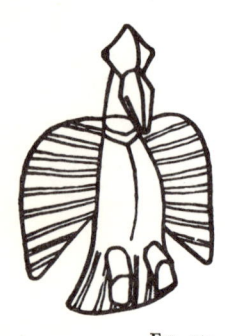

FIG. 27

FIG. 29

nar neck sprouts from a copiously-perforated cylindrical pedestal, the pattern of which is repeated on the head. The long pointed beak juts out, preserving the equilibrium of the figure as a whole (Fig. 32). The anok, too, is a requisite of the Simo society, and is honoured with masked dances at harvest time and at funerary rites; the head can also be lifted out of the pedestal and held in the hand during the rite. In the cavities of the head are affixed small horns, filled with magic medicine. In addition to these very important types of carving, there are a large number of others, such as huge stylized snakes, naturalistic female figures with voluminous breasts, posed standing, with legs astraddle. a stick with women's breasts, which is fixed in the roof, the sacred bird Foho, and many others.

A mysterious phenomenon dating from prehistoric times are the *nomori*, scattered far and wide over Sierra Leone and western Liberia: soapstone figures, found in fields and tumuli together with metal ornaments.[1] They are certainly of greater antiquity than the Mende, who inhabit this country today. The Mende believe them to be of supernatural origin, and for this reason ascribe to them magic powers. They place the nomori, protected by a roof of leaves, in their rice-fields, where they bring sacrificial offerings and come to invoke them. If they fail to produce the desired response, they are incited to act by being beaten with a stick. They are characterized by extreme variety and vitality, and are rendered in the most multifarious attitudes: riding, kneeling, sitting with legs crossed, hands placed upon the cheek or the decorative band framing the face, and equipped with a spear and shield. The head represents a drastically exaggerated, realistic negroid type, with flattened cranium, frog-like eyes, broad nose and heavily accentuated mouth (Fig. 33). The 16th-century Portuguese weapons, as Denise Paulme points out, indicate its probable age.

They have nothing in common with the Mende style of the present day. An old wooden kneeling figure of Mendeland origin, now in the British Museum, resembles in its essentials the nomori figure, and is thus linked to the old tellem sculptures of the Dogon, which are also posed kneeling and are decorated with a band around the chin.

The Mende live by fishing and hoeing the soil in the hot and humid jungle, and speak Mande-fu. The walls of their round huts are decorated with white and black engravings. Their social life

FIG. 28

FIG. 30

and art are dominated by omnipotent secret societies: the Poro society of the men, the Bundu or Sande society of the women. A special position is held by the Yassi society, which practises the art of magic healing. It employs numerous sculptured figures, known as *minsereh,* with slender rounded forms, rings on the neck, large head and high domed forehead. In the hands of the priestess, who goes into a trance, the minsereh figure, which has been rubbed with unguent and is charged with magic power, makes the will of the supernatural forces known by nodding distinctly (Fig. 34).[2] The large black Bundu helmet-masks, with rolls of fat round the neck (Fig. 35) – corpulence being regarded as a sign of beauty in a full-grown girl – extraordinarily high forehead and tousled fibre garment are so uniform that they are recognizable at first glance. And yet there is scope for countless variations in the treatment of the fine and compact faces, and especially the trimmings of the ornamental hair-dress (birds, horns, combs, etc.). The masks of the Vai resemble those of the Mende. Carved, it is usually thought, from bombax wood, they symbolize the guardian spirit of the female secret society, by whom young maidens are prepared for the functions they will have to fulfil as adult women. At the initiation ceremonies the spirit appears for the dance brandishing a whip, or carrying as a symbol a mace carved with figures.

KISSI The steatite and schist figures of the Kissi country, which are

FIG. 31

partly of phallic character, are columnar and much-simplified in form. They are found together with polished stone axes; the Kissi call them *pomdo*. In the belief that they are deceased persons resurrected once more to life, they afford them a place of honour on their graves or in their altar-huts, where sacrificial offerings are brought to them and their advice sought. The soothsayer ties a pomdo figure, by means of a supporting frame, on to his head, whence it replies to his questions by inclining sideways.[3] Clay figures in a similar style are still made today, but do not possess the power of the old specimens. The Kissi usually paint the walls of their houses in gay colours.

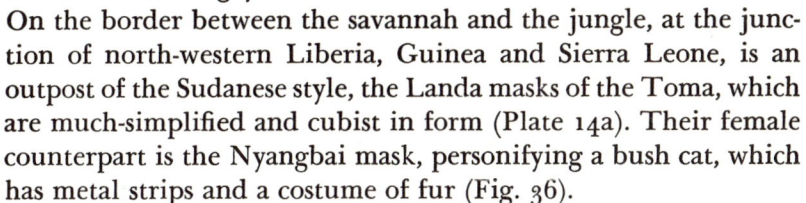

FIG. 32

On the border between the savannah and the jungle, at the junction of north-western Liberia, Guinea and Sierra Leone, is an outpost of the Sudanese style, the Landa masks of the Toma, which are much-simplified and cubist in form (Plate 14a). Their female counterpart is the Nyangbai mask, personifying a bush cat, which has metal strips and a costume of fur (Fig. 36).

Vast expanses of jungle in north-eastern Liberia and the western part of the Ivory Coast, as well as across the border in Guinea, are dominated by the all-powerful Poro secret society. Its sphere of influence, which takes no account of political frontiers, is responsible for the degree of uniformity that exists in the form and uses of the various types of mask. Thorough study of the copious material in collections[4] shows clearly that the stylistic variants are closely fused and interwoven with one another. The influence exerted by the Poro society is also facilitated by the fact that an extensive trade is carried on in these masks. A Poro artist does not consider it degrading to carve simultaneously several entirely different types of mask, varying according to the demand and the function they are designed to fulfil; it must, however, be emphasized that a mask serving a particular function need not always have the same form. Thus there is created a whole range of masks, from those that are portrait-like in their naturalism to those that are daringly abstract and cubist in form, in most cases both styles even being combined.

FIG. 33

With the *Dan* and *Kran* the centre of wood-carving is situated in the vicinity of the Upper Sassandra and Cavally. The Dan, with their sub-tribes the Yakuba, Geh, Gio, Uame, Kulime and others, inhabit the Cercle de Man and the subdivision of Danané. (The names Dan, Man and Mano are often confused; the last-

107

named live in the area to the east of the Nimba range in Liberia). The Mano, Kran, Shien, Kpelle (Guerzé) and Kono of Guinea are all within the sphere of influence of the Dan. In the eastern Kono villages there also live the Yakuba, who conduct their rites in the Dan language. In its pure form the Dan mask is oval and of stately simplicity (Plate 16). The eyes are either represented as slits evoking an impression of mystery, or as concentric circles, in which case they give a pronounced sense of movement (Fig. 37). The female mask, the symbol of maternal bounty, is more delicate and less animated than its male counterpart, which is often furnished with a moustache and beard of natural hair. The hairdress of plaited fibre is affixed by lateral holes. Within this basic form there are, however, great differences in quality and many special forms, for example: masks with a prominent forehead, eyes and mouth (sub-styles of Flanpleu and the Kulime); [5] masks which, as a result of continuous stylization, have become highly impressionist or cubist in style; surrealist masks with the nose projecting horizontally or curved like a beak (Fig. 38), with hinged jaws, tubular eyes, angular cheekbones (often interpreted as an ape motif), horns and inserted teeth. The creators of the other important style in the Cavally area, according to Vandenhoute, were the Kran, whom he calls Gere-Wobe, living to the south-west of the Dan tribe. Their style is thoroughly plastic and dynamic: their menacing masks, with their multiple horns, long projecting tubular eyes and accentuated cheekbones stand in striking contrast to the static Dan masks, and have often been imitated (Fig. 39). Where the Dan and Kran have been in close contact and have fused with one another, this has resulted in individualistic new forms and sub-styles with many different nuances, as seen, for example, in the Gio cubist mask in Fig. 40. Kran influence is also evident in the tubular-eyed masks made by the Kru tribes.

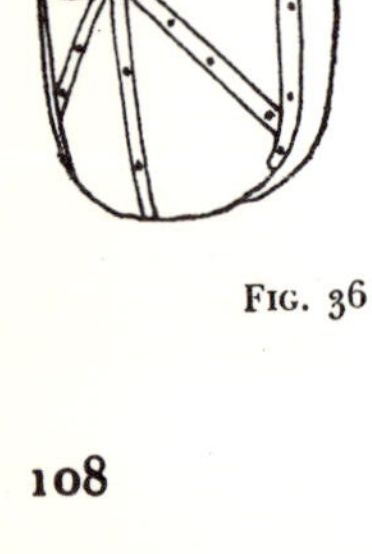

Kran masks give the impression of faces of humans who have become supernatural beings; they personify the spirit of the forest, as is indicated by the fact that they bear the characteristics of strong animals, such as the panther, wart hog or boar.

Detailed field studies [6] have led to most interesting findings concerning the function of the Dan and Kran masks, which are valuable to us from the religious and sociological points of view. They also corroborate the theories of Placide Tempels; namely, the idea

PLATE 29 — Bronze plaque, with king wearing beads, and musicians. Embossed plaques of this kind were affixed to the pillars and walls of the royal palace to glorify the ruler and his deeds. Benin, Nigeria. 17th century. *Ethnological Collection, Zurich (19¾ in.).*

a   b

PLATE 30a — An *oshe shango*, sacred wooden staff, used to invoke Shango, God of Thunder. His emblems are shown here: the Shango priestess, or his spouse, Oya, and the double thunderbolt. Thunderbolts are stone axes of earlier cultures, which the indigenous people believe to have dropped from the heavens during a thunderstorm, and therefore to be charged with magic. A staff of this kind can work miracles and ward off evil; from time to time the blood of a sacrificial ram is poured over it. Yoruba, Nigeria. *Rietberg Museum, Zurich, Von der Heydt Collection (19 in.).*

PLATE 30b — Rare standing figure, western Bapende. The style displays the same lyricism and introversion as that of the famous Minyaki masks. These figures formerly embellished the gable or entrance of the chief's hut, or were kept by the chief in his house as an emblem of power, upon which the fertility of all human beings and fields depended. South-western Congo. *Rietberg Museum, Zurich, Von der Heydt Collection (23¼ in.).*

PLATE 31 — An *otobo*, a hippopotamus mask of monumental force, the work of the Kalabari Ijo in the Niger delta. Once in 25 years the Sekuapu secret society invites the water spirits to the Owu play given in their honour. The mime wades up to his mouth in swampy water, wearing his mask horizontally on his head, so that it is turned upwards towards heaven, and moves across the water like a ghostly vision. Nigeria. *British Museum. (18⅜ in.).*

PLATE 32 — Death mask, spirit of a beautiful girl or of her mother. Together with a gaily-coloured costume with symbols applied, it is worn by northern Ibo men of the Mmwo society at ceremonies of the yam cult and at funerals of members. The departed speak through the mask with voices of spirits. South-eastern Nigeria. *American Museum of Natural History, New York (17 in.).*

PLATE 33 — Wooden mask with hinged jaw, as worn by members of the Ekpo secret society of the Ibibio, to exorcize demons at the yam harvest, and to ensure order. South-western Nigeria. *Lindenmuseum, Stuttgart (12 in.).*

PLATE 34 — Figure of a dignified bearded Ibibio man of the Oron clan, 18th-19th centuries. The figure is highly stylized and columnar in construction. Sacrifice is offered to it at the various phases of the agricultural cycle and in illness. South-eastern Nigeria. *Warner Münsterberger Collection, New York.* (28¼ in.).

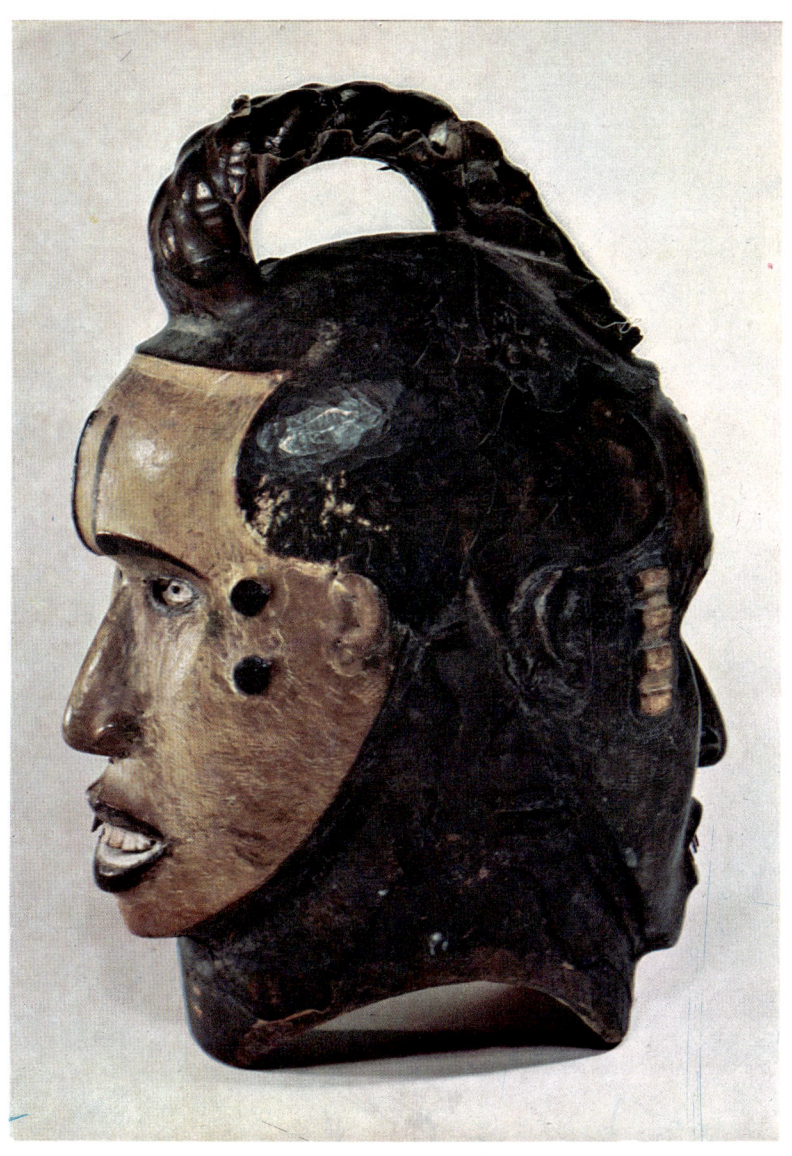

PLATE 35 — Helmet-mask, Ekoi, covered with antelope skin, representing deceased members of the powerful Ekpo society, which exercises judicial authority. The marks on the temples indicate the rank of nobility held in the society. The stark realism is further emphasized by inlaid eyes of iron and teeth of bone. The Janus head (on one side male, black and with closed eyes, on the other female, light and with open eyes) looks into the past and future, and is omnipotent and omniscient. As Talbot recorded in 1926, Ekoi head-hunters used to tie heads of vanquished enemies to their own heads, and then, intoxicated with victory, perform a dance similar to a Red Indian scalp dance. Cross River area. *Ethnological Collection Zurich (19¼ in.).*

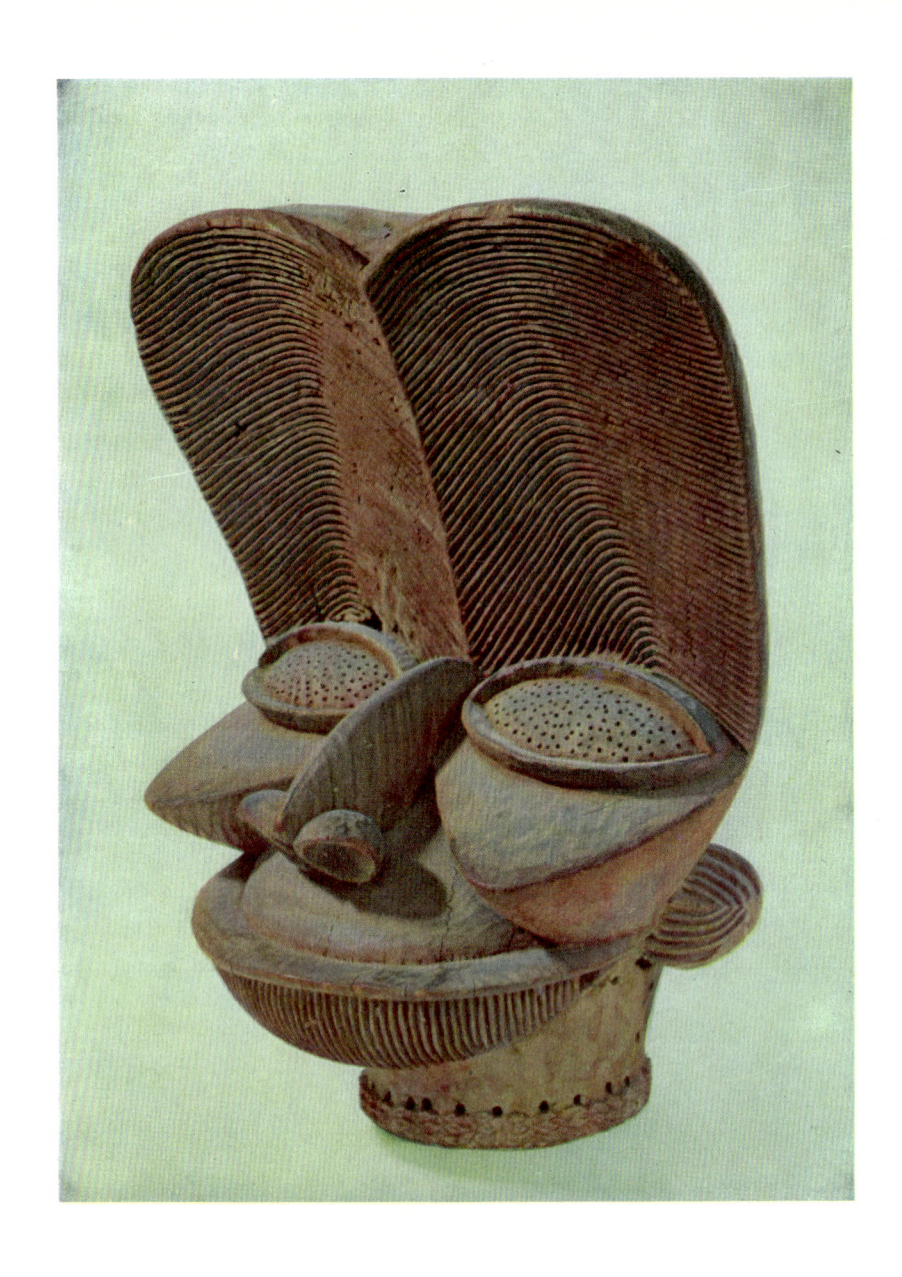

PLATE 36 — Large dance mask of the Bacham (Bamileke group), in Bamenda. Its artistic significance lies in the dynamism and energy of the cubes and striated planes. Cameroun grasslands. *Rietberg Museum, Zurich, Von der Heydt Collection (26⅜ in.).*

of regeneration, of the ancestors as partial emanations of the force, derived from the supreme god, Zlan, which enters into the mask. The older a mask is, and the more sacrifices that are offered to it, the greater its power and value, irrespective of its form. The amount of power it possesses determines the rank within the Poro society which it serves, and whether it is feared or regarded merely as a means of entertainment. The power transmitted to the mask from the ancestors differs greatly according to the function which it fulfils. An enumeration of some of the masks gives us an insight into the hopes, needs and demands of the African, and enables us to understand his character. Certain masks serve as judges, debt-collectors, and soothsayers in war. They settle quarrels, influence the course of wars and bring them to an end, and direct the lightning and the thunder. They are the protectors and patrons of fishermen (crocodile), smiths, twins and travellers; they forestall evil-doers, devourers of babies, and adulterers; they keep guard over the household, protect expectant mothers, help childless women and cure illnesses, such as gangosa (rhinopharyngitis), stammering or facial paralysis (through the crooked mask!). Some masks are portraits of beautiful women or effigies of persons absent on a journey. The ape mask plays the part of a clown. A special mask with round eyes and metal edges acts as guardian of the fire, and keeps watch for the dangerous bush fires; when one breaks out, he runs from one village to another to give warning. On hearing his call, the young men compete with one another to be first on the scene; for each seeks the honour of being the fastest. To the war masks sacrifice used formerly to be made in the form of prisoners taken in battle; but nowadays they are constantly fed with cola-nuts, chicken's blood and palm-oil. Owing to the importance of the function they fulfil, the utmost care has to be taken in making them. The Dan strive instinctively to create well-balanced, harmonious forms; for the image, as the abode of power, ought to be as beautiful and attractive as possible. Finally, as special types of mask, mention must be made of the *ma,* tiny masks of wood or stone, three to four inches long, copies in miniature of the large Dan masks, which include examples of the minor arts at their most charming. They are regarded as particularly sacred; for this reason they are worked with the greatest care, and serve as badges worn by those initiated into the secret societies. They act as ancestral guardians against illness, and

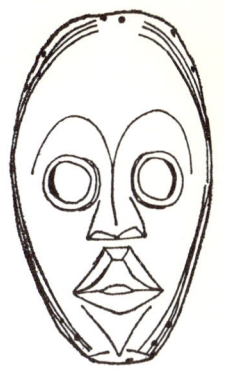

FIG. 37

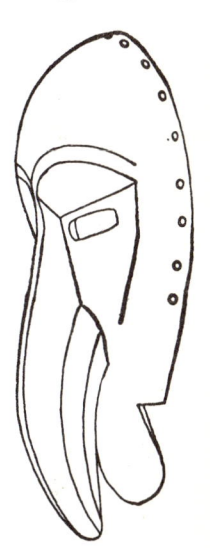

FIG. 38

FIG. 39

117

Utensils

FIG. 40

are honoured with offerings of rice and palm-oil.

If one bears in mind the important function fulfilled by the Dan mask, one will readily understand that the Dan devote less time and attention to carving whole figures. Where these exist, it is only in rudimentary form.

In contrast, it is a characteristic of the Kran that they sometimes carve whole figures on their implements. In addition to ancestor figures with short legs and the typical Dan face, which serve as guardians or simply to amuse their owners, we find many utensils decorated with heads: rice- and tobacco-pounders, seats for newly-circumcised persons, boards for the game of mankala, hair-pins and combs, dancing-staffs, etc. The handle of the large spoon known as *po* is formed by a human head (Fig. 41). The po spoons are honorific emblems of the chief's mother or wife, who controls initiation into female secret societies. When her son, the successor to the chieftainship, returns home from the bush school and has been initiated, she dances a proud dance in a public ceremony, holding the spoon and scooping up the rice, which is then consumed by the villagers in the invisible yet tangible presence of the ancestor spirit. Each clan possesses only one po spoon, which is handed down from generation to generation.

The shackle ring shown in Fig. 2, the emblem worn by the chief's wife, gives us an idea of the fine cast brass work produced by the Dan and Kran.

Other anklets and armlets consist of several rings, are furnished with little round bells and decorated with spiral patterns in wax. The small cast brass secular figures made by the Kran, although of little artistic value, are nevertheless engaging.

Paintings of figures found on the interior and exterior walls of their huts bear witness to their spontaneous narrative talents: among secular subjects, they include legendary scenes and animals, burlesque mask bearers and stilt-walker birds (Fig. 6).

Lit.: [1] Rütimeyer; [2] Sydow, Handbuch; [3] Paulme. Gens du riz; [4] Donner; [5] Vandenhoute; [6] Harley.

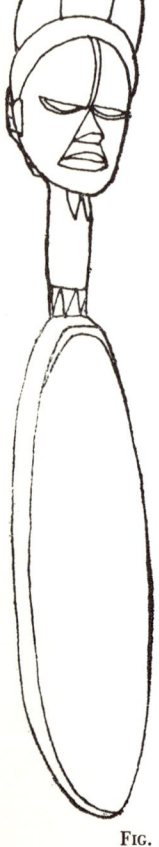

FIG. 41

IV. THE EASTERN LANDS OF THE ATLANTIC COAST

IVORY COAST

On the Ivory Coast, more or less exactly at the point of intersection of Lat. 5° N. and Long. 5° W., the river Bandama flows into the Atlantic Ocean. It forms the border between the western and eastern zones of the Atlantic coastlands of Africa. To the east of the Bandama the jungle recedes, giving way to rainy savannah, with its considerably less arduous conditions of life, thus imparting to the Guinea lands a different aspect. In this area, as in Ghana, Dahomey, and Nigeria, elements of the advanced civilizations outlined on p. 71 ff. come into contact with West African cultures. The foremost tribe of the Ivory Coast is the Baule, an Anyi people who speak a Kwa language. Owing to dynastic dissension in the kingdom of Ashanti, they left the Gold Coast about the year 1730 and, led by Queen Aura Poka, moved to the area between the Nzi and Bandama, on the Ivory Coast, where they intermingled with the peoples settled there, the Guro and Senufo, and founded a noteworthy kingdom. Their myths and legends tell of Alurua, God of Creation, and his pantheon, Nyamye, God of Heaven, Assye, Goddess of the Earth, Gu, God of the Wind and at the same time Organizer of the World; also of the sons of Nyamye, the demigods Kakagye or Guli, spirit of the dead, and Gbekre, the baboon. A great number of lesser gods are subordinate to them. The ram is a heavenly demon or a spirit of agriculture. The Wind God, Gu, is personified in a bearded human mask; Guli, son of Nyamye, is given a bull's head as an attribute. All these figures are reflected in art — in an ingenious art in which the cultured Baule and the talented Guro exercised a beneficial influence upon one another. The Baule brought with them from their old homeland the art of brass casting, but no tradition of wood-carving. The cultivated and distinguished style of carving of the Baule and Guro has not underservedly become world-famous. With it a fine poetic element enters into African art: a lyricism equalled only by the Ogowe tribes and the Baluba.

Here are no images of dread terror or fear of demons, no affecting outburst of feeling. Animal force is tamed, translated into cubist

Baule

FIG. 42

119

decoration, or suggested symbolically. If one may sometimes feel repelled by the powerful, primitive forms of other styles, one can find in the cultivated art of the Baule an avenue of approach to the whole of African art.

Statues We have seen that the Baule and Guro have strongly felt aesthetic requirements which they have to satisfy. Sculpture serves to provide their gods and ancestors with as fine and well-formed an abode as possible. When the Baule portray important persons and beautiful women, they endeavour to render them in a manner true to life. Observance of tradition does not inhibit the artist from making his portraits so personal that the subject is easily identifiable and not only by his scarification marks (Plate 17). In order to meet the continuous demand, many wood-carving centres have established veritable craft industries. Even among these rather standardized products works stand out which manifest fine aesthetic feeling; the local population hold their carvers in highest esteem, and strangers come to visit them.

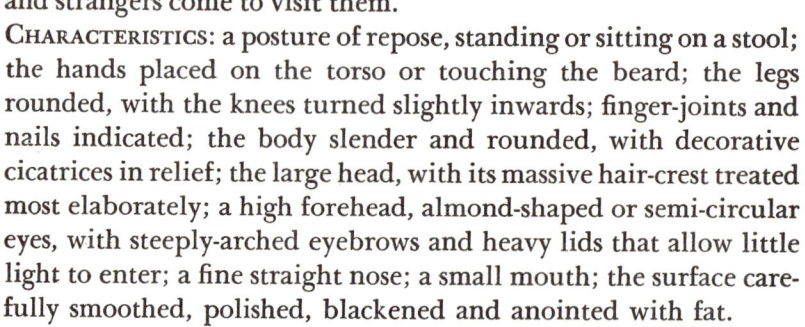

CHARACTERISTICS: a posture of repose, standing or sitting on a stool; the hands placed on the torso or touching the beard; the legs rounded, with the knees turned slightly inwards; finger-joints and nails indicated; the body slender and rounded, with decorative cicatrices in relief; the large head, with its massive hair-crest treated most elaborately; a high forehead, almond-shaped or semi-circular eyes, with steeply-arched eyebrows and heavy lids that allow little light to enter; a fine straight nose; a small mouth; the surface carefully smoothed, polished, blackened and anointed with fat.

FIG. 43 Gbekre, who sits in judgement upon the souls of the departed in the next world, is represented as a human being with the head of an ape: a composition executed with verve, yet evenly balanced. How appropriate are the large flat feet upon which the figure stands! (Fig. 42).

Masks Baule masks, too, are of dazzling charm, with the face serene and delicate, yet differentiated. The care taken over details is admirable: the fine strokes denoting eye-lashes, the decorative cicatrices on the smooth forehead, the striated hair-line, the zigzag contour of the face — all these details give an idea of the Baule wood-carvers' artistic sensibility (Plate 19, left; Fig. 43).

That the Baule also excel in vigorous and very abstract styles is shown by their polychrome animal masks, such as Guli, the mighty spirit of the buffalo, with its raffia costume (Plate 18; Fig. 44). The treatment of another charming Guli mask is also highly abstract: the face is small, round and disc-shaped, with the pupils like drops in oval eye-sockets (Fig. 45).

Utensils

A delight in art such as is possessed by the Baule also naturally finds expression in their utensils; indeed, the border-line between sacred and secular art may even come to be obscured. Today secular art predominates. Graceful heads and figures are combined in an ingenious way with loom pulley-holders (as in Fig. 48), ointment-pots (Plate 17, left), jars used for the mouse oracle, etc. Doors, drums and stools, resonating-tubes and maces, handles of fly-whisks and sword-hilts are covered with decoration in relief or with open-work patterns. Many of these reliefs show a clearly conceived, skilful disposition (Fig. 46), contradicting the frequently stated view that the negro is capable only of devising simple arrangements. Here, too, the fish and crocodile motif has a mythological import: it is designed to serve as a reminder of the human sacrifices which the Baule once had to make to the gods of the river Komoe, when crossing it during their trek to the Ivory Coast. The Baule brought with them from their former homeland small cast brass weights (cf. p. **123**) which can only with difficulty be distinguished from those of the Ashanti, and then only by their being somewhat cruder in form. Implements used at ceremonies were covered with thin sheets of hammered gold. The Baule and other Anyi tribes from the southern part of the Ivory Coast also cast gold, in the form of small decorative objects bearing human and animal figures. Small masks with human features, which warriors fixed to their swords, may be interpreted as trophies of a vanquished enemy. The mask with ram horns (Fig. 47) is the emblem of Nyamye, the god of fecundity; it bears croc-

FIG. 46

FIG. 44

Metal casting

121

odiles, fish and serpents, round decorative discs ('conveyors of souls') and other ornamentation. All these gold objects express cosmic and animistic forces. They are not worn for purely decorative purposes, but are reserved for the ritual festival of gold and fertility (Plate 18).

Even today many Baule wear their native cotton costume, patterndyed with indigo by the plangi technique.

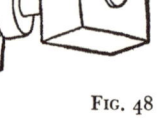

Guro The Guro style is perhaps even more ingenious and elegant than that of the Baule. Whole figures are rarely found here, although figured sculpture is used to embellish many utensils. Thus, for instance, on Guro looms there is a delightful little carving with a human or animal head, forming the holder of the pulley over which runs the string that supports the heddles (Fig. 48): a spirit of unparalleled delicacy and charm, keeping guard over the work.

FIG. 47

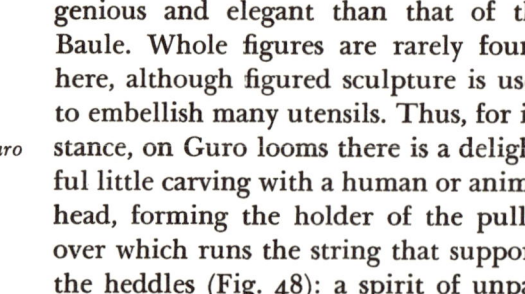

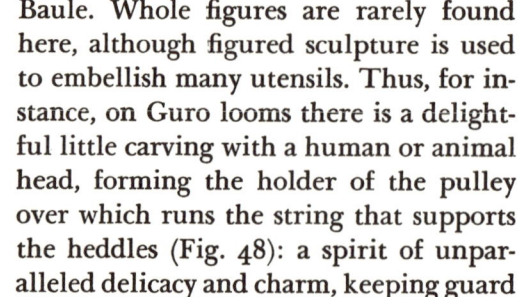

CHARACTERISTICS: slender face, deeply incised; forehead-nose line not broken up; chevron-shaped hair-line; the eyes sometimes slanting. Some of these features are already to be found amongst the Yaure, a sub-tribe of the Baule (Plate 19). Zoomorphic elements (horns, birds) identify the mask as that of a mythological being. The polychrome antelope in Fig. 49 joins in the dance of the Zamle secret society, and serves as a war-mask.

FIG. 45

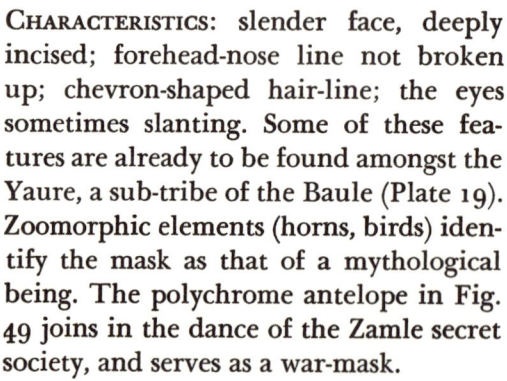

Ebrie In the densely-wooded lagoon of Ebrie we come across figures of a special character, related to Baule sculpture, with curved limbs, and the arms often raised to touch the head (Fig. 50). The Ebrie immigrated from the north and probably brought the art of carving with them.

FIG. 48

These sculptures have also frequently been ascribed to the Alladya (Alangoa), who share the lagoon with the Ebrie and other tribes.

Krinjabo In the Cercle d'Assinié, in the south-west of the Ivory Coast, are some abandoned graves from the time of the ancient kingdom of Krinjabo. Here clay figures have been discovered: sculptures, dating in part from the 17th century, with excessively large heads, protruding slit eyes, massive hair-dress, ringed neck and rudimentarily formed body (Fig. 51). These are thought to be likenesses of rulers, made by women sculptors immediately after their deaths. Clothed and ornamented, and protected by a thatched roof, they were placed on a stand over the grave.

Both terms, the Gold Coast and Ghana, recall a proud past. 'The Gold Coast' was the name given to the country by the Portuguese, because the Ashanti came to meet them lavishly adorned with gold ornaments. Ghana, the name of the former brilliant kingdom in the western Sudan, became the embodiment of African greatness.[1]

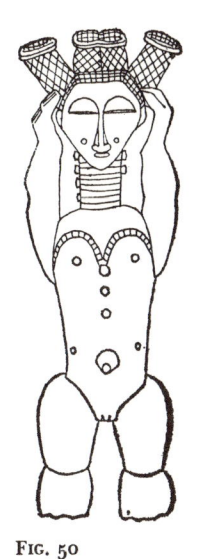

GHANA

In the 17th century, thanks to their strict military organization, the sacrosanct Ashanti rulers attained great power, and their court unheard-of pomp and splendour. The trade with Europeans in gold and slaves brought them much wealth. Gold was the monopoly of the court; it symbolized the sun, as the dynamic centre of the universe, and the king regarded himself as its representative. Goldsmiths constituted a highly-regarded and privileged caste at court. Today, however, the old wealth in gold has been scattered to the winds: lost, sold, re-cast — so that the magnificent gold mask from the treasury of King Kofi Kakari (Plate 20) is the sole object that has survived.

The charming small weights in cast brass, which served to weigh the gold dust, are very common, and famous. These weights were a speciality of the Akan and Anyi peoples, but especially of the Ashanti and Baule, which shows that this branch of artistic endeavour had reached a high level before the Baule left in the 18th century. The gold weights were at first of a symbolic character (animals, for example, regarded as representatives of the gods), and exclusive to the king and the queen mother. Later ordinary citizens were also allowed to use them; but at this time the royal weights were made 50 per cent. heavier than others of the same denomination, thus yielding a sort of tax in kind. In the administration

FIG. 50

FIG. 49

Gold weights

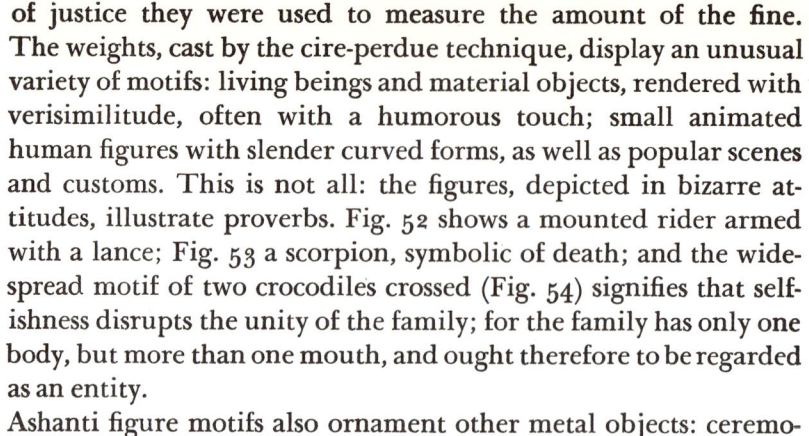

of justice they were used to measure the amount of the fine. The weights, cast by the cire-perdue technique, display an unusual variety of motifs: living beings and material objects, rendered with verisimilitude, often with a humorous touch; small animated human figures with slender curved forms, as well as popular scenes and customs. This is not all: the figures, depicted in bizarre attitudes, illustrate proverbs. Fig. 52 shows a mounted rider armed with a lance; Fig. 53 a scorpion, symbolic of death; and the widespread motif of two crocodiles crossed (Fig. 54) signifies that selfishness disrupts the unity of the family; for the family has only one body, but more than one mouth, and ought therefore to be regarded as an entity.

Ashanti figure motifs also ornament other metal objects: ceremonial implements and swords, small boxes for gold dust, and in particular the lid of the *kuduo,* the container for the souls of the deceased (Plate 21).

The great artistic sense of the Ashanti is not readily apparent from their wood-carving. The only objects really worth mentioning are the small *akua'ba,* fertility dolls (Fig. 55), which the women carry around wrapped up in their loin-cloths, in the hope of having good-looking children. When they hope it will be a boy, they choose a figure with a head highly stylized in the form of a flat disc and a figure with a rectangular head when they want a girl.

The Ashanti do not believe in ancestor figures, but in the divine power of the 'golden stool', which in or about the year 1700, according to legend, came crashing down from the heavens during a thunderstorm upon the knees of King Osei Tutu, the founder of the Ashanti kingdom, thereby sanctioning his authority. It is not simply a symbol of this miracle, but of the soul of the people given concrete form in the State. In the course of time the basic form of the sacred stool has been frequently copied, modified and ornamented with silver and gold covering, supporting figures, and pillars in open-work with the same function (Fig. 56). As conveyors of the souls of divine kings and their mothers, they serve as altars, upon which sacrificial offerings are made to the ancestors.

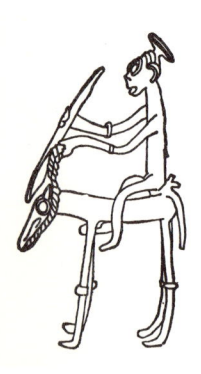

In addition to Ashanti arts and crafts, mention must be made of the magnificent textiles in silk and cotton (cf. p. 50), the designs on which always have some meaningful relationship to the wearer. The *adinkra* mourning garments, imprinted with stamps made from calabashes, are of symbolic significance. Like the Anyi, Ashanti women place clay figures on burial-places: impressive, almost lifesized renderings of the deceased. They used to preserve their hair in special head-bearing urns, and decorated ceremonial jugs and tobacco pipes with delicate figures and designs in relief.

The Bron, or Abron, who live to the north of the Ashanti, have developed an individual style for their terracottas and works in cast brass. The few wood and clay objects produced by the Ewe are quite 'primary', but expressive in form: clay fetishes used in the Legba cult, figured pot-lids, similar to that shown in Fig. 3, *aklama* wooden figures, and so on.

A certain amount of fame was gained in Kete Krachi by Ali Amonikoyi as an artist in brass casting. He was a Yoruba whose family had immigrated from Ilorin and had kept the technique a family secret. His masks, sceptres, animals and groups are rendered in a smooth naturalistic form, but the general impression gained from them is of a feeble echo of ancient tradition.

The crafts of northern Togo reach their climax in the particularly fine silver filigree jewellery produced there. The sultan's emblem shown in Fig. 57 represents an alligator with a fish in its mouth. In the 17th century one of the Ewe tribes, the Fon, established an absolutist kingdom which owed its wealth and power primarily to the slave trade — it was not in vain that this part of Africa was known as the 'Slave Coast'. The king concentrated at his court, and monopolized, several branches of artistic endeavour, particularly silver- and brass-working, as well as the weaving of gaily-coloured *appliqué* materials for wall-coverings. Only the crafts of woodcarving and calabash-carving remained open to ordinary people. In the capital, Abomey, interesting wall sculptures have been preserved in the royal palace: the finest are probably those made for Prince Agadja during the first golden age, at the beginning of the 18th century. They are clay panels, with the relief plaque-like but of low elevation; they depict historical and allegorical scenes, and victorious battles fought by the Fon against the Yoruba. An overpowering, and also intimidating, impression is produced by the great royal statues, with the upper part of the body in human and animal form (lion and shark). The realistic animal figures, covered with silver or brass plate, and the two lifelike statues of Gu, the war god, one of embossed copper plate, the other of iron, are famous; reproductions of them are common, although they cannot be considered great works of art. From the precincts of the

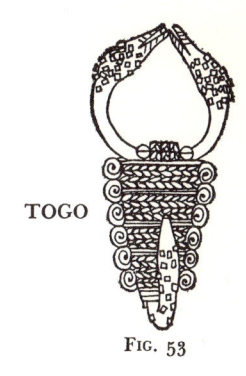

TOGO

FIG. 53

FIG. 54

DAHOMEY

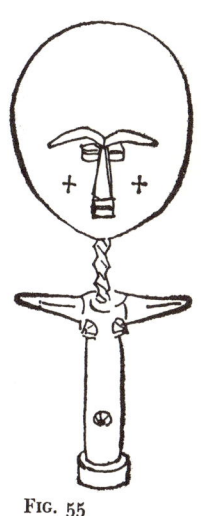

FIG. 55

FIG. 56

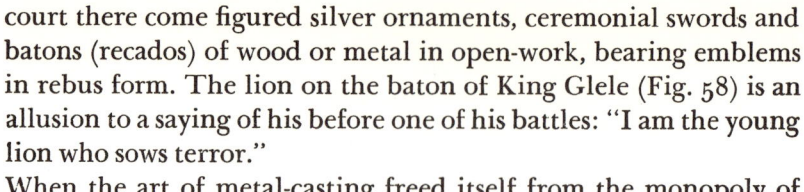

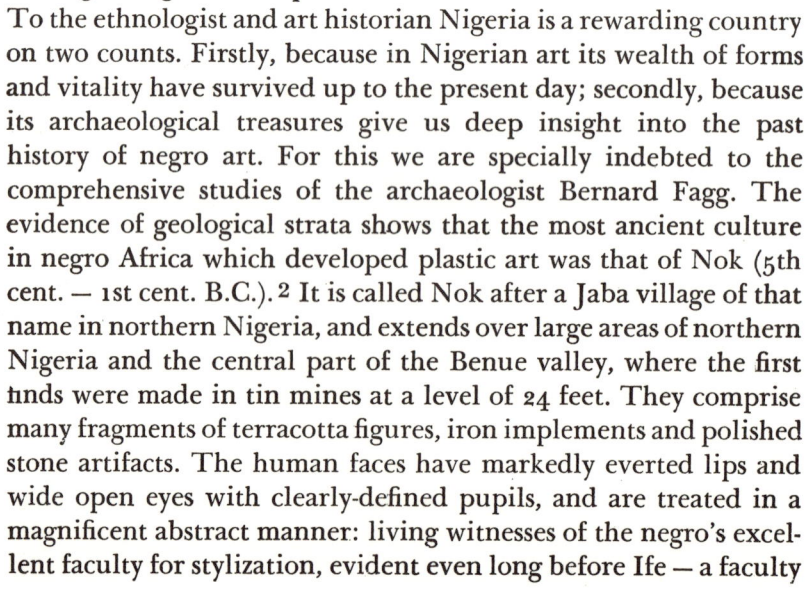

FIG. 57

EARLY CULTURES
OF NIGERIA

Nok

FIG. 58

court there come figured silver ornaments, ceremonial swords and batons (recados) of wood or metal in open-work, bearing emblems in rebus form. The lion on the baton of King Glele (Fig. 58) is an allusion to a saying of his before one of his battles: "I am the young lion who sows terror."

When the art of metal-casting freed itself from the monopoly of the court about the year 1900, there were made in Abomey secular brass figures and groups, cast in the cire-perdue technique, representing genre scenes and animals, which have since become a much sought-after article of export (Fig. 59).

CHARACTERISTICS: elongated cylindrical forms; schematized, slightly mannered naturalism; vitality, humour and verve; punched decoration to suggest the patterns of garments or skins of animals Of a different type is the folk wood-carving of the Nago (a Yoruba tribe): a crude unsophisticated style, which, inspired by the southern Yoruba, is found with the same figures of gods, Gelede masks, cult implements, figured bowls, ibeji and secular implements as we shall come across when dealing with the Yoruba (Plate 22). They make gaudy single- or double-tiered thrones for chiefs, stands of bowls, and masks upon which are many figures, placed close together. The Fon style is a little more rounded and simpler, approximating rather to that of primary art. Fig. 60 once stood in a shrine of the god Legba, and represents his consort.

To the ethnologist and art historian Nigeria is a rewarding country on two counts. Firstly, because in Nigerian art its wealth of forms and vitality have survived up to the present day; secondly, because its archaeological treasures give us deep insight into the past history of negro art. For this we are specially indebted to the comprehensive studies of the archaeologist Bernard Fagg. The evidence of geological strata shows that the most ancient culture in negro Africa which developed plastic art was that of Nok (5th cent. — 1st cent. B.C.).[2] It is called Nok after a Jaba village of that name in northern Nigeria, and extends over large areas of northern Nigeria and the central part of the Benue valley, where the first finds were made in tin mines at a level of 24 feet. They comprise many fragments of terracotta figures, iron implements and polished stone artifacts. The human faces have markedly everted lips and wide open eyes with clearly-defined pupils, and are treated in a magnificent abstract manner: living witnesses of the negro's excellent faculty for stylization, evident even long before Ife — a faculty

126

which still distinguishes him today (Fig. 61). Fragments from the Nok finds show that the statues were in part life-sized and asymmetrical, and were on occasion even constructed in spiral form. The figures are shown wearing abundant jewellery. There are also fine animal figures and plant motifs.

In the course of the political and ethnical changes brought about by the influx of new immigrants from the north and east, there developed around the court of Ife, the sacred Yoruba city in southwestern Nigeria, a culture which fostered a flourishing of the arts, and masterpieces that opened up completely new vistas. In the midst of the negro lands, in or about the 13th century, some hands unknown modelled heads, masks and figure groups in cast brass and terracotta, radiating such vital warmth, treated with such organic feeling, and of such perfect beauty in technique and form (that is to say, classical, without having undergone the stylization usual in Africa), that scholars for a long time believed that their origin must be ascribed to influences from the area of the Mediterranean or the Nile — especially since no corresponding primitive forms could be identified in Nigeria itself. It may indeed be the case that the technique of brass casting was introduced to Nigeria from without, but nevertheless the method employed is not to be found anywhere else. Why should one not assume in good faith that it springs from the negroes themselves? Have they not proved a thousand times over that they possess an outstanding talent for observation of nature, that they are accomplished masters of naturalistic expression, and that they also understand the art of excluding what is unessential and treating subjects in an abstract manner? William Fagg has clearly demonstrated the distinguished sensibility characteristic of Ife, which even nowadays finds expression in certain Yoruba wooden figures.

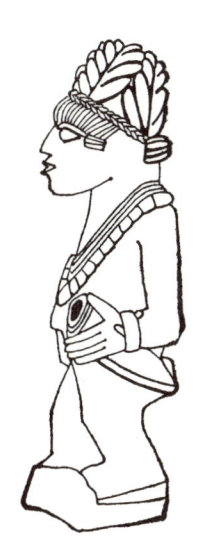

Ife

FIG. 59

FIG. 60

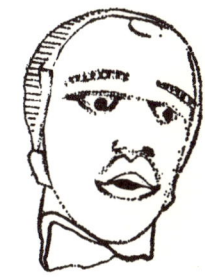

FIG. 61

FIG. 62

The first heads and fragments from Ife were discovered by Leo Frobenius between 1910 and

1912, and from the 1930s onwards new finds have continuously been made. Most of them are in the possession of the Oni, the ruler of Ife, and are exhibited to view in the fine local museum. The bronze head in Plate 23 is in the British Museum. The most remarkable ritual figure in Plate 24 was discovered only very recently, and remains in Nigerian safe-keeping. The human type represented is not always the same, emphasis being laid variously on the Ethiopian, the Semitic, or the negroid element. From the abundance of terracotta fragments and the variety of forms the conclusion may be drawn that many artists were employed over a considerable period of time. The casts are alloys of copper and zinc; the cire-perdue technique has been mastered to perfection.

Consummate skill is also shown in terracotta sculpture, which runs parallel to that in bronze (Plate 25).

The Yoruba also worked stone (a rare feat in Africa!), and outstanding examples of their art have been preserved in the magnificent granite ram's head, housed in the museum at Ife, and the monolithic mushroom-shaped stone seats of quartz, with a handle on the side, which can measure as much as 32 inches in height. We can see this form cast in bronze in Plate 24; it suggests Mediterranean influence.

FIG. 63

Benin

The cruder and more massive stone statues and columns of Idena-Ore, near Ife, seem to be of a different style or to have originated at a different stage of cultural development. They are deities, and sometimes also animals; the largest is three feet high, and the smallest, in a kneeling posture, has a distant resemblance to the figures of Esie. The powerful ancient kingdom of Benin, situated in the forest area of southern Nigeria, 106 miles south-east of Ife, has already been described in such detail that we need mention here only a few important facts. For a long time the Benin bronze sculptures were the only historical evidence dating back several centuries into the West African past, and both the level of technical accomplishment attained in bronze

FIG. 64

FIG. 65

128

casting, as well as the monumental vigour of the figures represented, were the object of great admiration — and no small amount of speculation. Today Benin is overshadowed by the classical art of Ife. By comparison, Benin art gives the sensation of a sacrifice of vital warmth for the sake of representation of externals. Tradition clearly states[3] that the art of bronze casting was introduced to Benin during the reign of King Oba Oguola (supposedly about the year 1280), and Ighu-igha, an artist despatched at that time to Benin from Ife, is venerated by smiths still today. Between that time and the arrival of the first Europeans (it was in 1472 that the Portuguese navigator Sequeira discovered Benin) the Benin kingdom flourished and evolved its own characteristic style. The accounts of the early travellers reveal their astonishment at the pomp and extravagance at the court of the king-god. Olfert Dapper's account (1668), in particular, conveys an impression of the great fortified city, enclosed by a rampart nearly 10 feet high, the royal palace, and the solidly built houses situated along thirty broad streets. These dwellings were of low elevation but extended over a considerable area, and had long interior galleries and courtyards, with smooth-polished marble-like clay walls and long rows of wooden pillars, covered with bronze plaques. The houses often had small turrets, on which were perched birds made of bronze, similar to the ibis shown in Fig. 63. The king had a complete monopoly of trade with the Europeans.

FIG. 66

Then Benin fell into oblivion. In 1704 Nyendael found the town in ruins, although subsequently it was re-built. In 1897 Benin was opened up again by the British, who undertook a punitive expedition, as a result of which 2000 bronzes found their way to Europe. The technique of Benin bronze casting is that of the waste form (cf. p. 48), in which a wax model is formed over a core of clay, and covered with a thin coating of gypsum paste and brick dust. The alloy of the plaques consists of 84 per cent. copper, 2.5 per cent. tin, and 8 per cent. lead, and that of the free-standing sculptures of 78 per cent. copper, 5 per cent. lead, and 14 per cent. zinc.[4] For further finish the cast was elaborately worked and chased. The most important bronze objects are: free-standing figures, commemorative heads, groups, plaques in relief, bells and rattle-staffs, small expressive masks and plaquettes worn on the belt as emblems of office; chests in the shape of palaces, animals (Figs. 63, 64), cult stands, jewellery, etc. Of objects in ivory: most elaborately

FIG. 67

decorated human masks, animals, beakers, spoons, gongs, trumpets, ornaments (Plate 27), and large elephant tusks covered with bands in figured relief. Although this list gives some idea of the abundance of forms, it is by no means exhaustive.

The representations on these objects served above all to exalt the king, the queen mother (Plate 26), the princes and royal household, army commanders, shown with their arms and armour and their retainers (huntsmen, musicians), or alternatively depicted important events (Plate 28). The kings had themselves portrayed in full regalia, occasionally with mud-fish for legs — to identify themselves with Olokun, the God of the Sea. Most of the bronzes are statically and symmetrically composed; the size corresponds to the rank of the person portrayed (Plate 29). In addition to these, there are bronze plaques with figures forming asymmetrical groups, in which no less than nine human beings are sometimes depicted, posed frontally and in profile, engaged in a violent brawl. Then there are all kinds of animals: leopards, crocodiles, snakes, birds and fish; also motifs of plaited bands. The background of the plaques is decorated with a rosette motif (Plate 29). The habit and costume of the Portuguese that are occasionally portrayed make it easier to date the bronzes more accurately. We also have the data clearly established by William Fagg, one of the foremost authorities in the field of African art.[5] The chronology put forward by Luschan and Struck is in his view inadequate. His investigations indicate that the early style, with its thinness of casting, and magnificently differentiated and naturalistic representations, continued far into the 16th century. The climax in the evolution of Benin occurred under Kings Ewuare and Esigie in the 15th and early 16th centuries. The magnificent head of the queen mother, with its narrow collar of bronze only three millimetres thick (Plate 26), and the noble artistic mask in ivory (Plate 27) date from the later part of this era. The intermediate period lasted from the end of the 16th century to the middle of the 18th, and introduced a monumental art with thick casting and highly schematized representations; this gave rise to the casting of bronze plaques in figured relief, amongst other objects. Even during the period of decline, in the 19th century (typified by hybrid casts, often treated in a perfunctory manner, and ill-proportioned works of purely extrinsic value), some remarkable work was produced. From this late period come the large heavy bronze heads with beaded 'wings' (Fig. 65), dating from

FIG. 68

the reign of Oba Osemwenede (1816—1848), as well as the huge elephant tusks in relief which were sometimes inserted into the large bronze heads.

Parallel to the art centring around the court there evolved a less refined folk art. Prosperous influential citizens commissioned for their private altars small heads in wood, with carved elephant tusks inserted, and other ornamental objects.

Many a rare work that found its way to Europe together with the Benin collections could well have originated in the workshops of neighbouring peoples, in Udo, Owo or other centres of craftsmanship.

Finally, there is in Nigeria an important group of brass castings, which can, however, not be linked either with Benin or Ife. Finds have been made among the Ijo and Andoni in the Niger delta,

FIG. 69

the Igala of Idah on the Niger, the Igbira and Gwari north of the mouth of the Benue, and finally, of animal figures in the Nupe villages Jebba Gungun and Tada, situated along the middle reaches of the Niger. The almost life-sized 'seated' figure stands out from other sculptures found amongst the Nupe: the ample naked body is represented with great forcefulness. Of this figure reproductions have often been made; it is assigned by William Fagg to the 15th century.

Esie

In Esie, in the province of Ilorin, some 60 miles north of Ife, there were discovered in 1934 about 800 fragmentary stone figures, some as much as 18 inches high (Fig. 62).

131

CHARACTERISTICS: either standing, on short legs, or seated on mushroom-like stools; women kneeling before a water-vessel; hat- or feather-like head-dress; negroid or Oriental types; tattooing, as on the Ife heads, but much cruder and more rigid, although typically African in the impression of vitality which they evoke.

These stone figures may have been carved in the pre-Islamic kingdom of Nupe about the year 1700. The inhabitants of Esie preserve them in a small grove, and hold a special sacrificial festival for them each year, for the stone spirits are a source of fecundity, giving the priests valuable advice whilst they sleep.

NIGERIA DURING THE LAST CENTURY

After this digression into the past history of Nigeria, which will still present us with many surprises and problems, let us now turn to Nigerian art of the present day. The main centres of wood-carving are situated in the south, on either bank of the Niger, where Islam failed to substitute itself for the deeply-rooted ancestor and mother cult, and where different styles co-exist in a treasure-house of creative talent. Little study has as yet been made of the bold abstract sculptures of the hill tribes of the so-called 'pagan belt' stretching along both banks of the river Benue, and including the Jos plateau.

Architecture: in the mountainous areas the Old Nigritic round hut, with a cone-shaped roof; in the towns of the north the neo-Sudanese Moorish-Berber mosque style and the clay box-shaped house; in the south, among the Yoruba and Ekoi, the multi-chambered construction with its impluvium, courtyard and gabled roof. The courtyards and living quarters are enclosed by protective clay walls or cactus hedges. The walls of the gable-roofed houses of the southern tribes are frequently covered with gaily-coloured geometric paintings or reliefs.

FIG. 70

Yoruba

The Yoruba, some five million strong, are one of the major African peoples. Together with their sub-tribes, they inhabit the south-western districts of Nigeria, and also extend far into Dahomey, Togo and Ghana. Although they are agriculturalists, many of them now live in the towns.

This highly-talented people, responsive to the influence of the more advanced cultures of the Mediterranean and Orient, conscious of the heritage of a great past (Ife!), and inspired by a rich mythology, produced an art of great splendour and vitality, which is still alive even today. It can be termed typically African, for in contrast to the classical portraiture of the court of Ife, inhibited by the cir--

PLATE 37 — Sumptuous beaded throne of the famous Bamum sultan, Njoya. The two-headed snake symbolizes the power of the ruler. The throne and stool correspond in size and shape to the rank held in the court hierarchy, and are chiefly used at assemblies of the council or judicial gatherings. Cameroun grasslands. *Ethnological Museum, Berlin (32¾ in.).*

PLATE 38 — Decoration of a Duala war canoe, brought to Europe as long ago as 1890. Ancient mythological motifs are combined with European ones in a grotesque way. This fanciful gaudy work has a note of decadence about it. The bark was 78 ft. 8 in. long and held 100 persons. Cameroun. *Statens Etnografiska Museum, Stockholm (37 in.).*

PLATE 39 — *Bieri*, reliquary figures placed by the Pangwe upon their bark boxes to personify the tribal soul, containing the skulls and skeletons of prominent deceased persons. The figure in the centre *(23 in.)* is probably of Mvai origin, that on the left *(19¼ in.)*, with its rigid posture and monumental simplicity, of Fang origin; in that on the right *(16½ in.)* the **neo-Sudanese crossed loop motif** has crept in: inset nails serve as eyes. Western Equatorial Africa. *All in the Rietberg Museum, Zurich, Von der Heydt Collection.*

PLATE 40 — This ingenious mask is worn by members of the Ngi society of the southern Pangwe when acting against sorcerers and criminals. Its artistic worth lies in its great simplicity, dignity and balance, in the tension between individual elements, and the contrast between white and black. The small eyes placed close together suggest mystery and introversion. Gabon. *Withof Collection, Brussels (25¼ in.).*

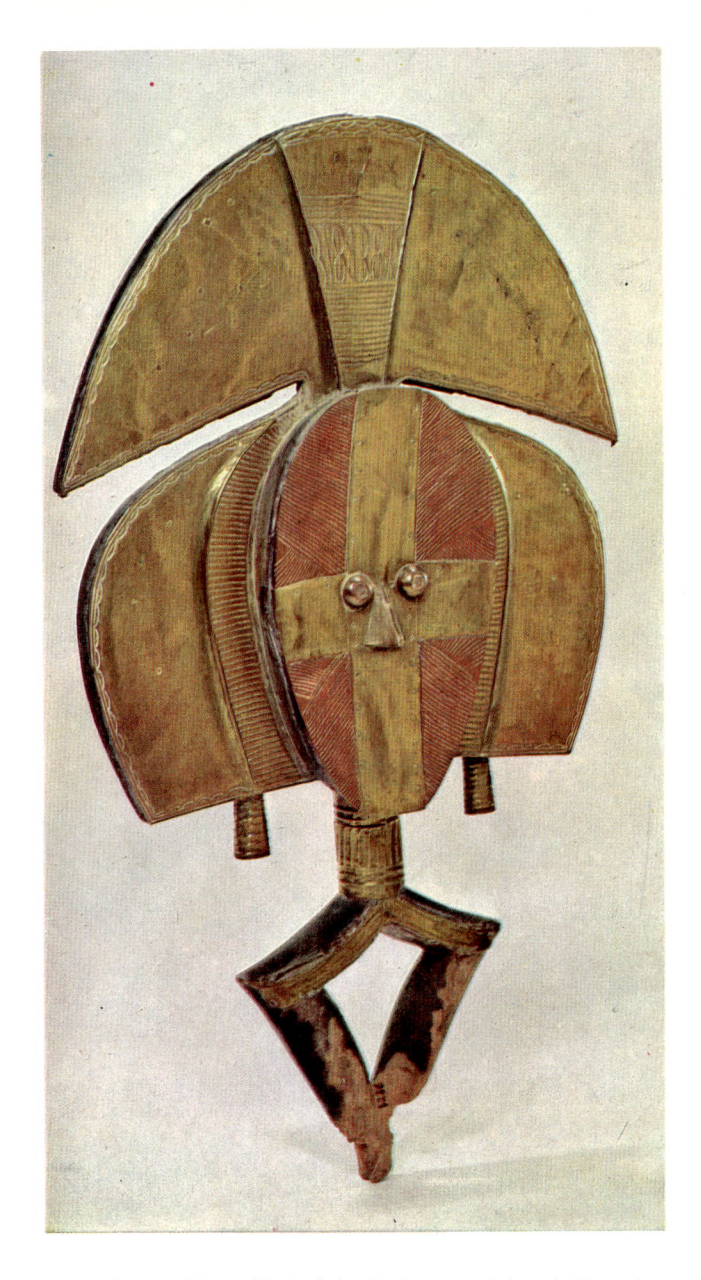

PLATE 41 — Spirit of the dead and 'guardian' of the basket containing skulls, Bakota. A balanced ornamental composition of engraved and embossed copper and metal sheet on a wooden base; the enormous crescent denotes a crest, and by some Bakota is termed a moon; the lateral areas are termed cheeks, but could equally well be plaits of hair or parts of ornaments. Local inhabitants state that the rhomb under the face corresponds to the arms (i.e. not 'head with feet'!), whilst the basket containing ancestors' skulls represents the body. Andersson considers this to be the Mother Goddess, who rules over the dead. Gabon. *Ethnological Collection, Zurich (30¾ in.).*

PLATE 42 — Impressive face of a spirit, from the Ogowe River area; symbol of a beautiful deceased woman. Although the slanting eyes and the white face have an Asiatic air about them, it is, however, a truly African work: for in Africa we often come across half-closed eyes with lowering gaze, mighty crests, white colouring denoting spirits, and pouting negro lips, serving as forceful media of expression. The initiate wears this mask with a raffia garment, and strides about on stilts, greatly enhancing the effect of weirdness. Gabon. *Ethnological Collection, Zurich (11 in.).*

PLATE 43 — Wooden dance head-dress, Kuyu. The mythical snake, *ebongo*, created the first man on earth; in its honour is performed the *kebe-kebe* snake-dance, with 6½ f.-high head-dresses, superimposed heads of wood, and sumptuous gaily-coloured fibre costumes with plumed tufts. Congo Republic. *Ratton Collection, Paris (14½ in.)*.

139

PLATE 44 — Abstract mask, Bateke. Despite the geometrical treatment it evokes a vigorous impression, not least by its delicacy of outline, the interplay of colours, and the cleverly-placed cunning little eyes inside the large oval double frame. Congo Republic. *Musée de l'Homme, Paris (13¾ in.).*

cumstance of its environment, it aspires to symbolism and surrealism, rendered in a stylized naturalistic manner and sustained by a pronounced dynamic sense. It is an art that makes use of gay colours and rich bead ornaments, combines human beings and animals into groups of figures, and continually emerges with new and original ideas.

CHARACTERISTICS: full lips, cut short vertically at the corners of the mouth; large eyes, oval and with pupils, the brows and lashes indicated by means of fine strokes; rows of teeth sometimes shown; the breasts heavy and pendulous.

The Yoruba pantheon, with some six hundred *orishas*, is headed by the almighty Olorun, the Just God, who is too sublime to be personified; his symbols and retainers must stand in his stead. Obatala, a mounted figure holding a lance, is the creator of the world, whose white colour marks him out as the god of purity (Plate 22). Odudua, the legendary king and founder of Ife, became one with the earth goddess, and is often represented as a mother with her children. Shango, grandson of Odudua, one of the first great rulers (*alafin*) of Oyo, was a cruel despot, and lives on in the imagination of later generations as the god of thunder. He is represented either as an armed rider or by the symbol of the thunderbolt (Plate 30). Other popular figures in mythology are: Eshu (Elegba), a sly demon, and for this reason often exorcized, represented wearing a cap with hanging flap and carrying a flute; Ogun, God of Iron; Olokun, God of the Sea; Ifa, God of the Oracle, and Orisha-Oko, God of Agriculture. Osanhim (Osanyin) is the god of medicine, and is symbolized by a bird on a perch. Shankpanna (Shopono), on the other hand, is the god who causes illness and smallpox. Finally, there is the god Ibeji, who created twins. Each son of god, each orisha, has a certain role to play and is allotted a certain emblem.

The delicate ibeji statuettes are very common among the Yoruba. They are carved when the death occurs of a twin, for the Yoruba believe that the souls of twins are indivisible, and that the soul of the deceased one requires an abode in order to be able to participate in everything in the same way as his living brother. Under the spell of this conception the mother, and later the surviving twin, carries ever afterwards a small figure on his or her person. At the same time as its twin brother or sister it is bathed, anointed with oil, dressed, adorned and fed. This 'counter-figure' is carefully

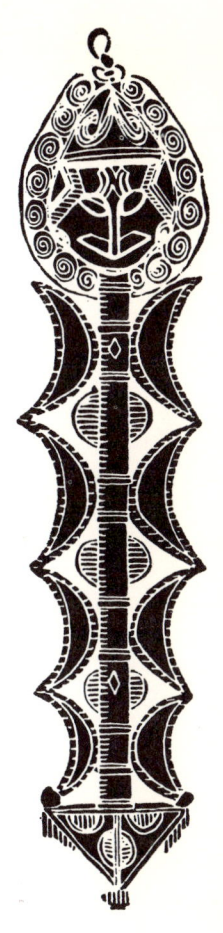

FIG. 71

Ibeji

141

preserved in a calabash, and once every year is blessed by the priest at the festival of twins. The cowrie-shell necklace shown in Fig. 66 indicates that the child has been consecrated to Shango.

Masks The masks, greatly venerated as incarnations of deceased persons, legendary heroes and magicians, may be divided into two main groups:

1. Gelede masks (Fig. 67), found in south-western Nigeria and Dahomey. These are roughly hemispherical, and are worn either on the head or at a slant on the forehead. They have a sharply receding forehead, complex hair-dress and open eyes with round pupils; are expressive, or else crudely painted in loud colours, and crowned by whole groups of figures. They always dance in pairs. Sometimes there appear as many as fifty masked couples with different forms and names.

2. The monumental Epa mask from the northern part of the Yoruba country (Fig. 68), which encloses the whole head. This has basically a barrel-shaped face, highly stylized and almost abstract. It is often carved as a Janus head, with a wide mouth and protruding eyes; above the forehead there towers a huge superstructure in loud colours, which encourages the most daring compositions, in a rather naturalistic manner. It was at ceremonial masks of this kind that Bamgboye of Odo-Owa, Nigeria's famous sculptor, excelled (cf. p. 34). The fact that one of these masks weighs some 110 lbs. and measures nearly five feet in height does not prevent the masked dancer from making great strides and leaps.

Ifa oracle Certain objects are appurtenances of the Ifa oracle, such as the following: a board with a border in relief, surrounded by a plaited band and symbols, depicting the countenance of Eshu (Fig. 69), which is placed in the grave of the Ifa priest; an ivory rattle, *iroke*, bearing a carving of a kneeling woman, used to invoke the god; small bone figures, and a vessel to hold palm-nuts. During the long and complex ceremony the priest shakes the palm-nuts and scatters them upon a board dusted with flour. From the way they fall and the figures they form in the flour, he seeks to interpret the message of the gods. These vessels in particular afford an opportunity for bold creative compositions, and many of them blaze in gaily-coloured splendour: genre motifs, such as mother-and-child groups, women at vertical looms, mounted figures, animals, etc.

The Ogboni society, which controls political life in every Yoruba village, disposes of two implements: firstly, the *agba* (Fig. 70), a large drum decorated in relief with mythical beings, with fish-fins, and aquatic animals, enclosed by bands of strap-work; secondly, the elegant *edan* rods, of copper or brass (Fig. 71), produced by the cire-perdue method, which are suspended in pairs from a chain and used in initiation as badges.

These typical cult objects do not by any means exhaust the artistic treasures of the Yoruba. Their art makes itself conspicuously felt in their daily life: on door-lintels, doors, and supporting pillars in the palaces (Plate 22); on handsome vessels, decorated with supporting figures and used for sacred cola-nuts; and on figured pots, clay lamps and ivory bracelets ornamented in relief.

The Ekiti in Owo, situated in the province of Ondo, in the eastern part of the Yoruba country, who have many cultural ties with the southernmost part of Benin, have developed a style of their own: bold heads in wood, used in the ancestor and yam cult, which surpass in forcefulnes even the wooden sculptures of Benin (as, for example, in the ram's head in Fig. 72). Owo was an ivory-carving centre, and many an object found in Benin may well have originated here. (Still today the Ekiti produce effigies of the dead which they make as close to nature as possible).

On both sides of, and to the east of, the Niger delta, in the humid jungle, live various agricultural tribes, of which the Ijo and Ibo speak the Kwa language of the Sudan, and the Ibibio and Ekoi a semi-Bantu tongue. In neither of these two groups have the tribes amalgamated to form unified states. Their political life is dominated by the powerful secret societies, which control everything connected with masks. Little research has as yet been done into the art of this forest land, which with some tribes takes a surrealist and cubist form, but in other cases is of a demonic naturalistic character. Each of these extremes can boast works of dramatic forcefulness. In addition to these four large tribes, with their numerous individual forms — not easily distinguishable, owing to the influence which they have constantly exerted upon one another — there are also smaller tribes that deserve to be mentioned because certain important works stand to their credit.

The *Ijo,* an Old Nigritic people who have been driven back to the swampy coastal region of the Niger delta, are fishermen and agriculturalists. They believe in the reincarnation of ancestors and in water spirits, which they render in the form of extremely bold abstract masks of fish and hippopotamuses (Plate

FOREST TRIBES OF SOUTH-EASTERN NIGERIA

FIG. 72

31). An impressive, though not particularly agreeable, effect is produced by their cubist ancestor shrines, consisting of many individual figures fitted together on screens; they are painted afresh for every festival.

The neighbouring tribe of Urhobo (Sobo) are a sub-tribe of the Edo who live on the right bank of the Niger. They have created some very valuable works in an abstract, though less extreme, style. The large tribe of the *Ibo,* some five million strong, and comprising about thirty sub-tribes, are agriculturalists in the fertile land behind the eastern part of the Niger delta (New Calabar). Many of the Ibo are itinerant traders, which accounts for the fact that their art has been greatly influenced by their neighbours. However, they have not simply copied these foreign trends, but have assimilated them and transformed them into an individual style of their own. Amongst their finest objects are the slender white faces of spirits: female death masks with helmet-like hair-dresses (Plate 32), to which the terrifying black male masks form an effective contrast. The so-called *maji* knife-masks of the Afikpo-Ibo (Ogoja province), treated in a wholly abstract manner and painted in bright red and black colours, are worn at the harvest festival and by young men after the initiation ceremony. The sickle curved upwards (Fig. 73) represents the ceremonial knife used to slice yams.

Very common are the life-sized statues of village idols and the *ikenga* of the province of Onitsha. They are to be found in almost every house, to bring prosperity and good fortune; they are consulted on every occasion, and destroyed at their owner's death. CHARACTERISTICS: crude, rigid forms; horns as a symbol of power; attributes held in the hand; painted in gay colours; some original figure combinations (Fig. 74, for example, carries an enemy's head and a sword); figures on doors and door-jambs of community houses; walls coloured, with numerous figures or geometric designs, reliefs in clay, paintings, or mosaics made of potsherds.

For the annual Mbari festival, in honour of the earth goddess, Ala, the Ibo model imaginatively conceived grotesque clay figures of human beings and animals, and even whole scenes from daily life, which are then placed in the temple dedicated to Ala. The figures of deities, often larger than life-size, with elongated torsos and necks and a tiny head, are frequently formed upon a mould of plaited palm-fibre.

144

Among the Ibo and Ibibio we hear of comedies being performed with marionettes, which originally had a religious function and symbolized spirits of the dead.

The Kwale-Ibo fashion interesting figure groups in red pottery: human beings and animals, in solemn attitudes (Fig. 75), which are placed in the yam shrine to serve as guardian spirits.

The Ibo and their neighbours, the *Abuan* (Abua), have adopted from the Ijo the rite of the water spirits; for their own part, they have created very interesting masks, carved in an abstract style, and worn horizontally on the head. The *ulaga* of the Ibo are combinations of human and animal elements, resembling the *anok* of the Baga. Fig. 76 represents Owu, the water spirit venerated by the Egbukere society of the Abuan, carved in a rounded and somewhat ornate style.

Among the Ogoni, a small tribe of the Opobo division, who live south of the Ibo, we find most ingenious and purely imaginary types of mask, which perform acrobatic dances during the *karikpo* harvest plays (Fig. 77).

The *Ibibio*, a people one million strong, living in Old Calabar, to the west of the Cross River, use masks and figures with hinged jaws and movable limbs, treated with an expressive realism (Plate 33). Those representing demons of destruction are macabre and fearsome: the gangosa (rhinopharyngitis) demon, for example, has a deformed nose.

All the more pleasant by contrast are the serene dignified columnar statues of the Oron clan (Plate 34), who have developed a unique style of their own.

From a stylistic point of view, the *Ekoi* group includes, in addition to the Ekoi themselves, the Anyang, Banyang, Keaka, Obang, Boki, and other tribes of the forest area on the middle and lower reaches of the Cross River, who speak a form of semi-Bantu. They are all dominated by the Ekpo secret society. This has six to seven ranks, into which the members are divided according to merit and standing, the various gradations of rank being denoted by skin-covered masks and crests, or by a combination of several faces and superimposed figures (Plate 35). With their stark, even demonic realism, they form

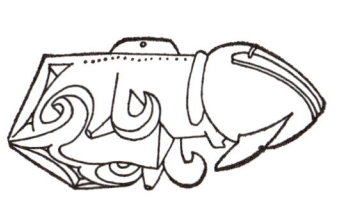

FIG. 75

FIG. 76

FIG. 77

a stronghold of naturalistic art, at the opposite end of the spectrum from the cubism of the western Sudan. Their skin-covered animal heads are no less gripping and aggressive. A basket-work cap serves to fasten the massive head to the crown of the wearer's head.

In this case, too, it is hard to distinguish between the styles of the different tribes, since an artist would cater for the needs of neighbouring tribes as well as his own. In general, the objects fashioned by the Anyang are said to be particularly wild and sombre, and those of the Obang smoother, with elegantly curved horns.

NORTHERN NIGERIA

From the little we know of the art of the hill tribes living on both banks of the Benue and on the Jos plateau, we can obtain an idea of the number of treasures that have perished, or that are kept hidden from us by the proud independent bush people in secret sanctuaries. We know of only a few outstanding daringly abstract sculptures carved by the Jukun, Chamba, Tiv and Afo, and by the Mama, Koro and the other tribes living near Wamba on the Jos plateau. The most common protective animal in northern Nigeria is the buffalo, represented in the form of a mask or a crude clay sculpture (Fig. 78, Mama buffalo mask). To the sound of the trumpet, masked bearers used once to accompany an Afo chief when he paid a ceremonial visit to a neighbouring village. I have seen with my own eyes how still today fertility statues, bearing figures of children, play a part in Afo ritual. The crests of their masks, a combination of rhinoceros, porcupine and other animal motifs (Fig. 79), resemble some of the chi wara of the Bambara. The masks are generally covered with red abrus seeds or painted red and white. The other tribes have not advanced beyond the stage of the primary style.

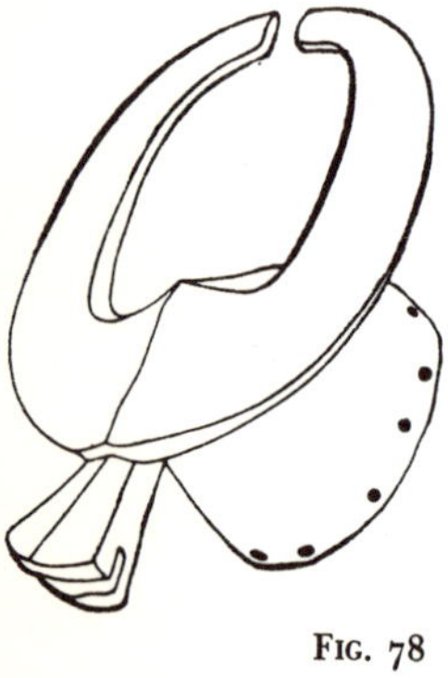

FIG. 78

The Hausa, Nupe and other tribes of the northern provinces of Nigeria, who are mostly Moslems, have developed, in lieu of figure sculpture, flourishing crafts that reveal the links between this area and the Mediterranean and Orient, particularly with the Byzantines and Copts. The Nupe are well-known for their glass beads, their work in hammered brass, with vegetable motifs and volutes, and the painted walls of their houses. The Hausa are agriculturalists and traders, but are also skilled in such crafts as forging, casting (cire-perdue), tanning, dyeing, plaiting, weaving and embroidering, and are particularly famous for their fine leather-work. Their higher cultural development is shown by the fact that they are fully clothed, and by the richly embroidered tobes (Fig. 7, p. 76) in which they trade.

Also worthy of note are the decorated pottery of the so-called pagan tribes (Fig. 3, Piri clay vessel), the ornaments and brass-casting of the Tiv, Bachama, Bata, Pabir and Bura. One may confidently assume that Nigeria still has many marvels and surprises to disclose.

Lit.: [1] Westermann, Geschichte; [2] Fagg, in: L'art nègre (prés. afr., 1951); [3] Egharevba; [4] Baumann, Völkerkunde; [5] Elisofon - Fagg; [6] Parrinder.

FIG. 79

V. CAMEROUN AND WESTERN EQUATORIAL AFRICA

SAO CULTURE

Once again we must turn back the wheel of history, to consider the graves in the delta of the river Shari, in the Chad region. Here many thousands of finds have been made, which may be dated to the period between the 10th and 16th centuries, and ascribed to the legendary people known as the Sao. Excavations have revealed human and animal figures in fine terracotta, of exceptional vitality and well-balanced, partly realistic and partly abstract in style (Fig. 80), as well as decorated libation vessels and utensils, and cast brass figures and ornaments. A conspicuous feature is the intensive use of the chevron pattern.

From north to south, from the Chad region to the Atlantic coast and the Congo, stretch five different cultural zones, distinguished mainly by climatic factors, and particularly by the gradual increase in rainfall as one moves towards the equatorial regions.

ADAMAWA AND CENTRAL AFRICAN REPUBLIC

The north is dominated by the Mohammedan Fulani, a preponderantly pastoral people with a feudal system. Their level of development is indicated by the fact that

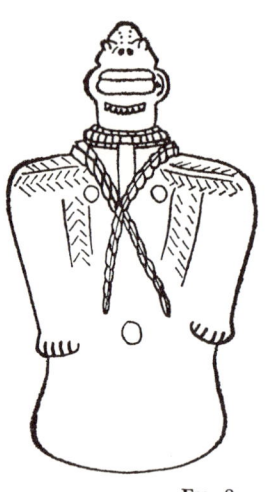

FIG. 80

they are fully clothed, and that they devote themselves (in view of the ban which their religion imposes upon the making of images) to the arts and crafts: decorated calabashes, leather-work, pottery and magnificent architecture (Fig. 11). Among the Musgu, on the Logone, we quite unexpectedly come across well-built dome-like dwellings and granaries, with ornamented surfaces, which represent an outpost of ancient Mediterranean clay culture. The Faro valley in northern Cameroun is famous for its wall-paintings. The negroes, driven back into the mountainous areas, have huts with cone-shaped roofs (Kirdi, Matakam, etc.), and pottery in an engaging primary style, as well as original wood-carvings (Mambila).

On this plateau, traversed by mountain ranges, dry areas are interspersed with fertile valleys. The inhabitants (semi-Bantu) are proud and self-assured agriculturalists and cattle-breeders; their womenfolk hoe crops of millet, maize and taro.

THE CAMEROUN GRASSLANDS

The Cameroun plateau has achieved great renown on account of its unusual artistic works. Under neo-Sudanese influence despotic kingdoms were established whose courts fostered the development of the applied arts, exercising a monopoly over certain branches. This is especially clearly shown in the architectural field: at this point of intersection between the West African and neo-Sudanese cultures, there were erected imposing palaces on a square plan and with large thatched cupolas (Fig. 81). The palace walls are made by plastering a frame of palm-frond midribs with red laterite clay. The supporting posts and door-frames invite colourful figured compositions, with the figures generally arranged in horizontal or vertical rows.

Wood-carving is inspired less by religion than by the monarch's need for representation and ornamentation. This may explain why it does not appeal so much to the emotions, but seeks rather to achieve spectacular effect. Carvings are large in size and bold in conception, and give a dramatic and dynamic impression, with their forceful, but simplified, realism, often infringing the laws of balanced proportion and disregarding the principle of frontality.

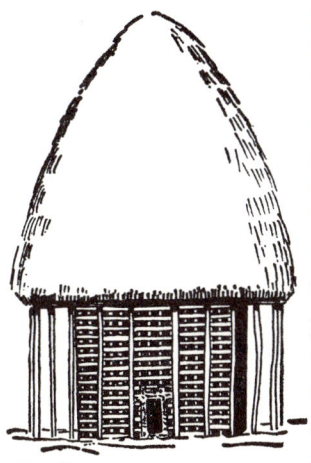

FIG. 81

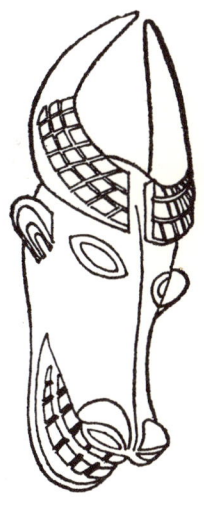

FIG. 82

FIG. 83

CHARACTERISTICS: puffed round cheeks, large open deep-set eyes, flared nostrils, ears standing out from the head, mouth open with white teeth showing; the head-dress fashioned with considerable imagination, and often derived from mythological beings, such as spiders, chameleons, frogs, lizards, or even humans. On most masks, including those worn as dance head-dresses, the expression seems to have been frozen in a smiling grimace (Fig. 82, from Bamum); there is a grin even on the face of the buffalo who, in Bamenda, appears at the dance performed before the commencement of the hunt (Fig. 83). On the impressive elephant mask of the Bali, which fulfils a function in their funerary rites, the consistent

149

simplification and the symmetry of form are especially worthy of note (Fig. 84). Other masks, by contrast, produce their effect through boldness of structure or through spontaneous humour (Plate 36). The innate dramatic quality of the figures, with ringed necks, standing with their legs astraddle, and carrying calabashes, pipes and bells, is still further enhanced by their asymmetry (Fig. 85: image of a Bamileke king, which, with its head-trophy, produces an extraordinarily dynamic impression). The sculptures are combined with supporting posts of houses and royal thrones (Plate 37). But the almost life-sized royal statues on the Bekom thrones (Fig. 86), on the other hand, give a sensation of majesty, with their near-classical proportions, their enhancement with copper sheet, beads and natural hair.

FIG. 85

Utensils, too, are distinguished by forcefulness and boldness of design, rhythmic sense of movement, and spirited ornamentation. Giant drums and food-bowls, as well as stool-seats, are supported by caryatids, by men squatting, strong animals or mythical beings, or are decorated in relief or in open-work. Fig. 87 shows how realistically the function of carrying can be expressed. Bead trimming was a privilege reserved for the court and was used for the royal insignia. The fortunes of the applied arts rose and fell according to the interest in and the demand for their products, and the relative power of the courts by which the skilled craftsmen were maintained. But still another factor was the craftsmen themselves, who kept certain techniques as family secrets. As they moved from one capital to another, so their arts became known in new localities.

FIG. 87

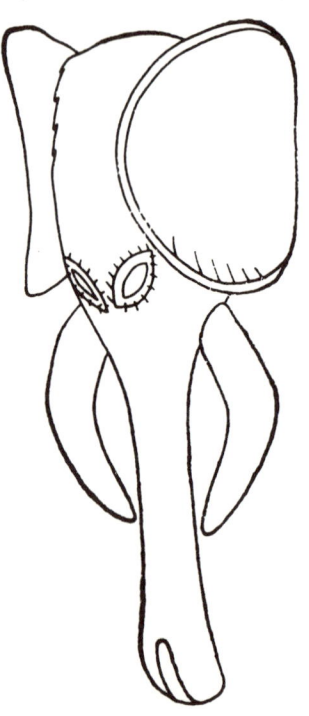

FIG. 84

This fact makes it difficult to establish the place of origin of the specimens in European museums. The Bali, who in the late 19th century were famed for their well-shaped figured red or black clay pipes, apparently obtained them from the Bamessing and Babungo.

150

But the very fine clay tobacco pipes, the stems often six feet long, may definitely be attributed to the Bamum (Fig. 88). They have the typical puffed cheeks and decorative cap with spider decoration; to the artist it was of no consequence if his bird-catching spider had six instead of eight legs; what mattered was that he had caught its essential character. The pipe used to be carried in the king's train by a servant as an emblem of his authority. The Babessi have established a centre for the production of ceramics which are of some interest. In the sphere of metal-casting, by the waste form process, it was first the Tikar, and later the Bamum who made a name for themselves. Sultan Njoya made gifts of lavishly decorated pipes of brass. The Bagam pipe-bowl, in the shape of an elephant's head, suggests, by its four tusks, the rank of a great ruler (Fig. 89) The royal pipes were smoked in the fields by the women of the court when carrying out ritual observances. There are magnificent brass stoppers for palm-wine vessels, decorated with ingenious animal motifs; the bracelet with a buffalo head in Fig. 1 also gives a remarkably graceful impression. Still today the craftsmen of the Cameroun grasslands cast brass bells, jewellery, sword-hilts, pipes, statuettes and decorative masks for the commercial market; unfortunately the styles seem to have become frozen in their present stage of development, and they are less elaborately executed.

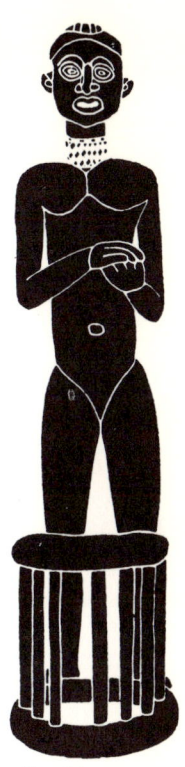

FIG. 86

FIG. 88

The cotton fabrics, woven by the men, were richly embroidered or dyed with indigo by the 'resist' technique, according to the plangi and stencilling methods. Sultan Njoya, who had numerous dye-works close to his residence, is said to have himself invented motifs and formulae for dyes.

The following places in the Cameroun grasslands are the most important artistically, or have special achievements to their credit: Fumban, the capital of Sultan Njoya of the *Bamum,* a distinguished monarch who reigned at the beginning of the present century and was a great patron of culture and the arts. The royal workshops supplied, in particular, masks, cast brass objects, patterned and embroidered textiles, drinking horns in relief and large tobacco pipes (Fig. 88). When the court was in mourning,

FIG. 89

neighbouring rulers sent envoys in masks to exorcize spirits. Figures, thrones (Plate 37) and calabashes were all decorated with magnificent bead trimmings.

The *Tikar* group, who live north of the Bamum, are also important from an artistic point of view. The Tikar, who once maintained a first-class centre of brass-casting, today produce comic heads in wood. The Bekom are known for the royal figures on their thrones (Fig. 86), and for their carved door-frames; the Bafum for their figures, which have a dramatic air about them, and for their greatly inflated masks; and the Bali for their elegant utensils, especially round stools and clay pipes.

In the area inhabited by the large *Bamileke* group (near Bafussang, Dschang and Bamenda) the most prominent features of the artistic landscape are the asymmetrical statues of the Bangwa, Batie and others (Fig. 85). Also worthy of note are the Bangwa's beaded thrones, giant drums, and bead-covered calabashes to hold the skulls of their kings, as well as their large face masks; Bagam brass work (Fig. 1), and the gigantic cubist mask of the Bacham (Plate 36).

FIG. 90

FOREST LANDS OF WESTERN CAMEROUN

To the south-west of Dschang the savannah gives way to dense rain forest, and, with the difference in natural conditions, so the cultural pattern also changes. In the western part the culture is ancient, and finds expression in crude pole sculpture (the Yabassi and others). Here and there the last echoes of the powerful Ekoi style are visible in masks, Janus-faced heads and busts with large horns (Ngutu and others). The Bafo, west of the upper Mungo, display in their groups of small-sized figures a marked contrapuntal and imaginative touch (Fig. 90); these sculptures are used in oath-taking ceremonies.

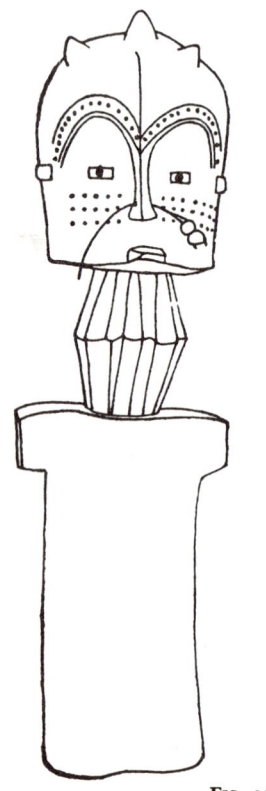

FIG. 91

The Ngolo, in addition to their sculptures, carve boards in relief with a combination of animal and other motifs.

Duala   On the coast of Cameroun, with its mangrove swamps (Duala), and in the hinterland (Bodiman and Wuri) an interesting hybrid style developed, as a consequence of many centuries of contact with European traders: spirited, imaginative, but somewhat grotesque and gaudy figure compositions are used to decorate their war canoes (Plate 38), dance-staffs and the thrones used by the Ekongolo secret society. They also make burial masks, which are strictly geometric in design, in the true African manner.

In the humid forest region of Gabon, Spanish Guinea and the Congo Republic, where the Bantu peoples, with a superimposed stratum of Sudanese, have preserved the old West African methods of agriculture (burning clearings by fire) and ancestor cult, a fresh artistic pattern unfolds. The centres of endeavour are to be found among the tribes living on the rivers Pangwe and Ogowe (Bakota, Balumbo, etc.), and among the Kuyu, Babembe and Bateke. The nearer we approach the Ogowe, the more pronounced become the abstraction and the sensitivity of their works.

EQUATORIAL FOREST

The Pangwe, who number about one million, migrated in or about the year 1800 from the eastern Sudan into the area between the Sanaga and Ogowe, reaching the Atlantic coast by about 1870. Their splendid art may be the result of a symbiosis between autochthonous forces and extraneous influences. The name 'northern Pangwe' will be used here to apply to the Bulu, Yaunde and Eton in southern Cameroun, 'central Pangwe' in regard to the Ntum and Mvai of Gabon and Spanish Guinea, and 'southern Pangwe' to denote the Fang of Gabon and others. The Pangwe have the custom of collecting in boxes, known as *bieri*, the skulls and bones of deceased dignitaries, together with substances possessing magical properties, crowning these bieri with a sculpture in wood, which they regard as the ancestor and guardian spirit of the family, the embodiment of their entire vital

Pangwe

FIG. 94

FIG. 92

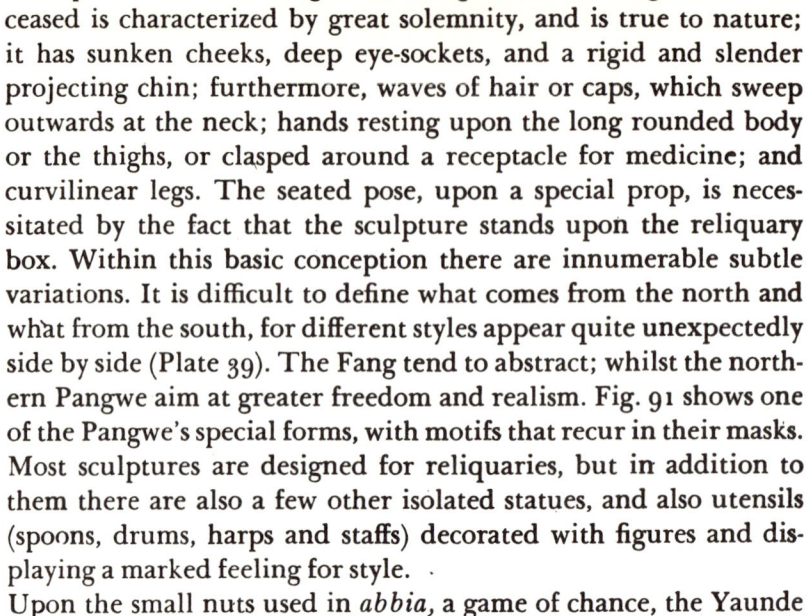

FIG. 93

FIG. 95

force. This belief led to a relatively homogeneous self-sufficient conception in the carving of these figures. The image of the deceased is characterized by great solemnity, and is true to nature; it has sunken cheeks, deep eye-sockets, and a rigid and slender projecting chin; furthermore, waves of hair or caps, which sweep outwards at the neck; hands resting upon the long rounded body or the thighs, or clasped around a receptacle for medicine; and curvilinear legs. The seated pose, upon a special prop, is necessitated by the fact that the sculpture stands upon the reliquary box. Within this basic conception there are innumerable subtle variations. It is difficult to define what comes from the north and what from the south, for different styles appear quite unexpectedly side by side (Plate 39). The Fang tend to abstract; whilst the northern Pangwe aim at greater freedom and realism. Fig. 91 shows one of the Pangwe's special forms, with motifs that recur in their masks. Most sculptures are designed for reliquaries, but in addition to them there are also a few other isolated statues, and also utensils (spoons, drums, harps and staffs) decorated with figures and displaying a marked feeling for style.

Upon the small nuts used in *abbia,* a game of chance, the Yaunde engrave ideograms and scenes, which are very adroitly adapted to the shape of the nut, profile and frontal postures being blended to form ingenious and original images (Fig. 92: female dancer in a raffia skirt).

Masks play a subordinate part with the Pangwe, although they too have demons who have to be exorcized, and thus also secret societies (Plate 40).

The *Bakwele,* who have long been settled on the upper reaches of the river Likwale, carve abstract non-realistic works (Fig. 93). The white perimeter and cheeks of their masks, together with the black mouth, form a heart shape, producing a high degree of intensity. A characteristic feature here are the arched and slightly protruding eye-slits. Some animal masks are of enchanting elegance. The Bakwele style exhibits certain similarities with that of the Pangwe, Wabembe and Balega.

The *Bakota,* under pressure from the Pangwe, moved from the upper Ivindo (a tributary of the Ogowe) westwards and south-westwards as far as Sibiti, where they spread out over the central Congo and western Gabon. Like the Aduma, Ambete, Ondumbo and the other tribes along the middle reaches of the river Ogowe, they also have the custom of keeping skulls of eminent deceased persons in baskets, crowned by an effigy. The ancestor spirit is roused by hand-clapping, rendered favourably disposed by sacrificial offerings, and then asked for its advice. Although they both set out from the same idea, there is a great contrast between the Pangwe and the Bakota as regards artistic realization: in the reliquary figures of the Pangwe the naturalistic form is always perceptible, despite the high degree of stylization, whilst the Bakota, on the other hand, give their sculptures an entirely imaginary countenance, which has no equivalent anywhere (Plate 41). The *mbulu-ngulu* (erroneously called 'head with feet') are flattened wooden faces covered with metal sheet, some of them concave, and others convex, decorative and symbolic at the same time — and ambiguous, which led to many absurd interpretations. The Janus-faced heads are called *mbulu-viti*. The smaller reliquary figures in Fig. 94, called *naja*, are striking on account of the particularly ingenious effect produced by the metal lamellae; they likewise belong stylistically to the Bakota group.

The Bakota masks, markedly cubist in style and painted black and white, correspond to the convex mbulu-ngulu in so far as they have a bulging forehead and eyes and noses at an acute angle, but are also reminiscent of Bambara masks. In one such mask, a phantom face beheld as in a dream, clad in raffia and adorned with feathers, the grotesque Yolo demon steals into the village while festivals and funerary rites are being held: but at once there appear on the scene heroes who exorcize it — and with it all evil.

The massive reliquary figures, statues and masks of the Ambete are cubist in structure (Fig. 95), the stepped hair-dress having clearly-marked gradations, and the face frequently being painted white.

It is preferable to call the style of the famous white masks, generally referred to as Balumbo or Mpongwe style, by the general regional term of Ogowe, and the river of that name, since this probably expresses more accurately their actual area of diffusion and supposed locality of origin (Plate 42). Many Gabon tribes, living far distant from one another, wear a white mask: the Balumbo, Mashango, Ashira, Galoa and Mpongwe. Andersson saw them among the Bakota, and suggests that they originate from the upper Ivindo. The coastal area of the Mpongwe is merely the terminus of their journey, the place where they are sold to Europeans.

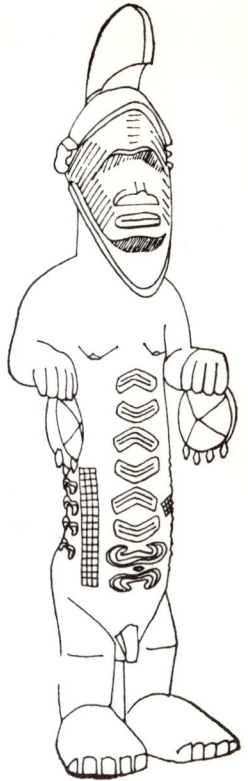

Fig. 96

Ambete

Ogowe style

Kuyu   The Kuyu (and the neighbouring Baboshi) of the Congo Republic carve for their snake dance club-shaped heads and statues in wood. They are usually very crude in form and gaudy in colour, with broad facial features and a barrel-shaped torso covered with cicatrices, the total effect being one of importunate realism. There are only a few specimens which constitute an exception, through their restrained forcefulness of expression (Plate 43).

Babembe   A further sculptural group is to be found among the Babembe (in the Congo Republic, north of Brazzaville, on the right bank of the Niari) — not to be confused with the Wabembe at the northern end of Lake Tanganyika, or with the Babemba of northern Rhodesia! Related to the Babembe are the Baladi, Batende, Babwende and other tribes in the cataract region of the Lower Congo. CHARACTERISTICS: figures and domestic fetishes in different postures; standing, seated, in part squatting, in part with the elbows resting on the knees; elongated cylindrical torso with tribal cicatrices in a decorative pattern, often highly polished; pieces of bone or glass inserted as eyes, the beard half-oval; the face naturalistically shaped, with soft features. They carry in their hands all manner

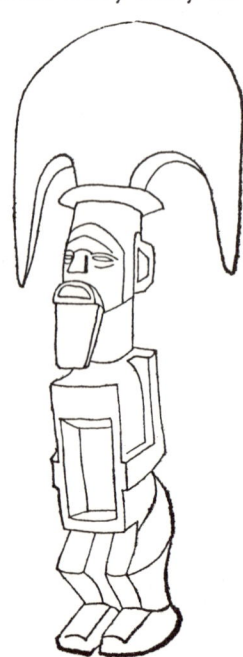

FIG. 97

PLATE 45 — Sepulchral monument, Basundi, 19th century. Tranquil posture, with cap of a high-ranking person and facial tattooing. Commemorative statues of prominent deceased persons, such as a great healer or famous midwife, stand in the sepulchral chapels as media of power, to ensure the continuity of the community. Before them the priests used to perform their oblations, make sacrificial offerings, and receive their counsel. Lower Congo. *Rietberg Museum, Zurich, Von der Heydt Collection (20 in.)*.

PLATE 46 — Looking-glass fetish, Bakongo. The expressive face stands out from all the magical paraphernalia from which fetishes derive their power. The raised hand probably held a knife or lance. In the looking-glass of the receptacle the magician discerns the image of the illness-giving demon or the malefactor who is to be traced; to guarantee his innocence the accused has to lick the looking-glass. Lower Congo. *Ethnographical Museum, Antwerp (19 in.).*

PLATE 47 — Painting with plastic bird on bark panel. The esoteric paintings are used in initiation of novices, in the initiation and circumcision hut. South-western Congo. *Musée Royal de l'Afrique Centrale, Tervuren (43¼ in.).*

PLATE 48 — Helmet-masks of wood and plaited raffia. Worn by the Bayaka and Basuku on the occasion of the concluding ceremonies of the Nkanda bush school. The newly-initiated *tudansi* spend a year isolated in camps to train in their various professions, such as hunting, singing and dancing; after passing their ordeals and becoming adult members of the society, they perform a dance in masks, always in pairs, and whilst in this disguise are allowed to seize everything they can lay their hands upon. An ovation is given to the artist who creates the best works, and he is awarded the honorary title of *Kimvumbu*. The motifs of the superstructures denote legendary animals, episodes or a particular rank. The Basuku mask with the bird is more subtle, the ghost-like white colour symbolizing the boys' death and re-birth. Both from the south-western Congo. *The Bayaka mask (22 in.), with its twilled plaited work, is in the Ethnological Collection, Zurich, and the Basuku mask (23⅜ in.) in the Rietberg Museum, Zurich, Von der Heydt Collection.*

PLATE 49 — Figure of hermaphrodite, Basuku, from the Kwango. Characteristic are the raised shoulders and the arms springing from the centre of the back. From the suspended medicine horns the figure can be identified as a healing fetish. South-western Congo. *Musée Royal de l'Afrique Centrale, Tervuren* (22¾ in.).

PLATE 50 — Commemorative statue of **Kata-Mbula**, 109th king of the Bakuba kingdom (1800—1810). **He** carries the emblem of peace, the knife which **Shamba** Bolongongo used in place of a weapon, as well as the royal drum bearing his favourite designs and the cowrie-studded cap, as a symbol of his divinity. From this realistically treated statue, carved from heavy wood and polished, there emanate dignity, power and energy: for it is an idealized portrait. **Central Congo.** *Musée Royal de l'Afrique Centrale, Tervuren (20 in.).*

PLATE 51 — Bakuba carvings. The head-shaped vessel was formerly used when ceremonially drinking palm-wine; or, if Hall is to be believed, used in the ordeal of poison. The apparently arbitrary proportions can be explained by the supreme magic significance of the human head. *Ethnological Collection, Zurich* (11½ in.).

The lidded jar *(left)* is used to contain camwood powder. On the lid is the scarab, creator of all animals; the pattern, derived from plaiting, is called 'the belly of Woto', the legendary fourth Baluba king and culture hero. *Rietberg Museum, Von der Heydt Collection (9¾ in.).*

The lidded bowl, resting on a base in open-work, has a crocodile-scale motif on the side and, on the lid, in addition to the Woto motif, the beetle (brachycerus), known as 'the Head of God'. *Rietberg Museum, Zurich, Von der Heydt Collection (width 11 in.).* Plush fabric, *musese,* of the Bashobwa (a sub-tribe of the Bakuba).

PLATE 52 — The *shene-malula* mask, with its copious painting, beads and cowrie-shells, manifests the Bakuba talent for decoration. The mask is said to have been introduced by one of the kings as an instrument of power for his secret police, the Babende society. All young men who wanted to join this society had first to prove their courage at the nocturnal appearance of the masked spirit by enduring tortures of all kinds. Central Congo. *Rietberg Museum, Zurich, Von der Heydt Collection (9 in.).*

of attributes: a gun, knife, staffs or bells (Fig. 96). They cover their calabashes with symbolic figured scrawls.

The *Bateke*, who live in the area north of Brazzaville, in the cataract region of the Lower Congo and Stanleypool, are characterized — along with other tribes (Wambundu, Bayanzi, Basundi, etc.)— by their *biteke*: fetish figures with inlaid magic substances (Fig. 97). Often there projects upwards from the 'magic parcel' a striking cubist head with a high-arched hair-dress or cap, straight eyes and mouth, angular beard, and vertical or oblique tattooing grooved on the face. The torso is treated without attention to detail, the arms are pressed in, and the knees are angular. A small receptacle in the centre of the body contains the placenta of a male child, which affords him protection until he reaches the age of puberty. The Wambundu, who are related to the Bateke, are reputed to be famous as wood-carvers, and to do an extensive trade in their biteke figures.

From the Bateke lands comes the polychrome face-disc (Plate 44), which testifies to their great capacity for abstraction. The Bateke are also famous for their delicate silk-like fabrics, clay heads and engraved neck-rings in brass.

VI. REPUBLIC OF THE CONGO

INTRODUCTION

The dense jungle and the hot and humid climate of the Congo basin, with its numerous rivers and streams, have always acted as a deterrent to cultural development. In the Ituri forest the small-statured Bambuti roam through the thickets as hunters and food-gatherers. But the jungle has also experienced extraneous influences, introduced by negro peoples who withdrew into its fastnesses under pressure from other tribes. Time and again whole groups of peoples have passed along the rivers Ubangi, Congo and Kasai. But it was only in the more elevated areas of the southern and eastern tributaries of the Congo, where the rainy steppe juts into the forest about 4° south of the Equator, creating more favourable conditions for human life, that culture could develop.

The stimulus towards a higher way of life came in the first instance from a neo-Sudanese ruling stratum, which immigrated from the north, subjugated the native Bantu peasants and united the small autonomous village communities into mighty feudal kingdoms. In the course of time many of these states collapsed again, either through being overrun by other tribes, or as a result of destructive internecine conflicts.

The best-known kingdoms are those of Congo and Loango, on either side of the mouth of the Congo, Bakuba, Baluba and Balunda in the south and south-east, and Azande and Mangbetu in the north. Certain characteristics that distinguish their absolute theocratic monarchies, their tribal myths and their ornamentation reveal cultural connections with the early kingdoms in the Nile valley, the interlacustrine area, Southern Rhodesia, Nigeria, Cameroun and elsewhere (cf. p. 15).

The northern Congo, with its patriarchal form of social organization, kept for the most part to pole sculpture, which the isolation of the jungle tended to preserve. The matriarchal Bantu of the southern savannah adopted round sculpture, a style in which they produced some imaginative works.

The regions most important from the stylistic point of view, with their countless sub-styles (of which only an outline can be given

FIG. 98

here), are situated in the area of the southern and eastern tributaries of the Congo and at its mouth.

In domestic architecture West African and neo-Sudanese elements meet and blend. The splendid great royal halls bear witness to the local rulers' desire to demonstrate their power.

As far as arts and crafts are concerned, there is an immense wealth of forms and variety in types of ornamentation, with the use of gaily-coloured beads, feathers, decorative plaiting and metals. Decoration is to be found on gourds, twilled mats and basket-work, ceremonial axes, weapons, beds, planks for houses, clay vessels with a lacquer-like coating, and jugs bearing effigies. Even the smallest utensil bears ornamentation, often inspired by ancient symbolic patterns. The plaiting motif prevails everywhere; animal motifs are rare, and plant ones not found at all.

When Diego Cão discovered the mouth of the Congo in 1482, he came upon flourishing kingdoms. Subsequently vigorous commercial relations were established between King Manikongo and the Portuguese court. Manikongo proved responsive to Christian teachings and was baptised under the name of Affonso I. He invited Portuguese artists to his capital, San Salvador, in northern Angola. Missionaries also arrived, bringing reliquaries and crucifixes from their homeland, and built monasteries and chapels. They succeeded in maintaining their hold for some two hundred years. Under their influence the native peoples made fine crucifixes from cast brass and chalices of ivory. But there were also conflicts: the Whites amassed profits from the slave and ivory trade, and upset the old customs by their insistence upon monogamy. Once the missionaries had been expelled, and relations with Europe broken off, the somewhat superficial features of Christianity also disappeared. It was not until the latter half of the 19th century that contact with the Whites was resumed.

In the course of its stormy history the kingdom of Loango in the Congo Republic temporarily won dominion over the southern Congo kingdom, with its peculiar hierarchical court ritual, which was later also exposed to raids by the Bayaka tribesmen. In the 16th century Hindus are also believed to have reached the Congo and to have settled there.

The term used to denote the style in the general area of the Lower Congo, between Leopoldville and the Atlantic, is Bakongo (not to be confused with the territorial designation Bas-Congo). The

LOWER CONGO

FIG. 99

Bakongo

most important tribes of the western Bakongo are: the Bavili in Loango, Congo Republic; the Bawoyo in the enclave of Cabinda; the Basolongo in northern Angola, and the Basundi of the district of Mayombe, a forest area north of Boma. The eastern Bakongo comprise the Bankanu, Bambata and Bazombo. There is comparatively little trace of European influence on early indigenous art. The Bantu cosmic conception stood in complete contrast to that of the missionaries, who demanded that they should destroy their 'idols'. If Christian trends are met with at all, it is only in the mother-and-child motif (cf. Madonna and Child), in fetishes with reliquary caskets, or perhaps in a realistic manner of representation; but the Bakongo have absorbed such foreign influences as they experienced, and fused them with their own conceptions.

CHARACTERISTICS: figures and groups, modelled in the round, often asymmetrical, with an attempt at lively movement; inlaid eyes, inserted rows of teeth, full lips, naturalistically formed ears, a masterly realism in the African manner, with the exclusion of all non-essentials, and a clearly-conceived style. The sepulchral monuments of eminent persons are of peculiar beauty (Plate 45); kneeling women are represented with tranquil dignity and great simplicity; mothers giving suck are rendered in an attitude of nobility, the child treated as a symbol of the continuity of the family (Fig. 98). Tattoos and jewellery display elaborate craftsmanship. The pointed or tiara-shaped hood worn by the nobility is typical of the Mayombe area. In the ancestor shrines human beings and animals are built up into complex groups. Certain European elements may be identified in the anecdotal trimmings.

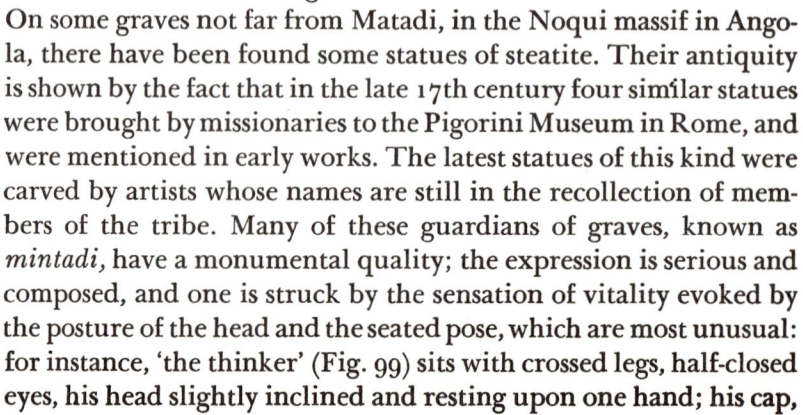

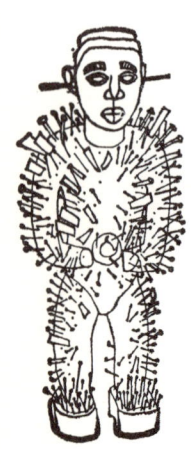

On some graves not far from Matadi, in the Noqui massif in Angola, there have been found some statues of steatite. Their antiquity is shown by the fact that in the late 17th century four similar statues were brought by missionaries to the Pigorini Museum in Rome, and were mentioned in early works. The latest statues of this kind were carved by artists whose names are still in the recollection of members of the tribe. Many of these guardians of graves, known as *mintadi,* have a monumental quality; the expression is serious and composed, and one is struck by the sensation of vitality evoked by the posture of the head and the seated pose, which are most unusual: for instance, 'the thinker' (Fig. 99) sits with crossed legs, half-closed eyes, his head slightly inclined and resting upon one hand; his cap,

FIG. 100

decorated with stylized leopard's teeth or claws, is an emblem of a consecrated ruler. Certain attitudes of the boy presumably correspond to rules of court ceremonial. The purpose of such figures as these is to give advice.

The *nkisi* fetishes are characterized by dramatic gestures, a lively sense of movement and accessories of various kinds.[1] From an aesthetic point of view they are only rarely objects of beauty; their function is essentially a magic one. But occasionally, where a talented artist is inspired by a vision of some active demonic force, an expressive work of art does come into being (Fig. 100). The nail fetishes used in judicial proceedings have to give an aggressive and threatening impression — and yet on the *konde* figure, above the nail-studded torso, there is an expressive face with wide-open eyes, resembling the face of an imposing sepulchral figure; for all sculptures are permeated by, and give effect to, the mighty tribal spirit. Each nail challenges the spirit to perform a magic action; for each nail denotes a ritual murder, and, in the ceremony carried out by the priest, represents a blow directed against malefactors and enemies: when divine judgement is pronounced, the accused drives a nail into the figure to prove his innocence. He knows full well what perils would befall him were he to commit a perjury.

The less formidable group of guardian and healing figures comprises numerous looking-glass fetishes in the form of human beings or animals (dogs, crocodiles, leopards, etc.) (Plate 46). The figure of a hunchback, for example, depicted with dramatic forcefulness, is supposed to ward off Pott's disease. When these special magic figures are made, the operation is always performed according to a definite ritual, controlled by the magician.

The *Bavili* give their masks a veritable expression of pathos by painting them black, white and red, and leaving the mouth slightly open, with the tip of the tongue showing (Fig. 101). The two-faced *ndungu,* an impressive mask in a massive attire of plumage, is worn by the medicine-man at the coronation of a prince, when invoking the gods to send rain, or pronouncing divine judgement. Other masks, by contrast, which have a symmetrical painted design in white and black, are employed in ritual by the Basundi of the Bakhimba sect, which runs the bush school. Their rattle-sticks, decorated with twin figures, are symbols of the serpent spirit and the double rainbow, and serve to combat sorcery.

The wooden pot-lids of the Bawoyo[2] constitute a parallel to the

Fig. 103

Fig. 104

SOUTH-WESTERN
CONGO

Bayaka

gold weights of the Ashanti. Their symbolic figured motifs, arranged in order and meaningfully, express a certain situation or desire. In this way a people's accumulated wisdom and experience are captured and gathered together in their images, in order to assist them in solving their spiritual conflicts, as the need arises. For example, to give a sign of warning to an obstinate husband, his wife covers the pot in which she brings him his food with one of these lids, which bears images. These lids are either inherited, or made specially by the medicine-man.

The small Basundi powder-boxes are also particularly beautiful in form, some having a plain surface, others being covered with a network pattern and crowned with an animal (Fig. 102); so, too, are their bells, sticks, the supporting posts of their houses, and many other objects.

Amongst their earthenware articles, as well as utensils of various kinds, there is a group of pottery vessels, topped by realistic heads or figures, clearly to be classed together (Fig. 103). They bear the name of the 19th-century Bawoyo artist Voania Muba, who did not found any school of followers.

The Bakongo once also produced some outstanding ivory work: for example, bells with kneeling women, resembling the *iroke* of the Yoruba. On the other hand, there is little of value in their elephant- and hippopotamus-tusk ivories, produced for export, worked in relief in spiral form, and showing Europeans and negroes in comic scenes.

Among the eastern Bakongo one's attention is caught by the *Bankanu*, with their huge masks and painted plaques of bark, similar to those of the Bayaka. The illustration in Plate 47 thus leads on to the next group of styles: the art of the Kwango-Kwilu region.

Along the fertile banks of the Kwango and Kwilu, the two great southern tributaries of the Congo, on the periphery of the old feudal states, there live highly talented hunters and agriculturalists, who worship ancestors and practise the custom of wearing masks.

The warlike Bayaka (their name means 'the strong') are said to have raided the Congo kingdom as early as the 16th century, obliging the ruler to call upon the Portuguese for assistance.

Their sculpture shows vitality and originality, with a touch of the grotesque. Their utensils, fetishes, neck-rests, divination implements, combs and whistles are decorated with human beings and animals; an exceedingly plastic effect is obtained by the disproportionately large nose, crest-like hair-dress, protruding abdomen and accentuated buttocks (Fig. 104). One conspicuous feature, besides the *retroussé* nose, frequently turned up like an elephant's trunk, are the 'spectacles': for such is the impression given by the hair-line, which describes a circle around the eye-sockets, from the forehead to the nostrils.

Most of the magic figures made by the medicine-men are of little aesthetic value, but in their masks the Bayaka display a keen artistic sense.

Trained professional artists endeavour to surpass one another in fashioning masks of an original imaginative quality for the *tudansi*, as the novitiates of the Nkanda bush school are called. The small wooden face is topped by a painted ornament plaited from switches and raffia, which depicts various village scenes and allows the artist to give full rein to his imagination. The mask is worn on the head or directly over the forehead, so that the fringe of fibre falls down over the face (Plate 48). The dancer, who sometimes holds on to the mask by a handle, wears a net-like costume and wields a rattle.

Completely different in character, and rarely met with, is the gigantic *kakungu* mask (Fig. 105), partly painted in red, with its puffed cheeks and flaccid forms. In contrast to the tudansi masks, it is made and consecrated by the magician, and thus imbued with a maximum of magic force. The effect it has is considerable: it aids barren women, drives away panthers, and cures the sick, who are put into the mask's own hut for several days. The great master of the initiation ceremonies wears it when new members are admitted. The walls of initiation huts are beautifully decorated with painted plaques in bark.

Basuku is the name given to the eastern Bayaka. For the sake of clarity, this name will be used here to apply to the region that differs in style from that of the western Bayaka. Among the Basuku there are statues with rounded heads and sharply defined forms. Characteristic are the raised shoulders and the arms springing directly from the shoulder-blades (Plate 49). The wooden masks known as *hemba*, with their raffia ruffs, and generally also bearing animal superstructures, are striking on account of the serene calm expressed by the white face (Plate 48, left.).

The Bambala figures from the middle reaches of the Kwengo have

FIG. 105

FIG. 106

Basuku

Bambala

a lively sense of movement. This is achieved by unusual postures or arrangements of groups: a drummer in action, a 'thinker' (similar to the mintadi of the Bakongo), figures squatting with their elbows resting on their knees, mothers with a babe at the breast, or at the hip, or worn pick-a-back fashion on the shoulder. On Bambala sculptures the faces are represented with a bulging forehead, projecting chin, and high median hair-crest, and are in general distinguished by their dynamic power. The statue of the mother shown in Fig. 106 gives the effect of a mighty natural force, and has none of the intimacy found in treatment of the mother-and-child theme in European art. Seated on a stool, the mother holds in her right hand an exorcizing rattle, whilst the child, with a head almost as large as its mother's, draws unconcernedly at the breast. The sculptures are patinated with the same camwood as is used for rubbing into the body.

FIG. 107

Bahuana

This small tribe of smiths, living on the Kwilu and Djuma, produce little in the way of wooden sculpture, but are past masters in the art of working ivory. This is evinced by their attractive little amulet figures, initiation emblems in kneeling posture, with enormous heads, and the hands touching the chin or breast. Some give the impression of an embryo (Fig. 107); others are projected on to a frontal plane (Fig. 108) or reduced to a mere head-disc. Double faces, in which one face is rendered with eyes open, and the other with eyes closed, probably suggest the novices' death and regeneration.

FIG. 108

The small tribe of the *Baholo,* on the upper Kwango, little known until they were studied by A. Maesen, have developed a surprisingly rich and impressive art. Their polychrome animal masks and cult figures with outspread arms and gigantic hands, bold compositions mounted on door-frames, display a very purposeful creative volition.

Bapende

The art manifested in their masks by the western *Bapende* (between the Kwango and Loange) is one of the most highly differentiated in the whole of Africa. Its effect is created by harmony of forms and glances shrouded by heavy triangular lids.

CHARACTERISTICS: the arched eyebrows join at the bridge of the nose in a depression and form a sharply defined unbroken line; the forehead has a pronounced bulge and is topped by a plaited hair-dress from which a flap hangs down; the cheek-bones are high and prominent, the chin pointed or with a notched beard attached to it; the tip of the nose is slightly *retroussé,* and the nostrils are shown. Like the Baluba, Bajokwe and other tribes with whom they engage in trade, the Bapende carve stools with caryatids and head-shaped cups (but rarely statues) [3] in a distinctive style (Plate 30b).

The fanciful *minyaki* masks, of charming elegance, are used by the Bapende at the mikanda dance (initiation ceremony) and in the N'Buya play. These plays are short comedies performed in masks, of which there are some forty different kinds, amongst them the ruler, who wears a beard, tribal heroes, a spirit dancing on stilts, and a clown. The performances are enthusiastically applauded by the audience. The fact that these masks are used for entertainment should not obscure their fundamental symbolic significance; they really relate to the death and regeneration of novices. This is shown by the custom amongst Bapende youths of copying the ivory mask in miniature and wearing it on their neck or arm for life, as a badge to show that they have undergone the *kimpasi* ritual, the test for admission to adult society (Fig. 109). In these small ivory masks the Bapende have produced objects of unique charm, and they become still more attractive when in use and in constant contact with skin dyed with tukula. When they are made of ivory they are reserved to initiates; but reproductions of them may be made by anyone in wood, lead or other material. Of the same delicate workmanship are the Bapende ivory statuettes, whistles and hair-pins. In addition to this they also plait abstract disc-shaped masks with large tubular eyes and rays projecting outwards like feathers, which have the purpose of keeping women and children away from the sacred places of ritual.

The masks of the eastern Bapende, between the Loange and the Kasai, are in general devoid of any lyrical quality. The characteristic features of eyebrows joining above the nose, broad cheekbones, and pointed chin indicate a trend towards an angular cubist type of mask, which is occasionally surmounted by sharply curved horns. These masks are of the type which the Bakete have adopted from the Bapende (Fig. 110).

The highly-civilized peoples who inhabit the heart of the Republic of the Congo, between the Kasai and its tributary the Sankuru, are of the utmost importance to our theme. In the first place, they undoubtedly deserve to occupy a prominent place in African art on account of their wealth of bold decoration. But in addition to

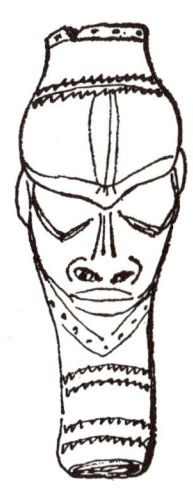

FIG. 109

CENTRAL CONGO

Bakuba

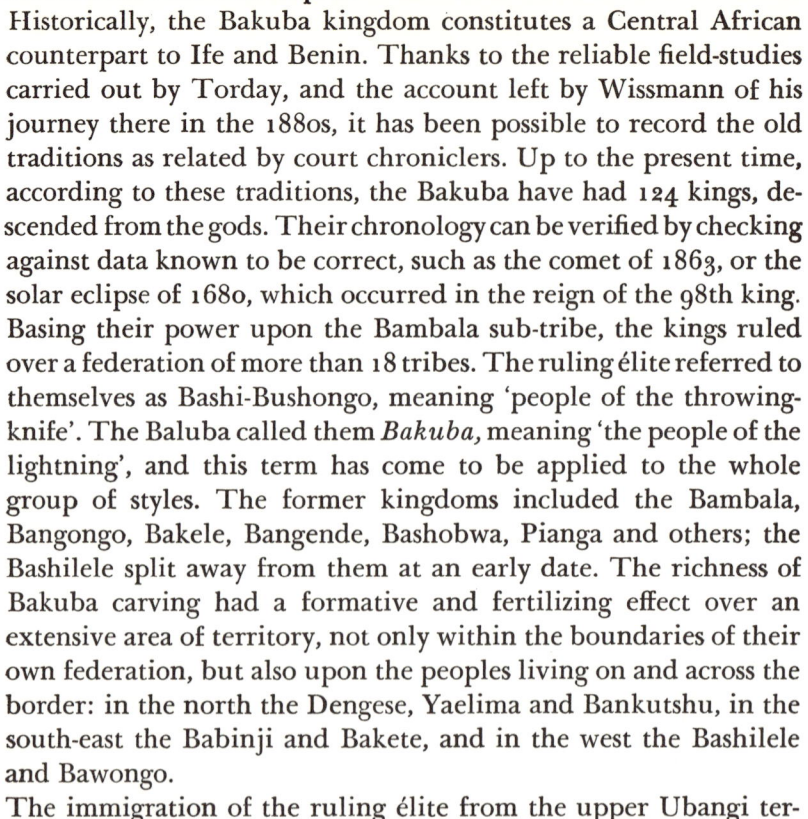

this, they belong to a kingdom of which the origins can be traced far back into the distant past.

Historically, the Bakuba kingdom constitutes a Central African counterpart to Ife and Benin. Thanks to the reliable field-studies carried out by Torday, and the account left by Wissmann of his journey there in the 1880s, it has been possible to record the old traditions as related by court chroniclers. Up to the present time, according to these traditions, the Bakuba have had 124 kings, descended from the gods. Their chronology can be verified by checking against data known to be correct, such as the comet of 1863, or the solar eclipse of 1680, which occurred in the reign of the 98th king. Basing their power upon the Bambala sub-tribe, the kings ruled over a federation of more than 18 tribes. The ruling élite referred to themselves as Bashi-Bushongo, meaning 'people of the throwing-knife'. The Baluba called them *Bakuba,* meaning 'the people of the lightning', and this term has come to be applied to the whole group of styles. The former kingdoms included the Bambala, Bangongo, Bakele, Bangende, Bashobwa, Pianga and others; the Bashilele split away from them at an early date. The richness of Bakuba carving had a formative and fertilizing effect over an extensive area of territory, not only within the boundaries of their own federation, but also upon the peoples living on and across the border: in the north the Dengese, Yaelima and Bankutshu, in the south-east the Babinji and Bakete, and in the west the Bashilele and Bawongo.

The immigration of the ruling élite from the upper Ubangi territory into the Congo basin is believed to have taken place during the first millennium A.D. According to ancient tradition, they crossed four large rivers, had a fair-skinned king as one of their first rulers, and reached the Sankuru during the reign of Minga Bengala, the sixth king, in or about the 6th century. This information is all the more valuable since it shows that the Bakuba had a common origin with the kingdoms of East and West Africa. These legendary kings are credited with certain cultural achievements: Mucu Mushanga, the 27th king, is said to have discovered fire and to have introduced clothing of bark cloth; Bo Kena, the 73rd king, to have invented certain masks, and so on.

The kingdom attained its climax between 1600 and 1620, during the reign of the distinguished Shamba Bolongongo, the 93rd king, who, whilst maintaining full political power, succeeded in keeping

Fig. 110

the peace and promoting cultural development. He was conqueror and philosopher in one, a sage who, in the midst of negro Africa, preached peace, love of one's enemy and high moral principles. He is still admired today as a model of humanity and a patron of the arts, and venerated and loved as a divine hero. It is a fact that, before he came to the throne, he travelled far and wide around his country, learning from the Bapende how to make plush-like fabrics, and from the Bakele how to embroider textiles; and also that he introduced into his kingdom manioc, palm-oil and tobacco. Indeed, Shamba Bolongongo, having summoned the greatest woodcarvers to his court, had a likeness made of himself in wood. By so doing he instituted a most important movement, the development of a particular kind of wooden sculpture; for the idea of depicting the king became a tradition, which was to endure for a long time (Plate 50). The nineteen known statues of kings are mounted on pedestals, seated with crossed legs, carrying the royal wooden knife, and personal emblems indicating their particular achievements: thus King Miele, the 86th king, who was a great smith and renowned for his iron figures, is shown carrying an anvil, Shamba Bolongongo a games-board, and so on.

The Bakuba also give expression to their great artistic sense in utensils: cups, boxes, weapons, tobacco pipes, drums, drinking-horns and textiles with ingeniously designed patternwork. The luxury articles made for the court are characterized by elaborate execution and rhythmically balanced form; for it was at court that the finest artists gathered, and here that they had an opportunity to gain prestige and renown. A good carver had the rank of a

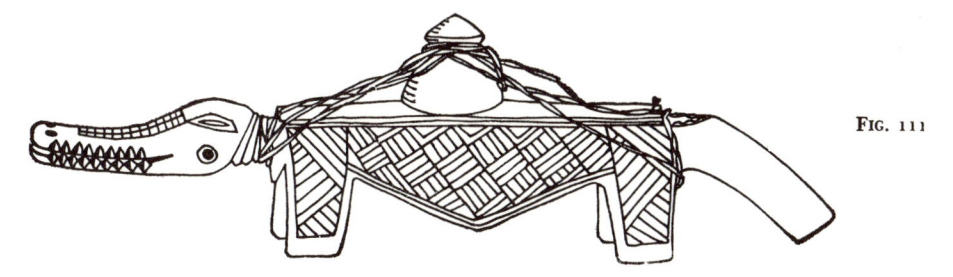

FIG. 111

senior official. The folk art of the Bakuba, although cruder and more angular in form, is marked by the same strong sense of style, and finds supreme fulfilment in the fashioning of masks.

Their wooden cups are masterpieces of craftsmanship: it is impossible to do justice in a few words to such a wealth of ideas, such ingenuity in composing figured and geometric patterns. The way in which technical problems alone are solved is outstanding: without a sketch, the most intricate patterns are incised and brought into rhythmic harmony. Unity between decoration and form is always observed, and there is real tension, for example, in the head-shaped cup (Plate 51), which is a portrait, as well as in cups with several heads, and in full figures, in all postures, with well-shaped backs. Some cups bear the insignia of the ruler or the emblem of the rank he held in the secret society. Members of the Yolo society who had cut off an enemy's head were allowed to affix a hand to the cup as their emblem. Motifs are also drawn from the animal world: beetles (Plate 51), antelopes, the shells of tortoises, the scales of reptiles, the foot-imprints of lizards and cats; and, from the heavens, the sun and the moon.

FIG. 112

Beauty of form and wealth of imagination are also characteristic of their geometrically decorated cups and boxes, with or without a handle or a base. Many motifs are borrowed from basket-work. Plaited bands, curls, angles, spirals, concentric circles and lozenges are dynamically and rhythmically modified, and are given names of mythological significance.

The fine old specimens were worked in hardwood; the rough parts of the surface have been worn down from handling.

In addition to the Bakuba, such tribes as the Dengese, Bashilele and Bawongo, as well as the Bapende, have also made some remarkably fine cups.

In their lidded boxes the Bakuba used to keep *bongotol:* the decorative little plaques of camwood, made by women, given to their friends on someone's death, and put into the grave. Red tukula, it will be recalled, possesses magical properties.

The singular divination implement known as *itombwa* deserves special mention (Fig. 111). This miniature narrow bench, decorated with human and animal heads, is used by the soothsayer when consulting the spirits — when, for example, a diagnosis has to be made or a thief identified. The soothsayer rubs a chewed magic medicine on the flat back of the implement, and allows the oracle knob to glide to and fro along it, whilst he puts his questions or enumerates names of suspects. If the knob sticks, the question is answered in the affirmative, or the person whose name has just been mentioned revealed as the culprit.

FIG. 113

There are three basically different types of mask in use amongst the Bakuba and the neighbouring peoples. All of them are characterized by a profusion of unusual ideas with regard to decoration and painting.

1. The *bombo* type is a large wooden helmet-mask covered with copper plate, and with a pronounced bulging forehead; the broad nose is joined to the triangular mouth by means of vertical lines; above the upper part of the nose a triangle can be made out, and woven bands studded with cowrie-shells and beads pass across the eyes, or from the nose across the mouth to the chin. The bombo mask is worn by the Bakuba at the initiation ceremony, and also at all *rites de passage*. They are supposed to represent pygmies, whom the Bakuba think of as weird gnomes. It is interesting to note that pygmies do in fact have a pronounced bulging forehead.

2. The *mashamboy* or *mokenge* mask consists of a cane frame, covered with raffia and decorated with sewn-on accessories, such as cowrie-shells, beads and pieces of hide. Only the nose, mouth and ears are made of wood. From the head there dangles a long flap, studded partly with cowrie-shells and partly with small bells or plumes. The mashamboy mask is the embodiment of an illness-bringing demon, and was at one time worn by the chief to compel obedience from the womenfolk. Today it is used only by the professional dancers who entertain people at the market.

3. The *shene-malula* mask is gaily painted and lavishly adorned (Plate 52). On this variant the eyes are represented as cones and surrounded by perforation. With the Bakete, too, we find this style in a marked form (Fig. 112).

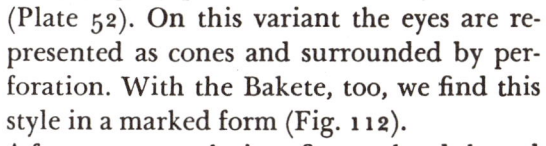

A few rare wrought-iron figures, head-shaped cups of clay and small ivory figures are Bakuba in origin. More common and famous are their textiles woven of raffia bast upon a hand-loom. Among these there are plain and patterned fabrics, fabrics with embroidery or of plush-like texture, *musese*, in red, violet, yellow and black (Plates 51, 59), mostly woven by the Bashobwa, and, finally, fabrics dyed by the 'resist' technique.

The *Dengese*, on the Lukenie, to the north of the Sankuru, are known for their solemn

FIG. 114

FIG. 116

FIG. 115

sepulchral figures (Plate 53). The elongated bodies are covered with ornamental cicatrices, have a large *membrum virile,* and break off abruptly at the buttocks. The unique hair-pin shown in Fig. 113 is of Bawoyo origin.

To the south of the Bakuba, on the river Lulua, the small tribe of the Bena Lulua, who derive from the Baluba, have developed a most impressive and distinctive style, combining liking for decoration (cf. Bakuba!) with lyrical elegance (Fig. 114).

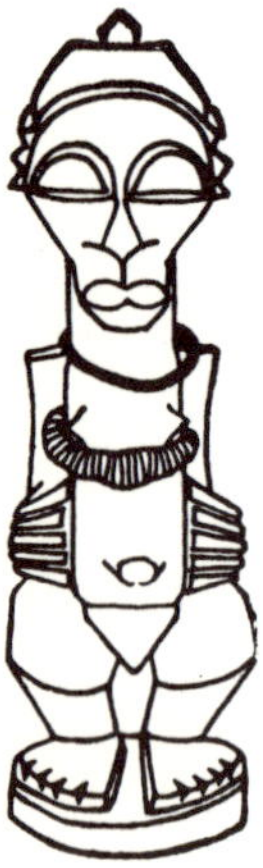

CHARACTERISTICS: elaborately plaited hair-dress; ornamental cicatrices on the head and body; ringed neck; concentric circles to mark the joints; protruding navel to represent the mystic centre of life. Attributes: beard, leopard skin, sceptre as symbol of authority, lance and shield. Mothers are portrayed carrying a child, lifting up a food-bowl, or standing with the pestle before the mortar for pounding manioc. The arbitrary proportions are highly effective. The heavy semi-closed eye-lids, the delicate nose and pronounced mouth give the whole figure an exceptional air of noble elegance. The origin of the Bena Lulua figures seems to lie in the far distant past; for as early as the 1880s Wissmann no longer found tattooing among the natives. Many statues taper at the bottom to a point, which serves to hold them erect when they are placed in houses or fields as guardian figures. They watch over their owner's property during his absence, and are looked upon as affording protection against illness and danger when hunting. One variant shows figures squatting; the hands touch the cheeks, the elbows rest upon the knees, and the backbone and ribs protrude (Fig. 115). The head is hollowed out, serving as a mortar for hemp or tobacco. Although the sculpture is bold in form, equilibrium is fully maintained. In their masks, with their pointed noses and deep eye-sockets, the Bena Lulua display a similar elegance (Fig. 116).

FIG. 117

Basalampasu

The Basalampasu, living far to the south of the Kasai, were until recently still cannibalistic. They wear extremely abstract smooth masks, resembling those of the Bakota and Bambara; whilst others, with bulbous noses and cheeks, constitute a link with the style of the Barotse masks in Rhodesia.

SOUTH-EASTERN CONGO
Basonge

The Basonge, who live in the district between the Lualaba and Sankuru, in the province of Lusambo, are a branch of the Baluba, who originated in an area to the north-east of their present whereabouts. Although, during the reign of King Kongolo, they participated in the foundation of the first Baluba kingdom in the 15th century, they occupy a special place from the cultural and artistic point of view. They have a patriarchal form of organization, which may lead them to prefer abstract pole sculpture.

CHARACTERISTICS: vigorous angular forms; the nose lozenge-shaped; the mouth open and protruding, often rendered as a horizontal figure-of-eight; the chin long and rectangular; the eyes open, their place occasionally being taken by cowrie-shells and metal nails; the neck ribbed; the shoulder area flat and broad; the hands placed on the abdomen, which often contains 'medicine', or has a sharply protruding navel; the hips sloping, and falling away evenly; the feet large but flat. The head may also be turned to one side, and the face covered with metal bands. Many figures are male and are shown wearing a beard.

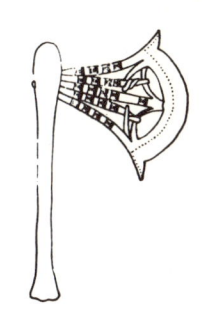

It is generally their fetishes, used for healing and magical purposes, which have a distinctly stereotyped form, despite the many magical attributes they bear (Fig. 117). According to legend, they are supposed to give the magician the power to influence leopards and the ability to identify culprits.

The Bekalebwe, a sub-tribe of the Basonge, have produced most of the figures, while the Bena Mpassa, another sub-tribe, have produced the massive grooved *kifwebe* masks depicted in Plate 54. The Batempe, who are related to the Basonge, make masks in the shape of a bishop's mitre, with protruding eyes and an abstract mouth, which are brought out at the end of the rainy season. In this connection attention may be drawn to Basonge armourers' work, an example of which is shown in Fig. 118: the blades of these fine wrought-iron ceremonial axes are decorated with heads, and the handles covered with copper plate.

Owing to their cubist tendencies and linear patterns, the masks of the Batetela (north-west of Lusambo) can be considered as a variant of the Basonge style.

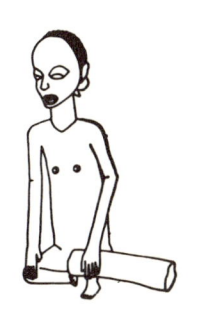

An individual style has also been developed by the *Bena Kanioka*, a Baluba tribe from the Kanda-Kanda area. Their sharply differentiated figures with slender limbs represent human beings in an unusual asymmetrical attitude: for example, a prisoner in the stocks (Fig. 119), or women with pestles, vessels, or a child carried laterally on the arm. The gentle inclination of the body and the gigantic feet serve to maintain the equilibrium of the figure, despite the dynamic posture.

CHARACTERISTICS: latticed *coiffure*, cascading on to the nape of the neck in knots; bulging forehead, heavy lids, open mouth with teeth and tongue, slender body.

The few masks of the Bena Kanioka are out of the ordinary and bold in form, with a globe-shaped protruding forehead and gnashing teeth.

Bajokwe-Lunda

The one million strong Bajokwe have spread out over a wide area in the southern Congo and northern Angola. They are vigorous and courageous hunters and agriculturalists, who used formerly to engage in the slave trade, and who in the 19th century even succeeded in conquering the then powerful Balunda kingdom. Their dynamic spirit is also reflected in their art. In addition to the folk art, somewhat rigid and giving no illusion of depth, there existed also the ancient refined culture of the court, expressed with conviction by professional artists.

CHARACTERISTICS: monumentality; the hair-dress forming a great curve; squat posture; vigorous facial features, with a broad mouth, deep eye-sockets, eyes shaped like coffee-beans, and a broad, frequently bearded chin; expressive hands, with nails; grooved spine; plastically formed ribs and collar-bones, the surface highly polished, and often trimmed with natural hair; a very life-like expressive realism (Fig. 120).

The figures supporting the stools are shown seated with their elbows resting on their knees, and hands touching the temples; some figures are posed asymmetrically or represented in movement. The Bajokwe keep their statuettes in their houses, in memory of deceased persons, and in case of illness make sacrificial offerings to them of manioc and meat. The figures give aid in pregnancy and help to track down thieves.

The existence of high-backed chairs in the European style need not surprise us, since in the 17th century the Balunda kingdom maintained lively contact with the Christianized kingdom of the Congo. These chairs, with their complex figure groups, are made from one piece, and draw their decorative motifs from the ideology of the negro: ritual customs, erotic scenes or healing ceremonies with drummers, or certain legends, or even striking events — for example, a traveller being carried in a hammock, or a European sitting in an armchair, drinking and smoking. In addition to these, there are countless animal motifs, and lavish ornamentation with plaited bands, wavy lines and concentric circles. This delight in decoration extends even to the smallest utensils.

FIG. 120

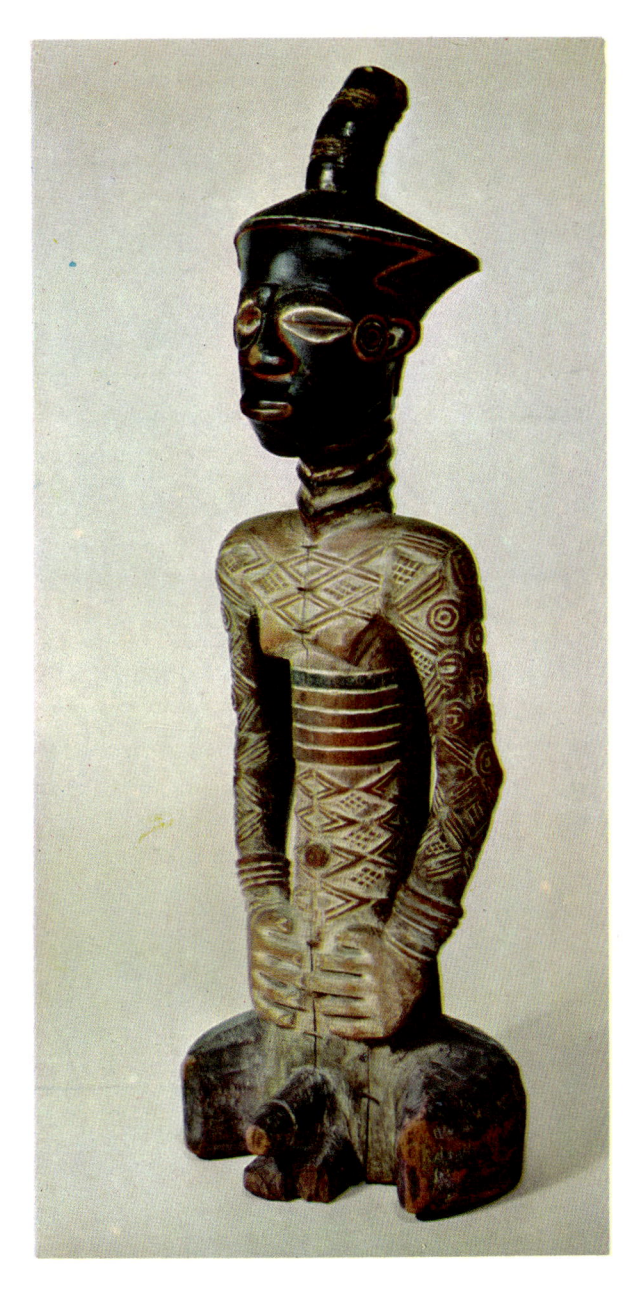

PLATE 53 — Commemorative statue of a Dengese chief, imposing in its austere solemnity, and with an expressive head. The elongated body bears decorative tattooings, often meaningful to the local population. Central Congo. *Ethnological Collection, Zurich (26¾ in.)*.

PLATE 54 — *Kifwebe* mask, Bena Mpassa, a sub-tribe of the Basonge, Lomami area. Characteristic is the ingenious interplay of smooth and striated areas. These lines filled with white colouring-matter, emphasizing the highly abstract treatment, evoke a singular tension of form. The smooth eyes seem to direct attention inwards. Frobenius has given an account (1898) of the operation of these masks: the priest-magician cut a slave into two, put a mask between the two parts of his body, and hurled it into the fire, so that it should be transformed into a powerful spirit. Later the priest wore it on very important occasions: when the village was plague-stricken, before military campaigns, and on the death of a king. Central Congo. *Rietberg Museum, Zurich, Von der Heydt Collection (13¾ in.).*

PLATE 55 — Wooden mask, Bajokwe, worn at secular games and entertainments, such as performances of folk satires. At these the most diverse types appear: magicians, hunters, and venerable old men; indispensable are the clown and the pretty girl, represented by the mask shown here. A certain lifelessness is noticeable, which ample accessories cannot hide; but the movements of the dancers give it its charm. Southern Congo. *Musée Royal de l'Afrique Centrale, Tervuren.*

PLATE 56 — The axe, emblem of the chief of the Baluba-Hemba, and the corn pestle, southern Baluba (cf. also Fig. 124) show a fine sensibility and sense of proportion. The balanced composition displays harmony; the eyes, under their heavy lids, express great restraint; the serenity emanating from them is both affecting and enchanting. South-eastern Congo. *Rietberg Museum, Zurich, Von der Heydt Collection (14⅜ in. and 9½ in.).*

PLATE 57 — Carved ivory neck-rest, Baluba, particularly precious. It probably belonged to a high-born princess, who slept on it to protect her splendid hair-dress. South-eastern Congo. *Charles Ratton Collection, Paris (7 in.).*

PLATE 58 — Famous large helmet-mask, north-western Baluba, with beautifully curved horns. Brought to Belgium as long ago as 1889. At the back a small bird is affixed. The proportion of form and fine harmony can induce a reverent spirit in a believer. South-eastern Congo. *Musée Royal de l'Afrique Centrale, Tervuren (25½ in.).*

PLATE 59 — Statue of a tribal progenitor, northern Baluba, in the so-called long-faced style. The cubist tendency enhances the dignified tranquillity of this fine figure *(29½ in.)*.
The raffia fabric originates from the Bahuana in the central Congo. The plush effect has been obtained by knotting loops close together in the material whilst weaving; these loops are then shorn off and dyed with camwood. Such *musese* came to Europe as long ago as the 16th century. South-eastern Congo. *Ethnological Collection, Zurich (19¾ in. x 53½ in.)*.

PLATE 60 — Stool of a chief, 'The Master of Buli'. Buli is a northern Baluba village on the Lualaba. The kneeling woman, the 'daugther of the spirit', has a forceful expression of exaggerated pathos. The seat and the arms frame the face, which is modelled with sensibility, and enhance its effect. South-eastern Congo. *Musée Royal de l'Afrique Centrale, Tervuren (20½ in.).*

The custom of wearing masks is still alive today. Large abstract structures of plaited bark, painted red and black, and attired in a net costume, appear as the embodiment of demons, spirits of the dead, and mock devils on stilts, who punish malefactors, cure those possessed of demons, and take part in initiation ceremonies. For games of a secular character wooden masks are thought sufficient (Plate 55).

The neighbouring Kaluena produce, among other things, urns bearing heads. The sepulchral style of the Ovimbundu in western Angola (Benguella) is related to that of the Bajokwe, but more refined, especially in their female figures.

Baluba style group

The vast Baluba territory, comprising the entire south-eastern part of the Congo, as far as Tanganyika and Lake Mweru, is uniform as regards language and culture, but racially mixed. The native Kiluba-speaking tribes have been subjugated by two different peoples from the north-east. It was on their initiative that a mighty and greatly-feared kingdom arose. The conquerors of the late 15th century were led by the cruel Basonge king Kongolo; the Baluba, who conquered Kongolo's kingdom in 1585, had a matriarchal form of organization. Their history is one of victorious wars and great extension of power, but also of dynastic and other internal trouble, which so weakened the state that at the end of the 19th century it fell victim to the invading Bajokwe and Bayeke. Many customs in this sacrosanct kingdom indicate the links with the Bahima states and the Monomotapa kingdom of Southern Rhodesia. It was the Baluba, too, who founded the Balunda and Bakuba kingdoms, and determined the political pattern as far afield as Northern Rhodesia.

FIG. 121

The splendid artistic achievements of the Baluba are due to a felicitous intermingling of different racial and cultural elements, and to the high standards prevailing at the court. Baluba art counts amongst the finest that Africa has to offer. There is no trace here of grotesque crude forms or troubling visions. Their most exquisite works are gently curved, organically conceived, rounded and soft in form; their simplified naturalism is of the utmost artistic compactness (Plate 56).

CHARACTERISTICS: intricate hair-dress, often in the form of a cross, or falling down like a cascade; a grooved diagonal band separating the hair-line from the forehead; eyes shaped like coffee-beans; small simplified 'cat's ears'; ornamental cicatrices in relief on the

FIG. 122

body, and cross-hatching on the mons Veneris; the surface elaborately worked and polished.

Of the female sculptures it is the Earth Mother who is chiefly represented, and of the male ones some brilliant tribal hero. The figure is the symbol of the tribal community, and, being endowed with power, is called upon to afford protection in every situation. The artist must reproduce the complex *coiffures* and cicatrice patterns with the greatest accuracy, for they are the distinguishing characteristics of the aristocratic upper class, of which he himself is a leading member. Each chief disposes of a seat of his own with supporting figure, a sceptre and decorated axes. The walls of the nobles' houses are painted red, black and white, and the beams are carved. Inside the house there are wooden bed-posts in relief, and innumerable neck-rests, water pipes, lidded bowls, three-pronged weapon-holders, fetishes and utensils, all fashioned with the same devotion and mostly combined with the Earth Mother (Plate 57). The neck-rest in Fig. 121 shows with what sureness of touch the female figure has been fashioned as a work of art, and also utilized as a functional element. Very common among the Baluba are the *kabila*, the so-called 'beggar women', female figures with vessels (Fig. 122).[4] In some tribes the magicians make use of them for medicinal purposes; the symbolic white colour in the vessel brings the invalid and the magician himself under the power of the spirit. Other 'beggar women' are reputedly buried under the threshold of the accouchement hut. On the Lomami, on the other hand, a pregnant woman places one of these vessels in front of her hut a few days before delivery, and every passer-by places a gift inside it, so that she shall not suffer any hardship through being unable to work during her confinement. Colle holds that this custom is an expression of their strong feeling of solidarity, based upon acceptance of the principle of mutual assistance in time of need, when, however, they also seek to invoke the power of the Earth Mother.

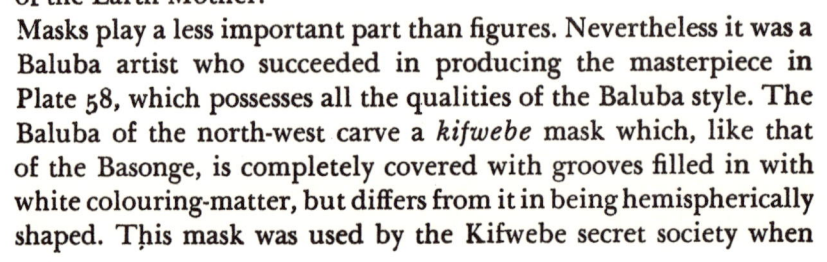

Masks play a less important part than figures. Nevertheless it was a Baluba artist who succeeded in producing the masterpiece in Plate 58, which possesses all the qualities of the Baluba style. The Baluba of the north-west carve a *kifwebe* mask which, like that of the Basonge, is completely covered with grooves filled in with white colouring-matter, but differs from it in being hemispherically shaped. This mask was used by the Kifwebe secret society when

FIG. 123

worshipping the souls of the dead, appointing an important chief, or visiting a distinguished person.

Let us now turn for a moment to consider the most important sub-groups in Baluba art:

The stronghold of the classical Baluba style is located in the district of Urua, between Lake Mweru and the lesser lakes. In this region live the highly talented Baluba-Hemba, who are widely renowned as carvers (Plate 56). In their sculptures the underlying mood is particularly elevated and lyrical: the rounded style, with the plastic joints, the short chin, and gentle flowing forms, is here executed to perfection.

The Bahemba make, as images of their ancestors, small figures of ivory or hippopotamus tusk (Fig. 123), which they wear in the arm-pit or on the arm. Frequent lubrication with oil and the rubbing of the surface through constant wear give them a wonderful patina. The small elegantly-shaped figures follow the natural curve of the tusk and are generally provided with a hair-dress in the form of a cross and a diagonal band.

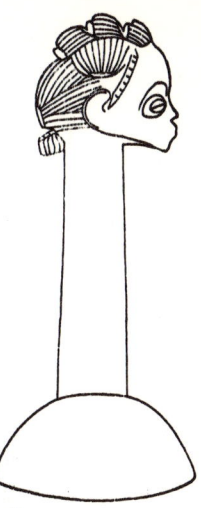

FIG. 124

The Baluba-Shankadi in Katanga, who live to the west of the lesser lakes and the Bahemba, deserve to be mentioned on account of their very graceful figures, which have a cascading *coiffure*. By their rhythmic interrelation two of these figures, supporting a neck-rest or stool, form a perfect spatial composition. The cornpounders in Plate 56 and Fig. 124 are examples of the southern Baluba sub-style.

The somewhat more rigid forms of the north-western Baluba betray Basonge influence.

Of special importance is the so-called long-faced style of the northern Baluba, who are settled partly in Katanga and partly in Manyema (Plate 59). As the name suggests, in this type of sculpture the face is less rounded; the nose is longer, and the eyebrows high-arched; the volumes of the body show a cubist tendency, which becomes more marked the further one goes towards the north and east. But they have created, at Buli, twelve sculptures which suffice to give this group an honoured place in African art: these are single figures, caryatid stools with one or two figures, and beggar women with vessels, all of which display very great creative talent (Plate 60).

FIG. 126

To the eastern Baluba group belong the *Wabembe* (northern end of Lake Tanganyika), Bangubangu (Manyema), Babuye, Baguha,

191

Batabwa, Babemba (Northern Rhodesia) and Baushi (Lake Bangweulu). Although the classical Baluba style, with its rich carving, can still be detected, the cubist tendencies of the adjacent lands to the north and east suit the negro artist so well that pole sculpture and round sculpture unexpectedly fuse, leading to interesting intermediary forms. This is shown particularly clearly in some *Wabembe* works (Fig. 125).

CHARACTERISTICS: large oval eyes, shaped like coffee-beans, with a horizontal line, which breaks up the forehead and face into planes that recede at straight angles; the nose long and straight; the mouth angular, with teeth; the chin roughly indicated; whiskers forming a frame around the face, which, with its large schematic eyes, produces a motionless effect, almost like that of an insect. The body is faceted and slender, the shoulders are thrust forward and broken up into horizontal planes; the limbs describe a zigzag line. Some Wabembe masks are wholly abstract, with only the eyes giving a sign of life.

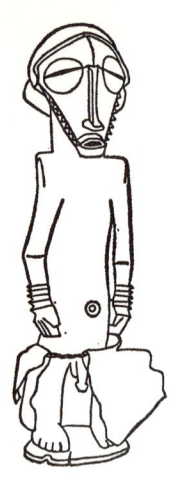

FIG. 125

NORTHERN CONGO

North of Lat. 3° S. there extends a vast area of jungle and river in which a few artistic centres stand out like small islands in an immense sea: in the east the Balega and Bambole; in the north-east the Azande, Mangbetu and Ababua; in the north-west the Bwaka and Mongala river tribes, and on the inner western bend of the Congo the Kundu-Mongo tribes. Once again we are leaving the domain of matriarchal organization for one where rigid pole sculpture predominates.

The patriarchally-organized *Balega* tribe, in the equatorial forest of the eastern Congo, demonstrates many times over how abstract treatment of form can lead to great artistic compactness. Once courageous elephant hunters, the Balega used to make figures and masks from hard ivory as emblems of rank for the members of the Mwami sects.[5] To the Balega these were symbols of power and dignity, continuity and vitality. For the highest rank, *lutembo lwa kindi,* was reserved the simple oval ivory mask, with a concave face alive with acute tension. Immediately beneath them in rank are wooden masks of the same style; diminutive masks, particularly delicate in form, serve as messengers and symbols of recognition. These figures are emblems of rank, *kindi,* or exert force in many ways. Often they symbolize some particular event, or are worn around the neck by a twin whose brother or sister has died, in the belief that it will have some magic effect. On ordinary working

FIG. 127

192

days all these objects are kept in a basket. But on festivals, and occasions for communal singing and dancing, the Mulega paints them white, spreads them out upon the ground, hangs them on a stand before the place of worship, or fastens them to his arm, forehead, or temples, or under his chin.

On the death of a member of the society, his mask passes into the possession of a relative, who assumes the same rank as the deceased. He wears the mask at the initiation ceremony, at which he recites certain cautionary songs and moral rules, and scoops up some banana beer with a handsomely decorated ivory spoon. In his carving the Mulega chiefly uses the dot-and-circle motif, which signifies youth and strength. The figures are crude and angular, pulsating with a rhythm of their own; the arms and legs are often suggested very rudimentarily by jagged projections, or omitted altogether; the mouth is cursorily treated, the eyes indicated by inlaid cowrie-shells, carved in the form of such shells, or represented by a dot and circle. Several masks have fringes of beard tied on, or are crowned by horns. The imploring gesture, with arms raised up above a slender body, eloquently expresses an appeal for aid to the celestial powers (Fig. 126).

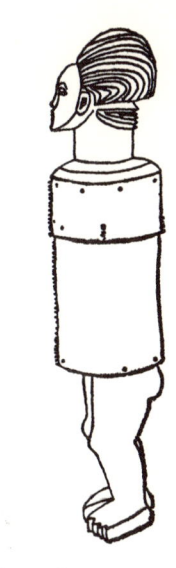

FIG. 128

The little-known *Bambole* tribe, on the river Lomami, south-west of Stanleyville, produces raffia mats with intricate patterns. Their wooden sculptures are highly abstract, with a large head; the concave white-painted faces give them a resemblance to the sculptures of the Balega and Pangwe. A striking feature are the dangling arms, which describe a single arc, like a horseshoe, with the shoulder as the centre (Fig. 127).

Bambole

Amongst the *Azande* and *Mangbetu* tribes (Welle and Mbomu region), whose styles are related, the stimulus to artistic endeavour came from the royal courts. People of neo-Sudanese culture, immigrating from the north, established themselves here as a privileged caste, exercising hegemony over the indigenous Bantu, and in the 19th century founded two kingdoms. In 1870 the famous Mangbetu sultan Munza welcomed the explorer Schweinfurth in a large palace hall over 150 feet long. At one time the Avungura sovereigns of the Azande also exercised dominion over the Mangbetu.

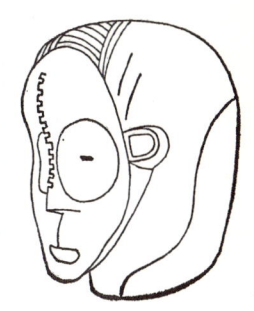

FIG. 131

Their utensils dazzle one with their fine harmonious forms, often combined with figures and heads, particularly when they serve to enhance the prestige of the ruling class, as is shown by the fol-

193

lowing examples: a box of bark in the shape of a human figure, serving as a receptacle for honey and other substances (Fig. 128), musical instruments (Plate 61), and drums in animal form. Characteristic of Mangbetu sculpture is the long slender head (Fig. 129). Their beautifully-shaped palm-wine and water jugs have rhythmically balanced plastic curves; their elegant angular knives are set in ivory hafts. They show a great deal of imagination in their decorated bark kilts *(milumba)*, worn by the men, and the oval seat-mats *(malembelembe)* of raffia leaves, worn by the women.

Ababua

The Ababua, a Bantu people who live in the area between the Welle and the Aruwimi, and who for a time came under the sway of the Mangbetu, have produced cubist masks, with planes broken up rhythmically by areas of black and white paint (Fig. 130).

NORTH-WESTERN GROUP
(Congo-Ubangi region)

Amongst the tribes that dwell in the swampy area of the outer bend of the Congo, it is the Bwaka (Ngbaka) who have developed an individual style; so also, amongst the tribes on the river Mongala, have the Ngbandi, Mbanza and Ngombe.

CHARACTERISTICS: as a rule, rounded heads, although among the Ngbandi and Ngombe, who practise the custom of head deformation, they sometimes taper to a point on top. Dotted lines of tattooing run across the forehead and nose, and in some cases also round the concave eye-sockets and the mouth; the body is heavy, and the arms rudimentary (Fig. 131).

In the western part of the inner bend of the Congo live the Mongo-Kundu peoples, who produce isolated sculptures in wood and clay. To this group belong the Dengese and Yaelima, already mentioned in connection with the Bakuba (cf. p. 177), as well as the Wangata, known for their coffins, bearing figures in pole style, and the Balolo group, whose masks are remarkable for their cubist tendency (Fig. 132). Due to their common origin, the peoples of the northern Congo have many similarities with the Pangwe across the border. This is shown by the frequency of bow-harps and slit-drums in animal form. The elegant Yangere drum (Fig. 133) has its counterpart in one found amongst the Welle peoples.

FIG. 129

FIG. 130

ARCHITECTURE: in this region the old West African gable-roofed house, sometimes with a tortoise-shaped roof, meets increasing competition from the Sudanese cone-roofed hut.

Lit.: [1] Maes, Figurines; [2] Gerbrands, Art....; [3] Sousberghe; [4] Maes, Soziolog. Bedeutung; [5] Biebuyck.

FIG. 132

FIG. 133

VII. EAST AFRICA

GENERAL SURVEY

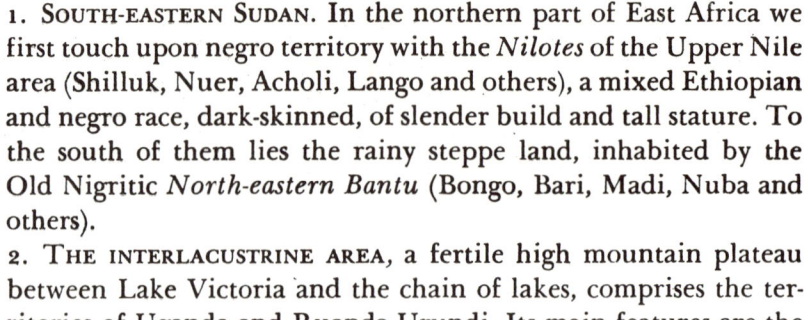

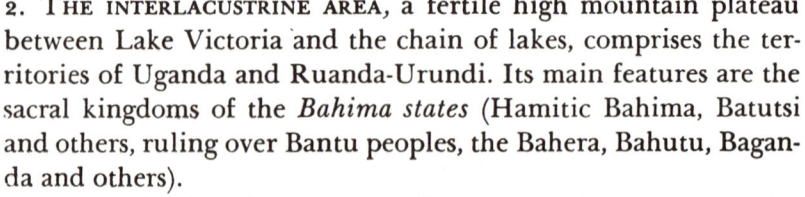

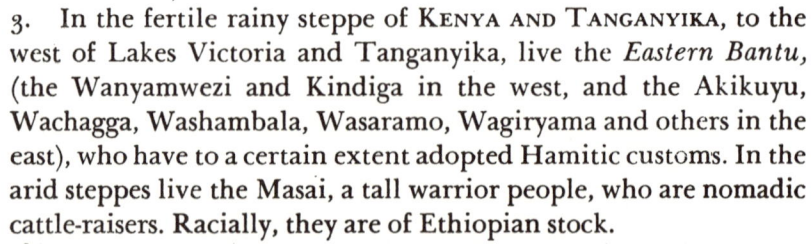

1. SOUTH-EASTERN SUDAN. In the northern part of East Africa we first touch upon negro territory with the *Nilotes* of the Upper Nile area (Shilluk, Nuer, Acholi, Lango and others), a mixed Ethiopian and negro race, dark-skinned, of slender build and tall stature. To the south of them lies the rainy steppe land, inhabited by the Old Nigritic *North-eastern Bantu* (Bongo, Bari, Madi, Nuba and others).

2. THE INTERLACUSTRINE AREA, a fertile high mountain plateau between Lake Victoria and the chain of lakes, comprises the territories of Uganda and Ruanda-Urundi. Its main features are the sacral kingdoms of the *Bahima states* (Hamitic Bahima, Batutsi and others, ruling over Bantu peoples, the Bahera, Bahutu, Baganda and others).

3. In the fertile rainy steppe of KENYA AND TANGANYIKA, to the west of Lakes Victoria and Tanganyika, live the *Eastern Bantu*, (the Wanyamwezi and Kindiga in the west, and the Akikuyu, Wachagga, Washambala, Wasaramo, Wagiryama and others in the east), who have to a certain extent adopted Hamitic customs. In the arid steppes live the Masai, a tall warrior people, who are nomadic cattle-raisers. Racially, they are of Ethiopian stock.

4. In the southern and eastern mountainous areas of ETHIOPIA, in addition to the Hamitic and Semitic peoples, and under their rule, there also live negro tribes, such as the Konso, Gato and others. (The advanced culture of Ethiopia will be dealt with in the volume on Egypt).

5. The central COASTAL ZONE of East Africa, an undulating lowland, constitutes a separate group of neo-Oriental culture. In this region the ancient negroid population has been continually exposed to racial and cultural influences from Arabs, Persians, Indians and Indonesians. The *Wasuaheli* call themselves Shirazi, for the Wasuaheli nobility from Shiraz in Persia came to the east coast of Africa in the first mill. A.D. Between the 10th and 16th centuries Kilwa was a thriving commercial centre inhabited by Persian immigrants, who controlled the gold trade even as far away as the Monomotapa kingdom in Southern Rhodesia and Mozambique.

FIG. 134

196

6. Finally, in the SOUTH, partly between Lake Nyasa and the coast, partly in Tanganyika, and partly in Mozambique, jutting into this patriarchal area, is a wedge of matriarchal culture, represented principally by the *Makonde*.

Since the peoples living near the source of the Nile were the most exposed to cultural influences from Egypt and Napata, it would be natural to expect their art to reach a high standard. But this is not the case. Although we find a great many attractive craft products, their sculpture, in the pole style, is uninspiring and poor in quality, rarely advancing beyond the primary stage. Its inadequacies cannot be accounted for merely by the fact that the Hamitic pastoral peoples did not look favourably upon the art of sculpture. For here, as in West Africa, alongside a Hamitic upper class there lives a settled Bantu peasantry, who continue to abide by their old ancestor cult. Moreover, in Egypt and Ethiopia a fusion between Hamitic and Semitic peoples led to great achievements in the cultural sphere. It may certainly be true to some extent that the patriarchal social structure of the Old Nigritic peoples creates a rather uninspiring artistic climate. But then almost the whole of the western Sudan also has a patriarchal form of organization, and yet it has become one of the greatest artistic centres in Africa! This riddle has yet to be solved. We are therefore justified in treating East African art in outline.

FIG. 135

FIG. 136

SOUTH-EASTERN SUDAN

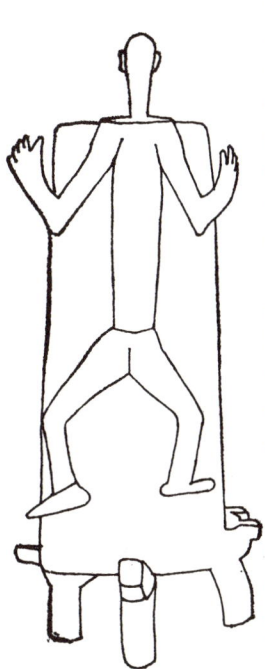

FIG. 137

ARCHITECTURE: cylindrical huts with cone-shaped roofs, fine granaries on piles among the Madi group, mural reliefs and paintings among the Acholi, Lango, Nuba and others. The Burun paint animals, in a naturalistic manner similar to that of prehistoric rock paintings, on their clay walls.

SCULPTURE: ancestor figures and fetishes in the primary style, undifferentiated, angular and clumsy. The Bongo, Bari (Fig. 134), Lango, Acholi, Shir and others living between them and the Sara place them on graves in the open or indoors, and pour sacrificial libations upon them to give protection against castration or to

endow women with fertility. The Shilluk make simple masks of the rind of gourds, to which they stick fish-bones and cow dung.
APPLIED ART: the Shilluk make simple neck-rests, resembling those of Ancient Egypt. Shilluk, Turkana and Karamojo men wear lavishly decorated *coiffures*. The Nuba enjoy particular renown as potters.

INTERLACUSTRINE AREA

ARCHITECTURE: cupola hut with an accentuated entrance; among royal buildings, the tomb of the absolute king Mutesa stands out, with its magnificently curved wide projecting roof (Uganda).
APPLIED ARTS: these reach their climax in basket-work: Batutsi women, using the coiling technique, weave baskets, with conical pointed lids, so closely-woven that they can be used as vessels for milk. The black rhythmically-proportioned patterns have specific names, for example, 'the large bird's tail' (Fig. 135). Ring-like pot-stands and trays are intricately woven and decorated. The Barundi weave pipes for sucking beer through, with a design, and shape the lids of their beer-containers, made of gourd, as tapering cones with flaps. Wooden vessels and implements are patterned by poker-work and scratching, whilst shields are painted. In Luzira (Uganda) prehistoric figured heads have been found. The Batutsi and other tribes wear lavish *coiffures* with striations and flaps; the Baganda wear garments made of bark, painted with mud, using stencils, fastening them across one shoulder in toga fashion.

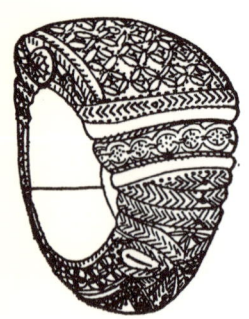

FIG. 138

ARCHITECTURE: houses with cone-shaped roofs and *tembe* (flat-roofed square houses).

KENYA, TANGANYIKA, SOUTH-WEST ETHIOPIA

PAINTING: thanks to the studies of Cory, we are now familiar with the initiation huts of the Wasukuma (a sub-tribe of the Wanyamwezi, to the south of Lake Victoria): they are used by the secret society of snake-charmers, and are painted with symbolic didactic pictures in ochre, black and white (Fig. 4).
POLE SCULPTURE is to be found among the Wakerewe, Akikuyu, Wasaramo, Wadoe, Wabondei, Wagiryama and Wanyika as ancestor and funerary figures, and among the Konso, Gato and others in south-west Ethiopia as sepulchral monuments (Plate 62), beside prehistoric ones made of stone. The Washambala, in Usambara, make crude figures to give strength in serious illness (Fig. 136), and the Wanyamwezi make ancestor statuettes as shrines, and slender figures with small heads, carved on thrones (Fig. 137). In all districts there is primitive clay sculpture, as, for example, in the vigorous figure groups used by the Wasukuma as symbols.

FIG. 139

APPLIED ARTS: notched staffs for initiation, simple iron animal figures from the kingdom of Karagwe, and very many ornaments made of metallic wire. The Masai boast leather shields painted with tribal emblems and marks denoting courage, milk vessels, and leather coats decorated with beads, and also fine iron lances.

ARCHITECTURE: as a result of extraneous influence, the square house with gabled roof; from the Shirazi, stone buildings with lime mortar (Kilwa and elsewhere).

APPLIED ARTS: Arabic and Persian ornamentation on carved doors, sandals, lecterns for reading the Koran, combs, etc., with many rosettes, arabesques and dot-and-circle motifs. In wood-working nails, lime and pegs are employed — aids of which the negro generally makes no use. The Wasuaheli are also noted for their techniques of metal-working: for punched, embossed, incrusted or filigree work in gold and silver (richly-decorated silver anklets with pin clasp [Fig. 138], Muscat daggers with silver sheaths, Lamu work (cf. p. 49, tin tarsias, spoons and vessels of all kinds). In addition they specialize in leather mats with mosaic pattern-work, and plaited mats with Arabic characters.

The Makonde group comprises the Makonde, Mawia, Makua, Yao, Wamuera, Matambwe and others.

ARCHITECTURE: round cone-roofed huts.

SCULPTURE: with the matriarchal Makonde tribes, living in an area under the influence of West African and Rhodesian cultures, pole sculpture gives way to a more organic rounded form. But there is still a trace of pole sculpture in the somewhat rigid and stiff figure of the primeval mother (with lip-plug and ornamental cicatrices). According to Makonde legend, the first man on earth made a wooden figure, which during the night miraculously awakened to life and became his wife.

MASKS: Their masks sometimes attain great expressiveness. Some are simple in form, with static concave planes (Plate 63); others display an organically sensed rounded style — for instance, in the Mawia mask in Fig. 139, hair and tattooing are represented by black beeswax and the adhesion of natural hair. This naturalism is exaggerated to an unpleasant extent in many masks from southern Tanganyika, with their full lips and ape-like receding cranium. Animal masks are provided with long ears and horns, and dancers in ape masks turn acrobatic somersaults. Male masks have beards, female ones lip-plugs and — a travesty of the male dancer — a

MAKONDE GROUP

SWAHILI COAST

separate plate with carved breasts. Famous, too, are the *mitete*: small wooden boxes for medicines, snuff or gunpowder, the lids of which bear pretty motifs of rosettes and animal figures.

VIII. SOUTH-EAST AFRICA AND MADAGASCAR

ZIMBABWE

In the dim and distant past the great north-south route of the East African steppe constituted a pathway for migrating Bushmen hunters, followed by Bantu peasants and Hamitic pastoralists. Along the coast Arabs and Persians, Indians and Indonesians carried on a lively trade with the African population. Bantu, Hamites, Arabs, Persians and Indians: here were many diverse influences and impulses, that led to the founding of flourishing kingdoms. Even today monuments of their existence remain scattered about Mashonaland, in the form of ruins of castles, temples, monoliths, mines, *thermae,* subterranean buildings and terraces. Ethnologists have named this culture after its most important centre, Zimbabwe. Its history lies shrouded in darkness; its chronicles remain unwritten. In her comprehensive study Caton-Thompson maintains that its mighty walls, built of smooth granite blocks in a herring-bone pattern, its massive conical tower and the gracefully curving flight of steps may be ascribed to an early kingdom, and that they originated some time in the latter half of the first millennium A.D. Subsequent buildings were erected in quarry-stone. The abandoned mines suggest that much copper and tin were excavated, that bronze was cast and gold melted.

It is still an open question whether any connection existed between the Zimbabwe ruins and the kingdom of Monomotapa (= lord of the mines), which abounded in gold and boasted great splendour, but which in the 16th century, when reached by Portuguese discoverers, showed signs of decadence. With its feudal institutions and royal rites it shows great similarity with other kingdoms, in particular with Baluba and Uganda.

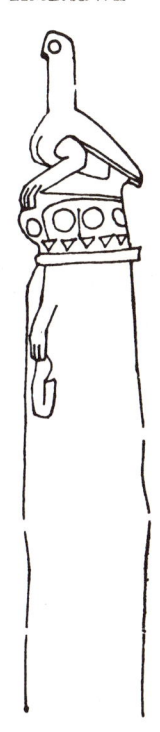

FIG. 140

Only a few specimens of plastic art have been found in the environs of Zimbabwe, such as, for instance, a proud bird made of soapstone, in a forceful simplified pole style (Fig. 140); stone bowls in relief, with plaited band and tendril motifs; a wooden vessel with signs of the zodiac; and simple vases, rigid in design and in the form of animal heads, in which to preserve the intestines of rulers.

FIG. 141

In the 17th century the Monomotapa kingdom was conquered by

BAROTSE

201

Barotse warriors, who then founded a kingdom of their own on both banks of the Zambezi, in which a Hamitic upper class ruled over Bantu tribesmen. Among the vanquished Bantu the Masubiya and Kwangwa have attained renown as wood-carvers. The Masubiya masks, with their furrowed brows and angular mouths with teeth (Fig. 141), and the Mambunda masks with their round cheeks, are brought out for the dance held to mark the new moon. The Masubiya and Kwangwa decorate their food-bowls (c. Plate on title-page), neck-rests and thrones with animal figures; they produce fine baskets and have added lustre to the court with their various arts and crafts.

In the whole area inhabited by the south-eastern Bantu pole sculpture is stiff and rigid; in recent times it has been subjected to European influence. But their utensils, on the other hand, display considerable taste and aesthetic sensibility: the neck-rest (Fig. 142) from Mashonaland (Southern Rhodesia) is an example of a fine, rhythmically measured composition with V-shaped indentations. Among other beautifully-formed objects are: wooden bowls with rims in open-work, calabashes (Fig. 143), a Manyakaze gourd from Mozambique with abundant poker-work, stools, shields, snuff-boxes, combs, and ceremonial weapons (many of them covered with an ornament of braided copper and brass wire), as well as ornamentation of gaily-coloured braided bead work, baskets intricately fashioned by the coiling method, and fine ceramics: pots, tobacco pipes, clay figures, etc. Animal figures are particularly popular.

ARCHITECTURE: all three basic types of dwelling are represented: the cupola hut, the so-called Kaffir kraal, made of switches and grass; the rectangular house; and that with a cone-shaped roof. Their lavish painting of clay walls and parapets in polychrome have earned the Ndebele and Basuto of the Transvaal a special place, and their paintings have brought them world renown (Fig. 5).

MADAGASCAR

The island of Madagascar occupies a position on the fringe of African art. The inhabitants are preponderantly Malays, who have fused with Arabs and Indians; in the remoter areas there live negroes. This variegated racial and cultural background has made for originality in artistic expression. The negroes of the south, the Mahafaly, Antandroy and others, erected upon their graves *aloala*, slender decoratively carved wooden posts six to twelve feet high (Fig. 144), their quantity and motifs depending upon the rank and wealth of the deceased. One royal grave is reputed to have as many as seventy of them! The motifs are of a mixed Arab and Oriental character, with arabesques, rosettes, half-moons, etc., arranged around human beings and animals. The aloala symbolize the link between heaven and earth. Similar grave-posts are also sporadically to be found among such northern tribes of Madagascar as the Tsimihety. The Madagascar Bantu decorate with carving posts and panels on houses, wooden bowls (with rosette motifs), and also many utensils. Among other Malagasy artistic endeavour is concentrated upon burial-places: for example, the stone sepulchral chambers and reliefs of the Hova, the pillars and lidded coffins of the Sakalava, the wooden sacrificial posts, shaped as figures, and menhirs of the Betsileo. In the secular field the Betsileo add decoration to houses, doors, window-casements and akalama ornamental discs, and the Hova to bed-boards, sceptres, and much else besides. The motifs of the older carvings have tendrils and torsades of an Arab or Indian character. Among the herdsmen of Madagascar the zebu is a common symbol of wealth and esteem. Indonesian in character are the horn and bamboo vessels and the sumptuous gaily-coloured ikat textiles, made by Hova noblewomen, who keep the technique a closely-guarded secret.

FIG. 144

ARCHITECTURE: rectangular gable-roofed houses, a few round huts, and royal palaces.

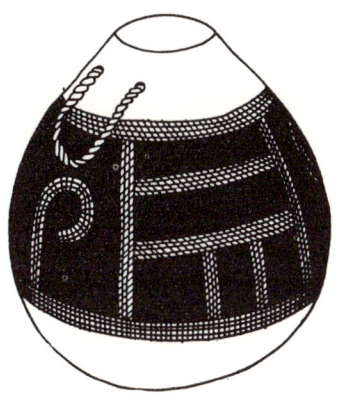

FIG. 143

IX. FUTURE PROSPECTS

Consequences of colonial rule

If we once again recall how closely interwoven negro art is with religion, and at the same time admit what a devastating effect White civilization has had upon it, the prospects for the future must inspire us with the utmost alarm. Africa is in a state of convulsion, and all accepted values are undergoing radical revision. Islam and Christianity are on the point of supplanting or assimilating traditional supernatural beliefs. This is undermining the basis of African art, and, indeed, depriving it of its whole *raison d'être*. For how can one venerate gods and sons of gods, and give them artistic form, if their very function is called in question? Anyone who faces up to these unpalatable truths must admit that the old established order has been completely destroyed. Colonial rule has temporarily brought in its train over-estimation of everything foreign. Missionaries have fought against the pagan cults and replaced their images by European ones. African markets are flooded with imported goods of all kinds, which are gradually ousting the time-consuming native handicrafts. The negro artist has found new patrons, to whose taste he is bound to conform. Where formerly it was the secret societies, priests and kings who assured his existence, today his customers are largely to be found amongst town-dwellers and missionaries, White settlers and tourists. In the hope of rapid and easy gain, the negro complies with their wishes. Thus there have arisen in the larger towns busy artisan workshops, producing *en masse* furniture, implements, ivory carvings and brass castings for the souvenir market. In Dahomey the entire village of Banamé is engaged in manufacturing carvings for export. If tourists want masks and sculptures, then they shall have them, as many as they wish! But what is produced is of most questionable value: works without any cultural roots or artistic content; elegant, perhaps, and ingenious, but at the same time plain, mannered and empty. The tribal sculptures exhibited in the superbly stocked museums make the African justly proud of his art; but they also show how false is the idea that he has merely to make use of traditional subjects in order to express himself in the modern idiom.

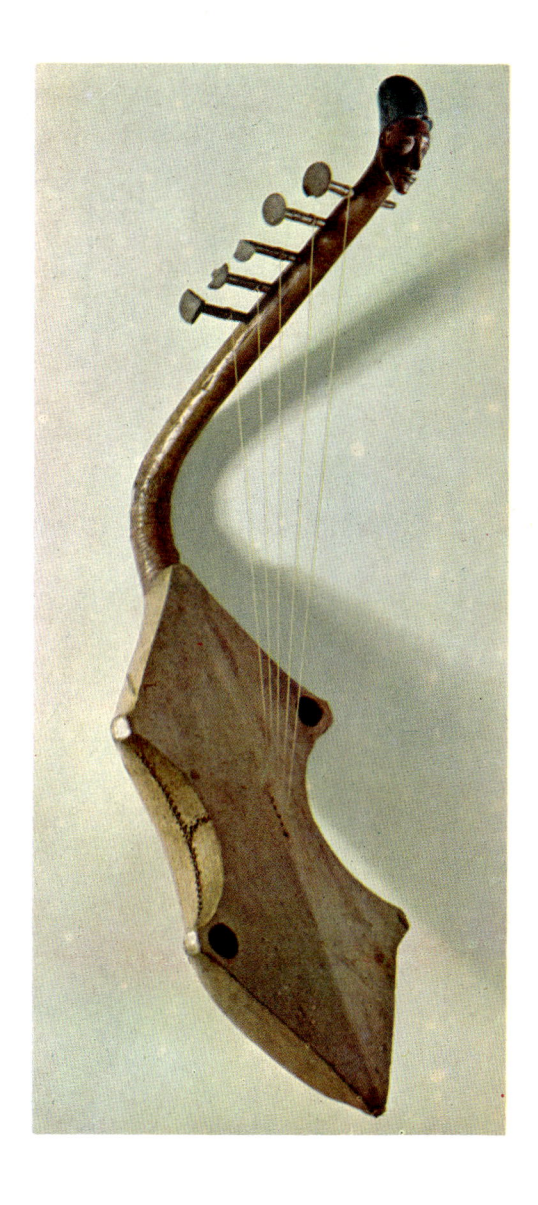

PLATE 61 — A *kundi*, a Mangbetu bow-harp, covered with the skin of an animal. The thick strings are made of giraffe hair; the fine ones of bast fibre. The instrument is plucked with the fingers by itinerant musicians to accompany the singing of nocturnal songs. The small head is integrated harmoniously into the figure as a whole. The head is oval-shaped in accordance with the Mangbetu custom of tying up the heads of their children to give them a pleasing form. North-eastern Congo. *Rietberg Museum, Zurich* (38½ in.).

PLATE 62 — Wooden figures, commemorating a deceased nobleman and brave warrior from the province of Gamu-Gofa. Pronounced pole style. In the graveyard the statue, distinguished by its tall cap, stood among figures of the enemies whom the warrior had vanquished; of these one, shown here, can be identified as Borana by its special hair-dress. South-western Ethiopia. *Ethnological Collection, Zurich (18½ and 16½ in.)*. The woven cloth is also of Ethiopian origin.

PLATE 63 — Wooden mask, Makonde, from the Rovuma River area, with beaded spirals and eyelashes of natural hair. The ears are simplified and their function particularly clearly brought out. This fine mask is worn at puberty ceremonies. Mozambique. *Lindenmuseum, Stuttgart (13½ in.)*.

PLATE 64: Balumbo dance mask, Gabon. This characteristic carved and painted wood dance mask, thought to represent the spirit of the dead, is the most typical art form of the Balumbo people. Musée de l'homme, Paris.

The African cannot meet the demands of the present and the future simply by taking up again the art of the past. The old ideas are being abandoned; the new ones have first to be identified and realized before the negro artist can set to work. At present he is in the act of breaking with the traditional content of his art. This makes it all the more impossible for Africa to turn back the wheel of history.

And yet we have no reason to succumb to pessimism about the future of negro art. The old gods are indeed doomed to pass away, but the negro's remarkable artistic sensibility is closely bound up with his nature, and cannot so easily be extinguished. His inexhaustible imagination, talent for abstraction, sense of rhythm and keen flair for penetrating to essentials — all these are inherent virtues which will stand him in good stead as he embarks upon his new course.

Contemporary art

The new era is dawning in a promising atmosphere. Africa is awake, and eager to acquire the fruits of civilization. From town and country, from remote bush villages, she sends her most gifted sons to Europe and America, to learn, to make up for lost time, to find a *point d'appui;* and this powerful spirit is reflected in the work of contemporary African artists.

The knowledge and training acquired in the artistic centres of Europe and America evoke a resounding echo in Africa itself. Governments, missionaries and groups of private benefactors are now founding in the larger African towns art schools and academies, run by European teachers who have recruited as staff Africans trained in Europe: for example, the Cyrene mission near Bulawayo in Rhodesia, the art academies of Elisabethville, Leopoldville and Kampala, the art studios of Desfossés in Elisabethville, of Pierre Lods in Poto-Poto near Brazzaville, and of Pierre Combes on the Ivory Coast and others. In these centres the negro's great artistic talents can be realized anew.

In plastic art his inborn sense of form and proportion is of great advantage. In painting it is remarkable with what skill and conviction he expands and enlarges upon the limited range of ritual colours formerly available to him, with what harmony — and yet with what verve — he combines elements of abstract art to form a unity.

He relaxes the background of his neo-impressionistic paintings with dabs and strokes; his poetic landscapes reveal his inherent sense of grace and rhythm, and his well-balanced groups are reminiscent of the ancient rock paintings.

Countless negro artists have achieved renown in Paris, London and New York, and made their presence felt at exhibitions: Jimoh Akolo, Oku Ampofo, Bandila, Bela, Djilatendo, Ben Enwonwu, Felix Idubor, Kiabelua, Lubaki, Mensah, Mtuze, Mwenze, Omaboku, Odongo, Pilipili, Sam Songo, Zigoma and many others.

The future All the ventures mentioned are as yet exploratory, but at the same time serious and positive, attempts to give new content to African art and to point its way to the morrow. We have no reason to give Africa up in despair. From the struggles and tribulations of the present, negro art will rise up again to new heights, like Phoenix from the ashes, to give new proof of the boundless artistic potentialities of the African.

SOURCE OF COLOURED PLATES

American Museum of Natural History,
New York: 32
British Museum, London: 1, 23, 26, 27, 28, 31
Ethnographical Museum, Antwerp: 46
Leuzinger, Elsy, Zurich: 5, 17, 18
Lindenmuseum, Stuttgart: 33, 63
Münsterberger, Warner, New York: 34
Musée de l'Homme, Paris: 8, 22, 44
Museé Royal de l'Afrique Centrale, Tervuren: 47, 49, 50, 55, 58, 60
Museum für Völkerkunde, Berlin: 37
Museum Rietberg, Zurich (Eduard von der Heydt Collection and others):
2, 4, 6, 7, 9, 10, 11, 12, 13, 14, 15, 17, 19, 30, 36, 39, 45, 48, 51, 52, 54, 56, 61, Title-page
Oni of Ife, Nigeria: 24, 25
Ratton, Charles, Paris: 43, 57
Sammlung für Völkerkunde der Universität Zurich: 3, 16, 18, 21, 28, 29, 35, 41, 42, 48, 51, 53, 59, 62
Statens Etnografiska Museum, Stockholm: 38
Wallace Collection, London: 20
Withof's Private Collection, Brussels 40

The following coloured plates were kindly supplied by:

W. Bruggmann, Winterthur: Title-page, 1, 2, 3, 4, 5, 6, 7, 9, 10, 11, 12, 13, 14, 15, 16, 17, 18, 19, 20, 21, 23, 24, 25, 26, 27, 29, 30, 31, 34, 35, 36, 39, 41, 42, 45, 46, 48, 49, 50, 51, 52, 53, 54, 55, 56, 58, 59, 60, 61, 62

J. A. Lavaud, Paris: 8, 22, 43, 44, 57
J. Skeel, London: 20, 28

LIST OF MAPS

Vegetation of Africa and Geographical Names 213
Tribes of Africa 214/215
Pole and Round Styles 216
Cultural Centres of Black Africa 217

For the sake of clarity the territory formerly known as the French Central Congo is referred to in this volume as the Congo Republic, while the former Belgian Congo is referred to as the Republic of the Congo.

I should like to express my gratitude to all the museums and private collectors who have kindly granted permission to reproduce works of art in their possession. I should also like to thank Dr. A. Maesen, of the Tervuren Museum, and Frau Margrit Hug, of Zurich, for their valuable advice, as well as Fräulein Greta Leuzinger, of Zurich, who is responsible for the figures in this volume.

MAPS

AFRICA: VEGETATION AND GEOGRAPHICAL NAMES

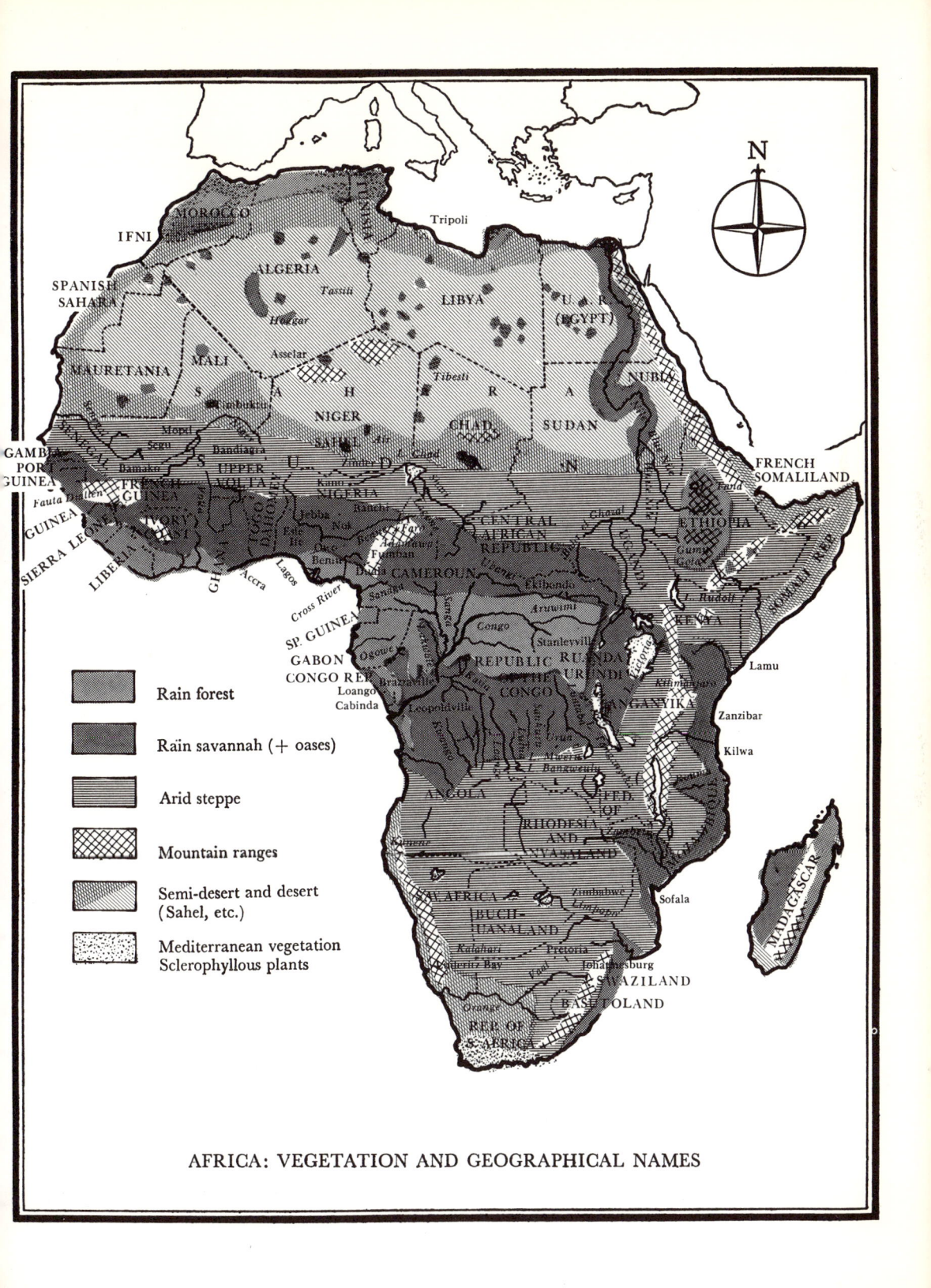

TRIBES OF AFRICA

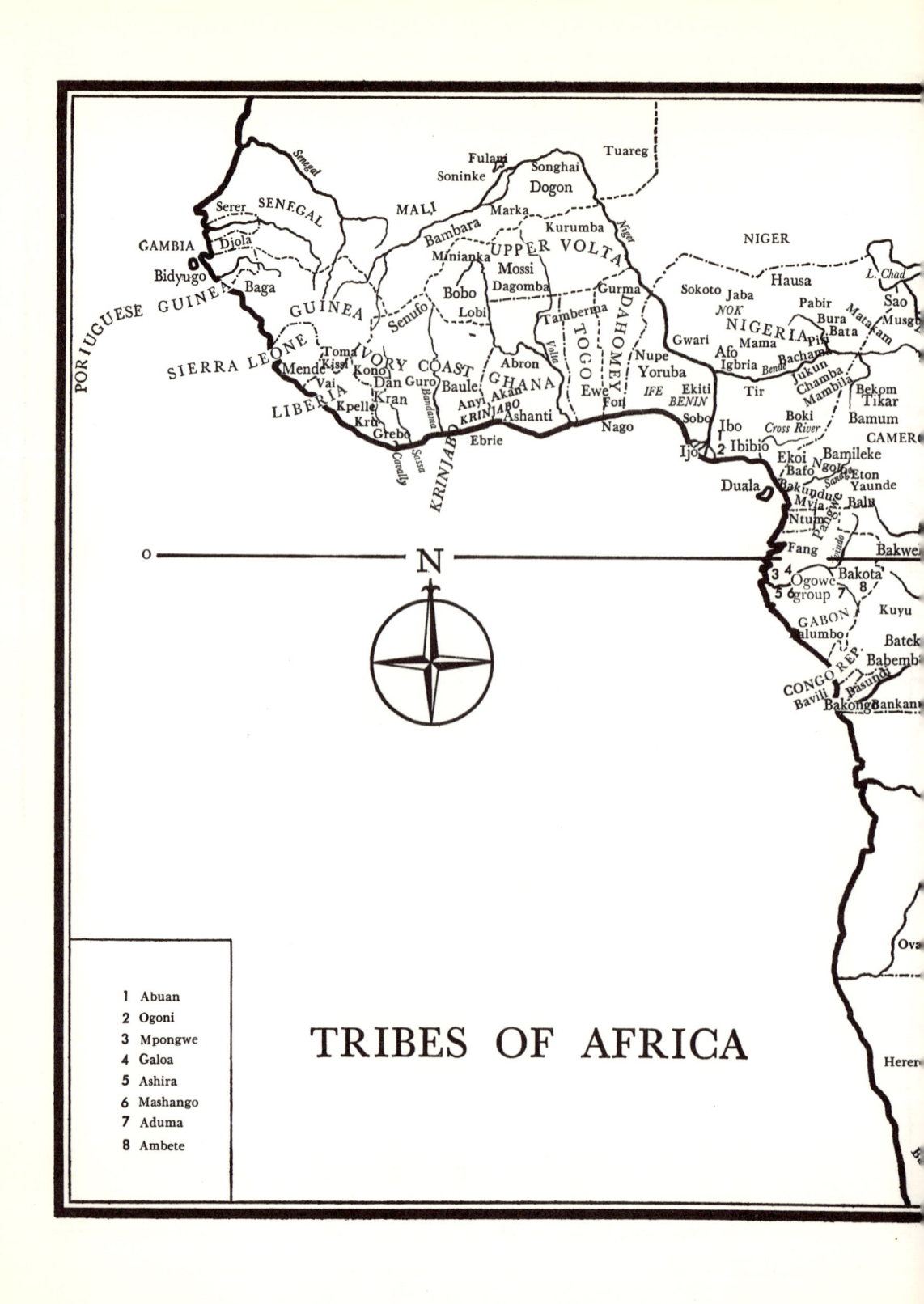

1 Abuan
2 Ogoni
3 Mpongwe
4 Galoa
5 Ashira
6 Mashango
7 Aduma
8 Ambete

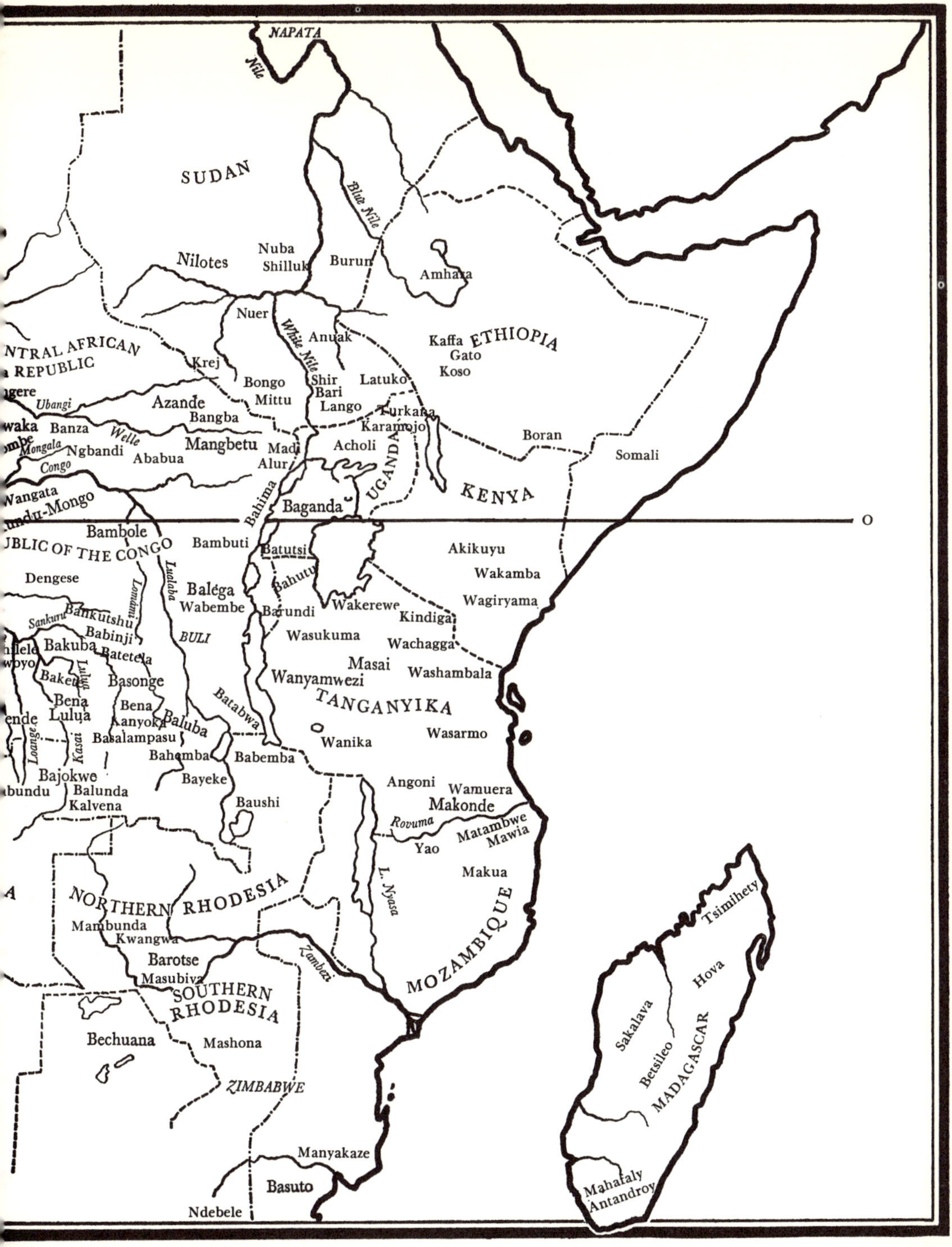

AFRICA

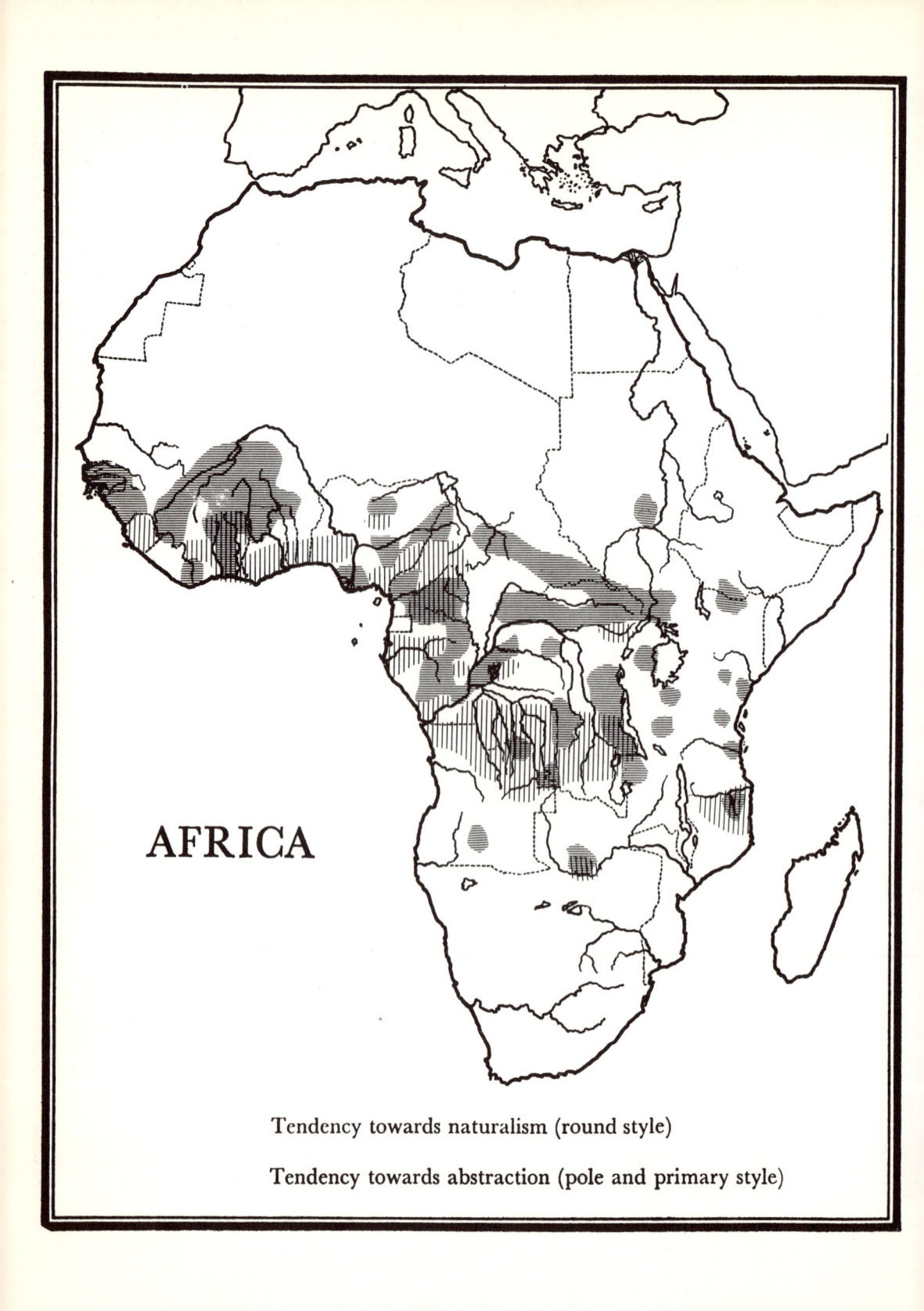

Tendency towards naturalism (round style)

Tendency towards abstraction (pole and primary style)

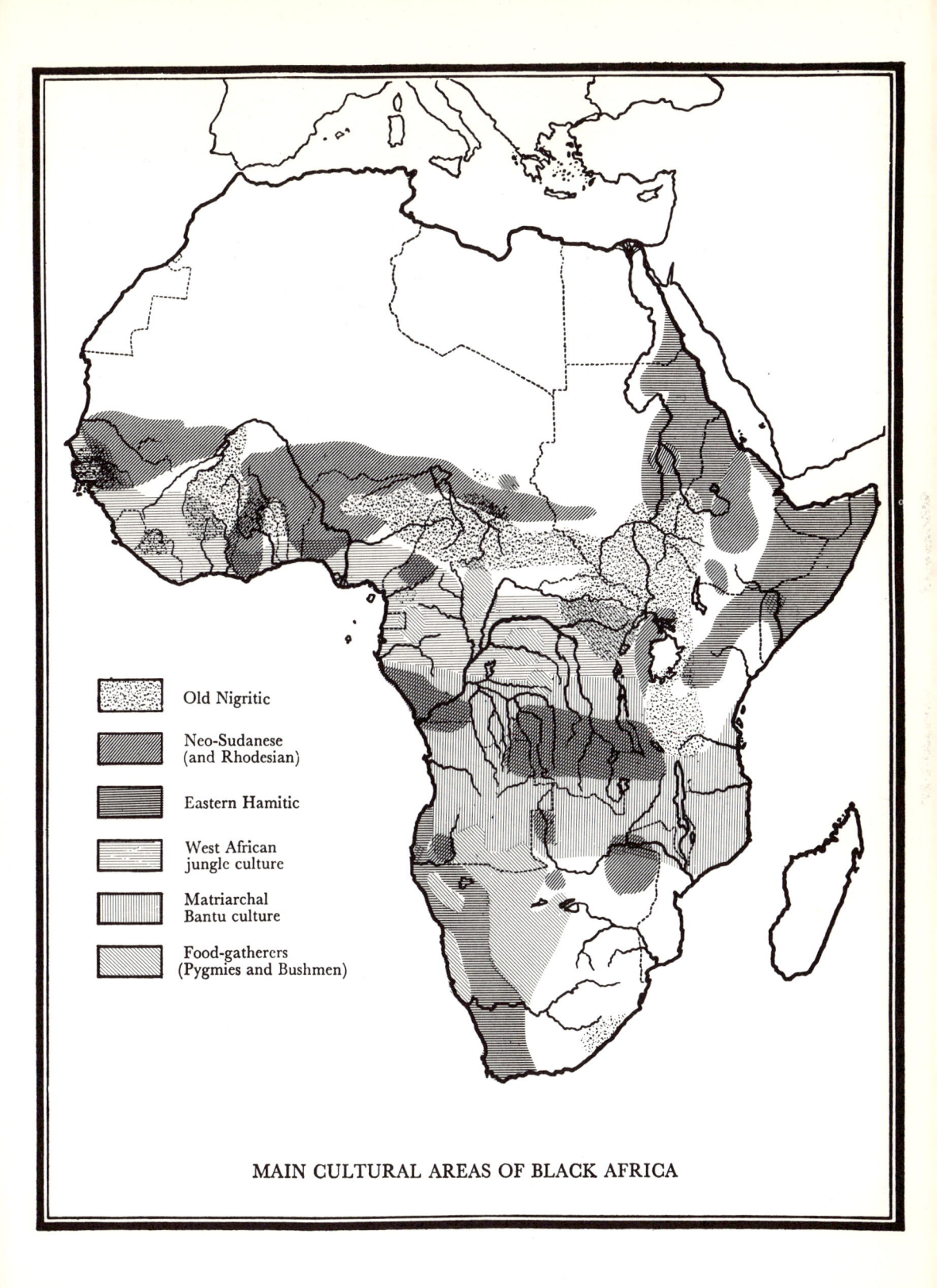

Old Nigritic

Neo-Sudanese
(and Rhodesian)

Eastern Hamitic

West African
jungle culture

Matriarchal
Bantu culture

Food-gatherers
(Pygmies and Bushmen)

MAIN CULTURAL AREAS OF BLACK AFRICA

APPENDICES
BIBLIOGRAPHY
GLOSSARY
INDEX

TABLE OF AFRICAN RACES AND CULTURES

(Based on H. BAUMANN, *Völkerkunde von Afrika, greatly simplified)*

I. WHITE AFRICA

Mediterranean, Ethiopian, Semitic and Cro-Magnon races.
Advanced cultures, oriented towards the Mediterranean and the Orient, in the sub-tropical region.
Egypt, the Sahara and area of the Atlas mountains: river valley, desert and highlands with mountain ranges and salt steppe.
Oasis agriculture with artificial irrigation, ploughing and hoeing; pastoral cultures.

II. BLACK AFRICA

A - *Negroes*

1. SUDANESE CULTURES *(from the border of the Guinea lands to the Upper Nile, and from the Sahara and Sahel to the Congo forests):*
Sudanese and Nilotic races, with an Ethiopian admixture.
Old Nigritic patriarchal culture, with a Hamitic upper class.
Arid and rainy savannah; during rainy season, cultivation of millet and maize; in the arid steppe, also cattle-raising.
A - WESTERN SUDAN: *(Mali, Upper Volta, Upper Niger):* Scattered Old Sudanese and Old Nigritic peoples (organized in family groups; tilling with the hoe, and some cattle-raising), overlaid by neo-Sudanese ruling races, bringing with them elements of advanced culture from the Mediterranean and Orient, and establishing states.
B - EASTERN SUDAN *(Upper Nile):* agriculture and raising of large-sized cattle in swampy areas and in the steppe.
North: predominantly neo-Sudanese and Asiatic colonial culture (Arabs);
South: Nilotes, Old Nigritic and Hamitic culture.

C - CENTRAL SUDAN *(Darfur, Wadai, grasslands of Nigeria, Cameroun and Central African Republic)*: Old Nigritic , neo-Sudanese and Old Mediterranean cultures, permeated by Arabic nomads and Islamic Fulani.

2. WEST AFRICAN BUSH CULTURE *(Atlantic coastlands, from Senegal to the Congo and the Equatorial forest)*:
Negroid and Palaenegrid races, with an Ethiopian infusion.
Old Nigritic and bush culture, with a neo-Sudanese and Mediterranean admixture.
Permanently humid, equable climate. Rainy forest zone with farming all the year round, agriculture in forest clearings, and cultivation of tuberous plants with hoe and planting-stick.
A - GUINEA LANDS: partly Semi-Bantu, partly Palaenegrid, overlaid with a Sudanese stratum.
Western Atlantic *(Senegal to the river Bandama in the western Ivory Coast)*.
Eastern Atlantic *(from the Bandama to the Sanaga in Cameroun)*. Rainy forest and rainy savannah. Old Mediterranean and neo-Sudanese ruling strata; feudal states with sacrosanct monarchies.
B - EQUATORIAL FOREST *(southern Cameroun, Gabon, Spanish Guinea, Congo Republic, northern part of Republic of the Congo)*. Palaenegrids, with some Sudanese immigrants; rainy forest.

3. MATRIARCHAL BANTU CULTURE *(From the mouth of the Congo across the southern Congo, from northern Angola to Rhodesia and the Indian Ocean, in the area of the rivers Zambezi and Rovuma)*:
Peoples of Bantu stock, with Ethiopian elements and Oriental strains; in the south, an admixture of steppe hunters.
Matriarchal Bantu; culture determined by the ruling groups, in part Sudanese, in part Rhodesian.
Savannah country, with agriculture during rainy season, and some cattle-raising.

4. EASTERN BANTU CULTURE *(East Africa, from the source of the Nile to South Africa and Madagascar)*:
Peoples of Bantu stock, with a strong Ethiopian admixture, permeated in part by Oriental and Pygmy elements.
Old Nigritic settlers, with eastern Hamitic pastoral culture, in Southern Rhodesia: culture determined by the Rhodesian overlords; in part, culture of Eurafrican steppe hunters. On the east

coast, neo-Oriental colonial culture, with subordinate Bantu culture.

Arid steppe, agriculture during rainy season with hoes, supplemented by raising of large-sized cattle.

B - *Non-negro peoples of Black Africa*

1. EASTERN HAMITIC CATTLE-BREEDERS *(East Africa, including Ethiopia, and scattered over the whole of South and West Africa):* Ethiopian upper stratum, pure or intermixed with negroids: Hamito-Nilotes.

Pastoral culture, with large-sized cattle (in part as overlords over Old Nigritic settlers and remnants of hunting peoples).

Salt and arid steppes; pastures in the high mountains *(Ethiopia)*. Nomadic cattle-raising, intermingled in the interior of East Africa with settled agriculture; in Ethiopia agriculture with ploughing during the rainy season and irrigated terraces.

2. HUNTERS AND FOOD-GATHERERS, the most ancient peoples, of small stature: Pygmies in the jungle, Bushmen in the salt steppes and semi-deserts of South Africa.

Primitive nomadic food-gatherers and hunters.

A - PYGMIES: Bambuti in the north-eastern Congo, Ituri area, Batwa in the Interlacustrine area, and others in Equatorial Africa.

B - BUSHMEN: culture of Eurafrican steppe hunters.

Kalahari of South Africa, and remnants in East Africa *(Rukwa province)*.

BIBLIOGRAPHY

GENERAL WORKS

Adam, L.: Primitive Art. London, 1954.

African ideas of God. Edited by Edwin W. Smith. London, 1950.

Afrikanische Plastik. Kunstwerkschriften 17. Baden-Baden.

African Worlds. Edited by Daryll Forde. London, 1954.

Baumann, H.: Vaterrecht und Mutterrecht in Afrika. ZfE. 1926.

Baumann, H.: Afrikanisches Kunstgewerbe; in: Bossert, Geschichte des Kunstgewerbes, Vol. II. Berlin, 1929.

Baumann, H.: Afrikanische Wild- und Buschgeister. ZfE. 1938.

Baumann, H., Thurnwald, R., and Westermann, D.: Les peuples et les civilisations de l'Afrique. Paris, 1948.

Bernatzik, H. A.: Afrika. 2 vols. Innsbruck, 1947.

Christensen, E. O.: Primitive Art. New York, 1955.

Einstein, C.: Negerplastik. Leipzig, 1915.

Elisofon, E. — Fagg, W.: The sculpture of Africa. London, 1958. (Recent and most reliable work).

Fagg, W., Afro-Portuguese Ivories. London, 1959.

Fagg, W.: On the Nature of African Art; in: Mem. & Proc. Manchester Lit. & Phil. Soc., 1953.

Frobenius, Leo: Das unbekannte Afrika. Munich, 1923.

Frobenius, Leo: Die Masken und Geheimbünde Afrikas, 1898; in: Nova Acta, Leopoldina, vol. 74/1.

Gerbrands, A. A.: Art as an Element of Culture. Leyden, 1957.

Germann, P.: Die afrikanische Kunst; in: Springer, Handbuch der Kunstgeschichte, Vol. 6. Leipzig, 1929.

Griaule, M.: Arts de l'Afrique noire. Paris, 1947.

Haselberger, H.: Die Wandmalerei der afrikanischen Neger. ZfE. 1957.

Hefel, A.: Der afrikanische Gelbguss und seine Beziehungen zu den Mittelmeerländern; in: Wiener Beiträge, Jg. 5, 1943.

Hermann, F.: Die afrikanische Negerplastik als Forschungsgegenstand. Berlin, 1958.

Herskovits, M. J.: Background of African Art. Denver, 1945.

Heydrich, M.: Afrikanische Ornamentik. IAE. Supplement No. 7 to Vol. 22, 1914.

Heydrich, M., and Frölich, W.: Plastik der Primitiven. Stuttgart, 1954.

Himmelheber, H.: Negerkunst und Negerkünstler. Brunswick, 1960.

Italiaander, R.: Neue Kunst in Afrika. Mannheim, 1957.

Kjersmeier, C.: Centres de style de la sculpture nègre africaine. 4 vols. Paris, 1935—38 (also Copenhagen).

Lagercrantz, St.: Contribution to the Ethnography of Africa. 1950 (Studia Ethnogr. Upsaliensia, I, Lund).

L'art nègre. Présence africaine, 10/11, 1951. Paris.

Lavachéry, H.: Statuaire de l'Afrique noire. Neuchâtel, 1954.

Leiris, M.: Les nègres d'Afrique et les arts sculpturaux. UNESCO, Paris, 1954.

Leuzinger, E.: Wesen und Form des Schmuckes afrikanischer Völker. Zurich, 1950.

Masterpieces of African Art. Catalogue. Brooklyn Museum, New York, 1954.

Münsterberger, W.: Primitive Kunst. Munich, 1955.

Murdock, G. P.: Africa: its Peoples and their Culture History. New York, etc., 1959.

Nuoffer, O.: Afrikanische Plastik in der Gestaltung von Mutter und Kind. Dresden, undated.

Parrinder, G.: West African Religion. London, 1949.

Paulme, D.: Les sculptures de l'Afrique noire. Paris, 1956.

Pedrals, D.-P.: Manuel scientifique de l'Afrique noire. Paris, 1949.

Pedrals, D.-P.: Archéologie de l'Afrique noire. Paris, 1950.

Plass, M.: African Tribal Sculpture. Univ. Museum, Philadelphia, 1956.

Radin, P., and *Sweeney, J. J.:* African Folktales and Sculpture. New York, 1952.

Schachtzabel, A.: Die Siedlungsverhältnisse der Bantuneger. IAE, Suppl. to Vol. 20, 1911.

Schilde, W.: Ost-westliche Kulturbeziehungen im Sudan; in: Mem. Weule. Leipzig, 1929.

Schmalenbach, W.: Die Kunst Afrikas. Basle, 1953.

Schurtz, H.: Das afrikanische Gewerbe. Leipzig, 1900.

Schweinfurth, G.: Artes Africanae. 1875.

Segy, L.: African Sculpture Speaks. New York, 1952.

Steinmann, A.: Maske und Krankheit; in: Ciba-Zeitschrift, No. 89, 1943. Basle.

Sydow, E. v.: Die Kunst der Naturvölker und der Vorzeit. Propyläen-Kunstgeschichte, I. Berlin, 1923.

Sydow, E. v.: Handbuch der afrikanischen Plastik, Vol. I. Berlin, 1930.

Sydow, E. v.: Afrikanische Plastik. Aus dem Nachlass herausgeg. von Gerdt Kutscher. Berlin, 1954.

Tempels, Placide: Bantu Philosophie. Heidelberg, 1956.

Trowell, M.: Classical African Sculpture. London, 1954.

Underwood, L.: Figures in Wood in West Africa. London, 1947.

Underwood, L.: Masks of West Africa. London, 1948.

Underwood, L.: Bronzes of West Africa. London, 1949.

Vatter, E.: Religiöse Plastik der Naturvölker. Frankfurt-on-Main, 1926.

Westermann, D.: Geschichte Afrikas. Cologne, 1952.

Wingert, P.: The sculpture of Negro Africa. New York, 1950.

BIBLIOGRAPHIES

Klein, Hildegard: Afrika südl. der Sahara. Ethnogr. Veröffentlichungen, 1945—50; in: Paideuma, Vol. V/3, 1951.

Mylius, Norbert: Afrika-Bibliographie, 1943—51. Vienna, 1952.

Wieschhoff, H.: Anthropological Bibliography of Negro Africa. New Haven, 1948.

REGIONS

Western Sudan:

Dieterlen, G.: Les âmes des Dogons. Paris, 1941.

Dieterlen, G.: Essai sur la religion Bambara. Paris, 1951.

Griaule, M.: Dieu d'eau. Paris, 1948.

Griaule, M.: Masques Dogon. Paris, 1938.

Lem, F. H.: Sculptures soudanaises.

Minotaure. Mission Dakar-Djibouti, 1931—33. Paris, 1933.

Pâques, V.: L'estrade royale des Niaré; in: Bull. Inst. Français de l'Afrique Noire, Vol. 15/4, 1953.

West Africa: From Senegal to Dahomey:

Bardon, P.: Collection des masques d'or baoulé de l'IFAN. Dakar, 1948.

Bernatzik, H. A.: Äthiopen des Westens. 2 vols. Vienna, 1933.

Bernatzik, H. A.: Im Reiche der Bidyogo. Innsbruck, 1944.

Creac'h, P.: Notes sur l'art décoratif architectural Foula du Haut Fouta-Djallon; in: 1 Conf. int. afr. de l'ouest, II, Dakar, 1951.

Donner, E.: Kunst und Handwerk in NO-Liberia. Bässl. Arch., Berlin, 1940.

Glück, J.: Die Goldgewichte von Oberguinea. Heidelberg, 1937.

Glück, J. F.: Die Gelbgüsse des Ali Amonikoyi. Jahrbuch Lindenmus. Stuttgart, 1951.

Harley, G. W.: Masks as agents of social control in Northeast Liberia. Papers of the Peabody Museum, vol. 32/2, 1950.

Herskovits, M. J.: Dahomey. 2 vols. New York, 1938.

Himmelheber, H.: Negerkünstler. Stuttgart, 1935.

Himmelheber, H. and U.: Die Dan. Stuttgart, 1958.

Holas, B.: Cultures matérielles de la Côte d'Ivoire. Paris, 1960.

Holas, B.: Masques Kono. Paris, 1952.

Holas, B.: Mission dans l'Est Libérien (Mém. IFAN, 14, 1952). Dakar.

Holas, B.: Portes sculptées du Musée d'Abidjan. Dakar, 1952.

Kjersmeier, C.: Ashanti Weights. Copenhagen, 1948.

Meyerowitz, E. L. R.: The sacred State of the Akan. London, 1951.

Paulme, D.: Les gens du riz (Kissi). Paris, 1954.

Rattray, R.: Religion and Art in Ashanti. Oxford, 1927.

Réal, D.: Note sur l'art Dahoméen. J. Royal Anthr. Inst., vol. 30, 1920.

Rütimeyer, L.: Über westafrikanische Steinidole. IAE. 1901.

Schwab, G.: Tribes of the Liberian Hinterland. Papers of the Peabody Museum, vol. 31, 1947.

Staub, J.: Beiträge zur Kenntnis der materiellen Kultur der Mendi. Berne, 1936.

Vandenhoute, P. J. L.: Classification stylistique du masque Dan et Gueré de la Côte d'Ivorie occid. Leyden, 1948.

Verger, P.: Dieux d'Afrique. Paris, 1954.

Waterlot, E. G.: Les bas-reliefs des bâtiments royaux d'Abomey. Paris, 1926.

Zeller, R.: Die Goldgewichte von Asante. Bässler Arch. Suppl. no. III, 1912.

NIGERIA:

Beier, H. U.: Sacred Wood Carvings from a small Yoruba Town. Lagos, 1957.

Daniel, F.: The Stone Figures of Esie; in: J. Royal Anthrop. Inst., Vol. 67, 1937.

Dapper, O.: Umbständliche und Eigentliche Beschreibung von Afrika. 1671.

Dark, Ph. and Forman, W. and B.: Die Kunst von Benin. Prague, 1960.

Egharevba, Chief J. U.: A Short History of Benin. Lagos, 1953.

Fagg, Bernard: Various articles in 'Man', 1946—48, 1956—59; in 'Africa', Vol. 15/1, London, 1945.

Fagg, William: De l'art des Yoruba; in: L'art nègre, Paris, 1951.

Fagg, William: L'art Nigérien avant Jésus-Christ; in: L'art nègre, Paris, 1951.

Luschan, F. v.: Altertümer von Benin. 3 vols. Berlin, 1919.

Marquart, J.: Die Beninsammlung des Reichsmuseums für Völkerkunde in Leiden. Leyden, 1913.

Meek, C. K.: The Northern Tribes of Nigeria. 2 vols. London, 1925.

Meyerowitz, E. L. R.: Ancient Nigerian Bronzes; in: Burlington Magazine, vol. 79, Sept. & Oct. 1941.

Murray, K. C.: The chief Art Styles of Nigeria; in: 1 Conf. int. africanistes de l'ouest, II. Dakar, 1951.

Murray, K. C.: The Stone Images of Esie and their Yearly Festival; in: Nigeria, vol. 37, 1951.

Murray, K. C.: Ekpu, the Ancestor Figures of Oron. Burl. Mag., vol. 89, Nov. 1947.

Pitt-Rivers: Antique Works of Art from Benin. London, 1900.

Read, C. H. and Dalton, O. M.: Antiquities from the City of Benin. London, 1899.

Roth, H. Ling: Great Benin. Halifax, 1903.

Talbot, P. A.: Life in Southern Nigeria. London, 1923.

Talbot, P. A.: Tribes of the Niger Delta. London, 1932.

Talbot, P. A.: Peoples of Southern Nigeria. 4 vols. Oxford, 1926.

The Art of Ife. Published by the Nigerian Antiquities Service. Lagos, 1955.

CAMEROUN AND EQUATORIAL AFRICA:

Andersson, E.: Les Kuta. Studia Ethn. Upsaliensia. Upsala, 1953.

Germann, P.: Das plastisch-figürliche Kunstgewerbe im Grasland von Kamerun. Leipzig, 1910.

Labouret, H.: Cameroun. Paris, 1934.

Lebeuf, J. P.: La plaine du Tchad et ses arts. Paris, 1946.

Lebeuf, J. P., and *Détourbet, A. M.:* L'art ancien du Tchad; in: Cahiers d'art, année 26, 1951.

Lebeuf, J. P., and *Détourbet, A. M.:* Les civilisations du Tchad. Paris, 1950.

Lecoq, R.: Les Bamiléké. Paris, 1953.

L'habitat au Cameroun. Paris, 1952.

Pervès, M.: Parmi les Fang; Le Jeu de l'Abbia; in: Revue Géogr. Hum. et d'Ethn., Paris, No. 3, 1948.

Plass, Margaret: The King's Day. Chicago, 1956.

Tessmann, G.: Die Pangwe. 2 vols. Berlin, 1913.

Congo and Angola:

Baumann, H.: Die materielle Kultur der Azande und Mangbetu. Bässler Archiv, vol. 11, Berlin, 1927.

Baumann, H.: Lunda. Berlin, 1935.

Biebuyck, G.: Function of a Lega Mask. IAE, 47/1. Leyden, 1954.

Boone, O.: Carte Ethnique du Congo Belge et du Ruanda-Urundi. Museum Tervuren, 1954.

Burssens, H.: The so-called 'Bangala'; in: Kongo-Overzee XX/3. Brussels, 1954.

Colle, R. P.: Les Baluba. 2 vols. Brussels, 1913.

Himmelheber, H. and *U.:* Die Dan. Stuttgart, leurs sculpteurs. Brousse 1939/1. Léopoldville.

L'art au Congo Belge (Les arts plastiques). Brussels, 1951.

L'art nègre du Congo Belge. Brussels, 1951.

Les arts au Congo Belge et au Ruanda-Urundi (CID, Brussels, 1950).

Maes, J.: Die soziale und kulturelle Bedeutung der Kabila-Figuren aus Belgisch-Kongo. Paideuma II/6-7, 1943.

Maes, J.: Les figurines sculptées du Bas-Congo; in: Africa, III/3, 1930.

Maesen, A.: Umbangu: l'art du Congo; in: L'art en Belgique, III, 1960.

Olbrechts, F. M.: Les arts plastiques du Congo belge. Brussels, 1959.

Scohy, A.: Ekibondo, ou les murs veulent parler; in: Brousse, 1951, 1/2. Léopoldville.

Sousberghe, L. de: L'art Pende; in: Beaux Arts, vol. IX, fasc. 2.

Torday, E.: Notes ethnogr. sur des populations habitants les bassins du Kasai et du Kwango oriental. Brussels, 1923.

Torday, E., and *Joyce, T. A.:* Notes ethnographiques sur les peuples Bakuba. Brussels, 1910.

Verly, R.: Les Mintadi. La statuaire de pierre du Bas-Congo. Louvain, 1955.

Wissmann, H. v.: Im Innern Afrikas. Leipzig, 1888.

East Africa and Madagascar:

Camboué, P.: Aperçu sur les Malgaches et leurs conceptions d'art sculptural; in: Anthropos, 1928.

Caton-Thompson, G.: The Zimbabwe Culture. Oxford, 1931.

Cory, H.: Wall Paintings by Snake Charmers in Tanganyika. London, 1953.

Cory, H.: African Figurines. London, 1956.

Emery, W. B.: Nubian Treasure. London, 1948.

Jensen, Ad.: Im Lande des Gada. Stuttgart, 1936.

Junod, H. A.: The Life of a South African Tribe. 2 vols. Neuchâtel, 1913.

Lormian, H.: L'art malgache. Paris.

Meiring, A. L.: The Art and Architecture of the Amandabele. South African Scene, vol. I. Pretoria.

Meyer, H.: Die Barundi. Leipzig, 1916.

Schebesta, P.: Die Zimbabwe-Kultur in Afrika; in: Anthropos, 1926.

Stuhlmann, F.: Handwerk und Industrie in Ostafrika. Hamburg, 1910.

Trowell, M., and *Wachsmann, K. P.:* Tribal Crafts of Uganda. London, 1953.

Weule, K.: Ethnographische Forschungsreise in den Südosten Deutsch-Ostafrikas. Mitt. dt. Schutzgeb., 1908, Supplement No. 1. Berlin.

PERIODICALS

Africa. Journal of the Int. Afr. Inst. London.

Annales du Musée du Congo Belge. Les Arts. III. 1902—6. Brussels-Tervuren.

Bulletin de la Société d'études camérounaises. Douala.

IFAN (Inst. Français de l'Afrique Noire): Mémoires, Bulletin, Notes africaines, etc.

IAE (Internat. Archiv für Ethnographie), Leyden.

Journal de la Société des Africanistes, Paris.

Journal of the Royal Anthropological Institute, London.

Kongo-Overzee, Brussels.

Man. London.

Nigeria. A Quarterly Magazine. Lagos.

Paideuma. Institut für Kulturmorphologie. Frankfurt-on-Main.

Zaire. Revue Congolaise. Brussels.

ZfE (Zeitschrift für Ethnologie). Deutsche Gesellschaft für Völkerkunde. Brunswick.

GLOSSARY

Amulet
Magical protection against misfortune.

Appliqué
Ornamentation of textiles, leather, etc., by sewing on gaily-coloured pieces of fabric or other decorative materials.

Bantu
Collective term used to designate the various negro tribes of the south and east of Africa on the basis of peculiar features of their language, with its class system: the type of word is indicated by prefixes. Subgroups: north-eastern, eastern, south-eastern and south-western Bantu, matriarchal central Bantu of the southern Congo, and the semi-Bantu in West Africa, who have a strong admixture of Sudanese negro elements.

Calabash
Vessel made of rind of gourd.

Cast brass
Works cast from an alloy of copper and zinc, occasionally with an admixture of tin or lead; the term thus comprises all intermediary grades from copper and bronze (copper and tin) to brass.

Chi wara
Antelope, tribal animal of the Bambara in the western Sudan and Mali, represented as a dance head-dress, modified in various ways.

Cire-perdue
Metal casting by the 'waste mould' process, melting out the wax. The wax model is covered with clay; when this coating of clay has dried, the wax is melted out and molten metal poured into the cavity. Casting is completed by breaking the mould in each case, and working up the surface accordingly.

Coiling technique
Building up baskets or clay vessels in coils with long ropes.

Cowrie-shell
Cypraea moneta, found mainly near the Maldives in the Indian Ocean, and exported from there in great quantities to Africa. They used to serve as currency and as a symbol of fertility.

Culture hero
Promoter of culture or welfare, semi-divine being or mythical hero, generally an emissary of the Creator, who gave to mankind valuable knowledge and fostered culture.

Dot-and-circle motif
Decorative motif, a small circle with a dot in the middle; in many cases derived from the Arab world.

Effigy jug
Vessel in human shape.

Embossing
Decoration on the surface of metal, leather, etc., by using a chisel or patterned punches. Depending on whether embossing is carried out on the front or the back, the design is either blurred or distinct.

Engraving
Working of metal with chisel, file and graver to produce an ornamental effect. Also finishing of cast metal objects.

Fetish
Object 'charged' with magical substances, and used for certain purposes.

Filigree
Fine wires, artistically plaited wires, or grains of gold or silver, soldered on to metal plates to produce an ornamental effect.

Food-gatherers
Nomadic hunters in remote areas, at a very primitive level of cultural development, e.g. the Pygmies and Bushmen.

Fulani
Nomadic cattle-herdsmen, of Hamitic culture, scattered over the arid steppe of the western Sudan; some have become settled.

Hamites
Linguistic and cultural term for breeders of large-sized cattle, Ethiopian in race

Head-shaped vessel
Wooden or clay vessel, part of which is fashioned as a human head.

Impluvium
A courtyard formed by four adjoining houses in a square, as in ancient Rome.

Incrustation
Ornamentation of planes by overlaying with a crust of a different, generally more precious, material.

Initiation
Ceremonies performed at puberty, after completion of instruction in the bush school, with tests of courage and ordeals of every kind, whereby young persons are admitted into the adult community.

Iron Age
Prehistoric era, which in Europe succeeded the Bronze Age in approx. 800 B.C. In Black Africa the Iron Age follows directly upon the Stone Age — in northern Nigeria, for example, about the middle of the 1st millennium B.C.

Lamu
A technique of inlaying gold plate. The term originates from the island of Lamu, on the Swahili coast of East Africa.

Libation
A drink-offering.

Matriarchy
Dominance of woman in social and religious life, conditioned by her important role in agriculture, and her fertility in general: cf. image of the Earth Mother. The man marries into the family of the woman, and the children belong to her clan (descent through the mother); inheritance of title, rank and property by the female line. Important position held by the maternal uncle.

Monoxylous
Made from a single piece of wood.

Napata Meroë
Nubian kingdom on the Nile, between Khartoum and the Ethiopian plateau; ruled over Egypt as the 25th dynasty in the 8th century. First capital Napata, but from the middle of the 1st millennium B.C. Meroë, on the Nile above Dongola. Eastern Hamitic population with negro elements. Important Egyptian and Ethiopian trading depot. In addition to ancient Egyptian influences, Byzantine, Greek and Christian, and later Arab, influences also made themselves felt here. The kingdom collapsed in the 13th century. Descent through the mother; many aspects of sacral kingship.

Neck-rest
A narrow support for the head, to protect the hair-dress whilst asleep.

Neo-Sudanese
More recent waves of immigrants, who brought elements of Oriental and Mediterranean civilization across the Sudan and into the Guinea lands. They encouraged the formation of large states and sacral kingship; they made ample use of clay for the building of houses, and for their implements.

Old Nigritic
Ancient negro culture in isolated areas of the Sudan (Old Sudanese), the northern Congo and East Africa. Characteristics: patriarchal organization in family groups; the smith and his craft held in high regard; cone-roofed dwellings with cylindrical substructure.

Patriarchy
The father is the head of the family. The mother enters his clan, and the children inherit the title and property in the father's line (descent through the father). Most widespread amongst cattle-raisers.

Plaited band motif
Decorative motif derived from plaiting, widely diffused already in antiquity.

Plangi
'Resist' or 'reserve' technique; patterns are obtained by tying off parts of the finished fabric before dyeing.

Pole sculpture
Sculpture in wood, highly abstract, cubist in style, its compactness of form suggesting the long rounded block or pole from which the figure is carved.

'Primary' art
Initial, undifferentiated, primitive phase in the art of all peoples.

Repoussé technique
Hammering of ornamentation into a thin sheet of metal from the reverse side.

Rites de passage
Ritual practices marking the various phases of life.

Round sculpture
Sculpture which is closer to naturalism, with supple, rounded, organically animated forms.

Sacral kingship
Sacred ruler appointed by the deity as the head of a large state. Certain customs are more or less common to such states, suggesting common sources: for example, the well-being of the king ensures the prosperity and fertility of the country. When his strength ebbs, he is ceremonially killed. He generally lives in isolation from his people, and may not be seen eating or drinking; he must refrain from much else besides. Attributes of the king are the sacred fire and the royal drum, lion and leopard. The horse is his mount; his sister is simultaneously his wife. The queen mother holds a high position. The state is administered by a hereditary nobility, and there is a hierarchical court ritual. The king is accompanied by his bodyguard and pages, sons of nobles who receive their instruction at court. The sacral kingship is related in many respects to Hamitic and neo-Sudanese cultures.

Savannah
Tropical grassland (rainy and arid steppe), interspersed with shrubs and sparse forests, particularly along the rivers; the so-called 'bush'.

Secret society
Body of adult men (in rare cases, women) to ensure power and order, administer justice, and educate young people.

Stone Age
Earliest era in human history, before the use of metal. Dating for Europe:

1. **Old Stone Age** (palaeolithic), comprising the glacial periods, and ending circa 5000 B.C. Nomadic hunters and food-gatherers. Chipped stone implements.
2. **Middle Stone Age** (mesolithic), approx. 5000-4000 B.C., characterized by microliths, i.e. small chipped stone implements.
3. **Later Stone Age** (neolithic), 4000-1800 B.C.; beginning of simple hoeing and pottery. Typical are the polished stone implements. The stone axe is widely diffused.

Tembe
Rectangular house with flat roof. In contrast to the clay dwelling proper, the tembe consists of posts and brushwood, coated with clay.

Tukula
Camwood powder, mixed with oily substance obtained from the bark of the pterocarpus. It is termite-resistant, and has a symbolic significance by reason of its red colour. Natives rub tukula into their skin, and also treat their deceased, and ancestor figures, with it.

West African culture
Collective term for culture of the patriarchal jungle tribes, on one hand, and the matriarchal Bantu of the southern Congo on the other.

Yam
Tuberous root of the dioscorea, similar to a potato. Important foodstuff for inhabitants of the tropics.

INDEX

The figures in italics refer to the plates and figures. The letter (G) indicates Glossary.

Ababua 59, 192, 194
Abomey 125, 126
Abron 125
abstraction 39, 40, 41, 53f., 60, 62, 63, 66, 95f., 99f., 101, 103f., 107f., 126f., 132, *140*, 145f., 153, 154, 178f., *182*, 192, 209
Abua (*Abuan*) 145
Acholi 196f.
Adamawa 148
adinkra 124
Aduma 154
adze 36
aesthetics 56, 57, 120, 202
Afikpo Ibo 144
Afo 23, 56, 146
Affonso I 167
Agadja 125
agba 142f.
agriculture 81, 153, 219f.; agricultural rites 29, 37, 101, 104f., *113*, *114*, 151; agriculturalists 81, 100, 146, 149, 170, 180, 201
Akan 123
Akikuyu 196, 198
aklama 125
akua'ba 124
alafin 141
Alangoa 122
al-Bakrî 48, 82
Ali Amonikoyi 125
Alladya 122
aloala 202
Alurua 119
Ambete 154
amulet (G), 102, 172
ancestor cult 21f., 83, 117, 132, *137*, 155, 170, 180, 197; figure 24f., *38*, *39*, 53, 60, *65*, 71, 99, *135*, 153f., 197; shrine 144, 168, 198
Andoni 131
Angola 167, 180f.
Angoni 74, 77
animal fetish 169; figures 26f., 71, 104, 125, 131, 145, 170f., 194, 199, 201f.; masks 94ff., 99, 120f., 145f., 149, 154, 172, 199; in paintings and relief 74, 197
anok 27, 104, 145
Antandroy 202
antelope 20, 27, 31, 37, 40, 41, 58, 61, 85, 95f., *115*, 122, *123*
Anyang 145
Anyi 49, 119, 121, 123, 124
ape 27, 117, *119*, 120, 199

appliqué work (G), 50, 125
Arabs 47f., 53, 73, 76, 81f., 196, 199, 201f., 220
architecture 46, 73, 75-80, *82*, 83, 129, 132, 148, 195, 197, 198, 199, 202, 203
Aribinda 40
art 15, 26, 30, 204f.; folk art 131, 175, 180; modern 53, 204f.; art schools 209
artist 32f., *160* 175, 204f.
Ashanti 45, 46, 49, 60, 71, 73, 83, 119, 121, 123f., 170
Ashira 155
Askia 82
Asselar 14
Assye 119
asymmetry 56, 130, 150, 168, 180
Aura Poka 119
Avungura 193
Azande 78, 166, 192, 193

Babemba 156, 192
Babembe 153, 156
Babessi 151
Babinji 174
Baboshi 156
Babungo 150
Babuye 191
Babwende 156
Bacham *116*, 152
Bachama 147
Bafo 152
Bafum 29, 152
Baga 27, 59, *62*, *63*, 103, 104, 145
Bagam 48, 151, 152
Baganda 51, 76, 196, 198
Baguha 191
Bahemba 191
Bahera 196
Bahima 189, 196
Baholo 172
Bahuana 27, 45, 172, *187*
Bahutu 196
Bajokwe 47, 59, 173, *180*, 180, *183*, 189; Bajokwe-Lunda 180
Bakele 174, 175
Bakete 173, 174, *176*, 177
Bakhimba 169
Bakongo 27, 46f., 56, 59, 70, *158*, 167-170, 172
Bakota 45, 59, *137*, 153, 154f., 178
Bakuba 26, 27, 34, 45, 47, 60, 72, *162*, *163*, *164*, 166, 174-178, 178, 189, 194
Bakundu 25

230

Bakwele 59, 154, *154*
Baladi 156
Balega 31, 45, 57, 59, 154, 192, 193
Bali 149, 150, 152
Balolo 194
Baluba 33, 45f., 56, 59, *163*, 166, 173f., *178*, *184*, *185*, *186*, *187*, *188*, 189-192, 201; Baluba-Hemba *184*, 191, *186*; Baluba-Shankadi 191
Balumbo 153, 155
Balunda 166, 189
Bamako 96
Bambala 171f., 174
Bambara 20, 27, 29, 37, 51, 58f., 73, 76, 79, 94-97, 101, 104, 155, 178
Bambata 168
Bambole 192, 193f.
Bambuti 156, 221
Bamenda *116*, 149, *149*, 152
Bamessing 150
Bamgboye 34, 142
Bamileke 73, *116*, 150, *150*, 152
Bamum 48, *133*, 149, 151, *151*
Banamé 204
Banda mask 27, *63*, 104
Bandila 210
Bangba 74
Bangende 174
Bangongo 174
Bangubangu 191
Bangwa 152
Bangweulu, Lake 192
Bankanu *159*, 168, 170
Bankutshu 174
Bantu (G), 13, 21f., 33, 145, 153, 166, 193, 194, 196, 197, 201ff., 220; philosophy 21f., 168
Banyang 145
Banyoro 77
Banyun 103
Bapende 45, 78, 110, *164*, 172f., *173*, 173, 175, 176
Bari 196, *196*, 197
bark *159*, 170, 171, 174, 189, 194, 198
Barundi 198
Barotse 15, 178, 201f., *201*
Basalampasu 178
Bashi-Bushongo 174
Bashilele 174, 176
Bashobwa *163*, 174, 177
basket-work 50, 146, *160*, 167, 173, 189, 193, *197*, 198, 202; cf. plaiting
Basonge 28, 32, 59, 178f., *179*, *182*, 189, 190, 191
Basolongo 168
Basuku *160*, *161*, 171

Basundi 156, *157*, 168, 169, 170
Basuto 74, 77, 202
Bata 147
Batabwa 192
Bateke 59, *140*, 153, *156*, 165
Batempe 179
Batende 156
Batetela 179
Batie *150*, 152
batik 51
Batutsi 196, 198
Batwa 221
Baule 27, 36, 45, 49, 51, 60, *65*, *66*, 67, 71, 72, 75, 84, 119-122, *119*, *120*, *121*, *122*, *123*
Baushi 192
Bavili 168, 169
Bawongo 174, 176
Bawoyo 168, 169f., *178*
Baya 47
Bayaka 33, 56, 70, *160*, 167, 170f., *170*, *171*
Bayanzi 156
Bayeke 189
Bazombo 168
bazu 97f.
beads 34, 45, 75, 82, 91, *133*, 141, 146, 150, 152, *164*, 167, 177, 199, 202, 207
Bechuana 47, 74
Beja 12
Bekom 150, *152*, 152
Bela 210
Ben Enwonwu 210
Bena Kanioka 179f.
Bena Lulua 56, 78, *177*, 178
Bena Mpassa 32, 179, *182*
Benguella 189
Benin 17, 34, 45, 48, 59f., 70, 75, 83, *90*, *91*, *92*, *109*, 128-131
Benue 47, 83, 126, 146
Berbers 14, 50, 81f.
Betsileo 203
Bidyugo 59, 74, 103, *106*
bieri *135*, 153
Bini 71
Bisharin 12
Bissagos Is. 103
birds 27, 99, 102, *104*, 104f., 129, 130, 141, *160*, *186*, 201, *201*
biteke 165
Bobo 59, 75, 79, *91*, 100; Bobo-Fing 42, 100
Bodiman 153
Bo Kena 174
Boki 145
boli 95
bombo mask 177
Bongo 196, 197
bongotol 176

231

Borana 206
Bornu 51, 83
Bron: cf. Abron
bronze casting 35, 48, 71, *87*, *88*, *90*, *92*, *109*, 128, 129, 201
buffaloes 43, *46*, 120, *121*, *146*, 149, *149*
Buli 79, 191, *188*
Bulu 153
Bundu 28, 106, *108*
Bura 147
Burun 197
bush school 31, 52, 73, *160*, 169, 171
Bushmen 14, *19*, 146, 201, 220
Bwaka 192, 194
Byzantines 14, 48, 76, 146

Cabinda 168
calabash (G), 45, 124, 148, 152, 165, 167, 198, 202
Cameroons 46f., 48, 59, 74, *116*, *133*, 134, 148-153, 166, 220
caryatids 150, 173, 191
cast brass (G), 48f., *48*, 75f., 82, 84, *85*, *87*, *88*, *90*, 102, 119, 121, 123, 125, 126, 127, *128*, 129, 130f., 146f., 151, 152, 167, 204
cattle-raising 11, 149, 196, 219f.
Cavally 107
Cercle d'Assinié 122f.
Cercle de Korhogo *44*, 101
Cercle de Man 107
Chad territory 15, 48, 51, 83, 148
Chamba 146
chameleon 27, 96, 102, 149
Chelles-Acheul culture 14
chi wara (G), 31, 37, 95f., *98*, 146
Christianity 83, 167, 180, 204
cire-perdue technique (G), 48, *68*, 75, 84, *85*, 124, 126, 128, 129, 146, 151
clay buildings 35, 77, 79, 83, 132, 149; clay culture 148; clay figures 123, *124*, 165, 194, 198, 202; cf. pottery
climate 12, 81, 84, 148, 219f.
clothing 75f., 122; of bark 174, 194, 198; of leather 50, 76, 199; on masks 95, 99, 120, 155; on sculpture 72, *92*; cf. tobes
coiling technique (G), 50, *197*, 198, 202
colours 45, 50, 52, 71, 74, *138*, *160*, *171*, *187*, 190; cf. painting
Congo 15. 51, 56, 59, 70, 83, 180; Belgian Congo 166-195; Central 154f., *162*, *164*, 173-178, *181*, *187*; eastern 192; Lower 46f., 60, 165, 167-170; northern 78, 84, 166, 192-195; south-eastern 178-192, *184*, *185*, *186*, *188*; south-western 74, *110*, *159*, *160*, *161*, 170-173; southern 56, 59, 167, 180, *183*; French Congo *140*, 165, 167f., 220

Copts 146
corroding technique 37, 51
courts 72, 82f., 123, 125, 126, 127, 150, 151, 152, 175, 180, 193, 202, 204
cowrie-shells (G), 35, 50, 95, 97, *162*, *164*, 177, 179, 193
crocodiles 99, 121, 130, *163*, 169, *175*
Cross River 145
cubism 20, 55, 59, *62*, 106f., *116*, 146, 152, 155, 165, 173, *187*, 194
culture heroes (G), 23, 26, *163*, 174
cups, head-shaped (G), 72, *163*, 173, 176, 177

Dagomba 83
Dahomey 34, 45, 47, 51, 56, 59, 79, 83, *86*, 125f., *126*, *127*, 132
Dan 57, 59, *64*, 71, 107-118, *117*, *118*
Danané 107
dance 20, 37, 58, *61*, 95, 104, *115*, *116*, 118, 122, *139*, 145, 149, 156, *160*, 173, *183*, 193, 199, 202
Dappert, Olfert 129
Darfur 49, 220
death masks *112*, *138*, 153, death rite 28, *39*, *40*, 104, 149
deble mask *44*, 101
decadence 33, 102, *134*, 204
degele mask 101, *103*
demons 24, 28, 141, 145, 154, 155, *158*, 189
Dengese *163*, 174, *181*, 194
Desfossés 209
divination implements 27, 107, *131*, 170, *175*, 176
Djilatendo 210
Djola 103, *105*
Djuma 172
Dō *42*, 100
Dogon *38*, *39*, 58, 59, 71, 74, *74*, 75, 97-100, *98*, *102*, 105
doors 27, 72, 80, *105*, *121*, 144, 149, 199
drama 29, 95, *111*, 145, *145*, 173, *183*
Duala 71, 100, *134*, 152
dyeing 37, 50f., *66*, 146, 151, 177, *187*

Earth Goddess *41*, *44*, *86*, 141, 144
earth-hog 95
Earth Mother 60, 72, 190
East Africa 12, 16, 33, 45, 47, 59, 70, 74, *174*, 196-200, 220f.
ebengo *139*
Ebrie 122f.
edan 143
Edo 144
Egbukere 145
Egypt 73, 197f., 219; cf. Nile valley
Ekibondo 74

232

Ekiti	143
Ekoi	31, 45, 46, 51, 56, 59, *115*, 132, 145, 152
Ekongola	153
Ekpo	*113*, 145
Elegba	141
elephant	149, *150*, 151
El-Hadj-Omar	83
Elmenteita, Lake	14
emblems 20, 33, 72, 87, 90, 91, 110, 126, *133*, 162, *167*, 168f., 199	
embossing	(G), 49, 84, *137*, 199
embroidery	51, *75*, 76, 146, 151, *175*, 177
engraving	(G), 48
Epa mask	34, 70, *130*, 142
Eshu	141
Esie	46, 70, 131f.
Esigie	130, *190*
Ethiopia 12, 14, 46, 81, 83, 128, 196, *206*, 219f.	
Eton	153
Etruscans	14, 48
Europe	74, 129, *134*, 153, 167, 180, *187*, 202, 204f.
Ewe	125
Ewuare	130
Fang	*135*, 153f.
Faro	95, 148
fertility 25f., 35, 37, 60, 62, 74, 95, 97, 101, 104, *110*, 121, 122, 124, 132, 171, 197f.	
fetish	(G), 26f., 60f., *156*, *158*, *161*, 165, *168*, 169f., 179, 190f.
Fezzan	15
filigree	(G), 49, 84, 125, 199
fish	121, 130, 143
Flanpleu	108
Foho	105
Fon	125, 126
food-gatherers	(G), 166, 219f.
Fouta Djallon	13, 74
French Congo: cf. Congo	
French Guinea: cf. Guinea	
French Equatorial Africa 59, 84, *135*, *137*, 153-165, 220	
French Sudan: cf. Sudan	
frogs	149
Fulani	(G), 12f., 45, 50, 77, 83, 148
Fumban	151
funerary figures 26, 46, 60, 107; funerary rites 41, 67, 97, 102, cf. sepulchral figures	
Gabon	*136*, 153, 154, 220
Galla	12
Galoa	155
Gambia	103
Gamu-Gofa	206
Gato	196, 198

Gbekre	27, 119, 120
Gbon	*61*, 101
Geh	107
Gelede mask	70, 126, *129*, 142
Gere: cf. Kran	
Ghana	48f., 79, 82, 119, 123ff., 132, *168*
Gio	29, 107, *118*
Glele	126
gods	119, *127*, 130, 141
gold 45, 49, 81, 121, 122, 123, 124-170, 196, 199	
gourd: cf. calabash	
granaries	74, 78, 83, 148, 197
Great Britain	129
Gu	119, 125
guardian figures	45, *169*, 178
Guinea 50f., 56, 59, 74, 78, 83; French Guinea 20, 62, 74, 107f.; Portuguese Guinea 103; Spanish Guinea 153, 220	
guli	66
Guli	119f.
Gundam	48
Guro	67, 119f., 122
Gurunsi	74f.
Gwari	131
Habbe	97
hair-dress 70, 90, 94, 102, 106, 108, *137*, *138*, 149, 155, 178f., 190f., *185*, 198	
Hamites	(G), 12f., 33, 49, 81, 196f., 201f., 219f.
hand-axe	14
Hausa	47, 50, 75f., 83, 146f.
head-dress 37, *40*, 95f., 103, *139*, *160*, *171*, 171	
hemba mask	171
Herero	77
Hindus	167
hippopotamus	46, 103, *111*, 143, 170, 191
history 14f., 46, 81f., 119, 128f., 167, 174f., 178f., 193, 196, 201f.	
horse	95, 98
Hova	203
hunting 97, 149, *160*, 166, 170, 180, *183*, 192, 201, 220	
ibeji	58, 126, 141f.
Ibibio	29, 56, 59, *113*, *114*, 143, 145
Ibn Batûta	82
Ibn Khaldun	82
ibis	*128*, *129*
Ibo	29, 46, 70, 74, *112*, 143, 144, 145
Idah	131
Idena Ore	128
Idia	*90*
Idubor, Felix	210
Ifa 141; Ifa oracle	*131*, 142

233

Ife 46, 59, 71, 83, 87, 88, 89, 126, 129, 141
Igala 131
Igbira 131
Ighu-igha 129
Ijo 25, 59, *111*, 131, 143
ikat technique 51, 203
ikenga 70, 144
Ilorin 131
impluvium (G), 78, 132
incrustation (G), *40*, 48, 73, *91*, 199
India 15, 47, 196, 201f.
indigo 51f., *66*, 122, 151
Indonesia 196, 201, 203
initiation (G), 30f., *44*, 52, 97f., *159*, *164*, 177, 189, 192, 199
Interlacustrine area 166, 196f., 225
iroke 142, 170
iron 47f., 126, 175, 177, 179, 199; God of 141; Iron Age (G), 14
Islam 49f., 74, 79, 82f., 94, 100, 103f., 132, 146f., 204, 220
itombwa 176
Ituri 166
Ivindo 154, 156
ivory 172, *185*, 191f., 204; figures *17*, 45f., *91*, 177, 191; jewellery 45, *91*; mascot 45f.; masks 45f., *91*, 173; objects 170, *185*; ornamentation 131; trade in 72, 170
Ivory Coast *44*, 59, *61*, *64*, *65*, 84, 100, 107, 119-23

Jaba 126
Janus head 56, *115*, 142, 152, 155
Jebba Gungun 131
jewellery *19*, 45f., *48*, 49, 71, 75f., *91*, 127, 129, 151, 165, 168, 199
Jimoh Akolo 210
Jos plateau 132, 146
Jukun 48, 83, 146
jungle 11, 84, 93, 143, 152, 166, 192
justice 28f., 117, 120, *133*, 169, 179

Kaarta 82
kabila 190
Kaffa 15, 46
Kakagye 66, 119
kakungu mask 171
Kalahari 14, *19*
kalebue mask 179, *182*, 190
Kaluena 46, 189
kanaga 99, *102*
Kanda-Kanda 179
Karamojo 198
karikpo 145
Kasai 51, 166
Kasamanka 103

Kata-Mbula *162*
Katanga 191
Keaka 145
kebe-kebe 139
Kenya 196f.
Kete Krachi 125
Khassonke 94
Kiabelua 210
kifwebe mask 190; Kifwebe secret society 190f.
Killi 48
Kilwa 46, 196, 199
kimpasi 173
Kimvumbu 160
kindi 192
Kindiga 196
Kirdi 148
Kissi 25, 46, 106-107
Koba *41*
Kofi Kakari 49, 68, 123
konde 169
Kongolo 178f., 189
Kono 108
Konso 196, 198
Kore 20, 95
Koro 146
Kpelle 108
Kran 49, 56, 59, 107f.
Krej 78
Krinjabo 46, 122f.
Kru 108
kuduo 85, 124
Kulime 107f.
kundi 205
Kundu 192
Kurumba *40*
Kuyu 71, *139*, 153, 156
Kwale Ibo 70, 145
Kwango *161*, 170, 172
Kwangwa 202
Kwengo 171
Kwilu 170, 172

Lamu (G), 49, 199
Landa mask 20, 106
Landuman 104
Lango 196f.
languages 108, 119, 145, 189
leather 49f., 76, 146f., 199
Legba 125f.
leopard *17*, *85*, *91*, 130, 169, 179
Leopoldville 46, 209
Liberia 28, 31, 84, 105, 107f.
Likwale 154
lion 95, 126
lizard 27, 149

234

Lō	102
Loango	166f.
Lobi	48, 109
Lods, Pierre	209
Logone	148
Lomami	*182*, 190, 193
Lubaki	210
Lukenie	177
Lulua	178
Lusambo	178
lutembo lwa kindi	192
Luzira	46, 198
ma mask	117
Madagascar	201-203, 220
Madi	196f.
magic 22f., 35f., 67, 94, 105, *110*, *136*, 153, *158*, *163*, 165, 168, 171, 176, 179, *182*, *183*, 190f.; cf. fetish	
Mahafaly	202
Makonde	59, 71, 197, 199, *207*
Makua	199
Malagasy	203
Malays	202
malembelembe	194
Malinke	94
Mama	59, 146
Mambila	148
Mambunda	202
Mande	82
Mandebele: cf. Ndebele	
Mande-tan	94
Mandingo	50, 94, 104
Mangbetu	46, 51, 72, 76, 166, 192, *205*
Manikongo: cf. Affonso I.	
Mano	107
Mansa Musa	82
Manyakaze	202
Manyema	191
marionettes	29, 95, 145
Marka	45, 94, 95
Masai	12, 45, 49, *196*, 199
mashamboy mask	177
Mashango	155
Mashonaland	201f.
masks 28-9, 30, 31, 34, 45, 53f., 56f., 107f., 125, 142, 174; Ababua 194; Abuan 145; Ashanti 49, 60, 68, 71, 123; Bacham *116*, 152; Bafum 29, 152; Baga 62, 104; Baholo 172; Bajokwe *183*, 189; Bakuba 45, *164*, 177; Bakwele 154, *154*; Balega 31, 45; Bali 149; Baluba *186*, 190; Bamum 151; Banda 27, 63, 104; Bankanu 170; Banyun 103; Bapende 45, 172, 173, *173*; Basalampasu 178; Basonge 28, 179, *182*, 190; Basuku *160*, 171; Basundi 169; Bateke *140*, 165; Batelela 179; Batempe 179; Baule 67, 120f.; Bavili 169; Bayaka 70, *160*, 171; Bena Kanioka 179f.; Bena Lulua 178; Bena Mpassa 179, *182*; Benin *91*, 129; Bundu 106, *108*; Dan *64*, 71, 107f., *117*, *118*; Djola 103, *105*; Dogon 58, 98, *102*; Duala 100; Ekoi 31, *115*, 145f.; Gio 29, 108, *118*; Guro 67; Ibibio 56, *113*, 145; Ibo *112*, 144; Ife 127; Kran 56, 107f.; Kru 108; Makonde 199, *207*; Mambunda 202; Marka 45, 95, 95; Masubiya *201*, 202; Mende 105, *108*; Ngolo 152; Nuni 94; Ogoni 145; Ogowe *138*, 155; Oron-Ibibio 145; Pangwe *136*, 154; Senufo *61*, 100f., *103*; Shilluk 198; Toma 20, 107; Vai 106f.; Yoruba 70, *130*, 142; Wabembe 192; cf. head-dress	
Massa	101
Masubiya	*201*, 202
Matakam	148
Matambwe	199
matriarchy (G), 16, 60, 103, 189, 192, 197, 199, 220	
Mauretania	103
Mawia	199
Mayombe	168
Mbanza	194
Mbari festival	74
Mbomu	193
mbulu-ngulu	*137*, 155
mbulu-viti	155
medicine-men	23f., *157*, 169, *171*, *182*
Mediterranean 58, 78f., 81f., 127f., 132, 146f., 219f.	
megaliths	46
Melli	49, 82
Mende	28f., 46, 49, 56, 70, 105f., *108*
Mensah	210
metals 45, 71, 121f., 125f., 199; cf. smith	
Miele	175
mikanda	173
milumba	194
Minga Bengala	174
Minianka	37, 94, 96, 100
minsereh	30, 106, *108*
mintadi	*167*, 168f., 172
minyaki mask	*110*, 173
mitete	200
Mmwo	*112*
Mohammedanism: see Islam	
mokenge mask	177
Mongala R.	192, 194
Mongo R.	192
Monomotapa	15, 49, 189, 196, 201f.
Moors	12, 49, 81f., *132*
Mopti	46, 95
mosques	79, *82*, 83, 132

Mossi *41*, 83, 100; Mossi Dagomba 82
mother-and-child statue 31, 56, 141, *166*, 168, *171*, 172, *177*, 178
Mother Goddess *137*
motifs: animal 96, 121, 124, 146, 151, 152, *160*, *163*, 176, 180, 200; arabesque 199, 202f.; crossed loop *135*; dot-and-circle 73, 193, 199; geometric designs 74, 84, 148, 176, 179f.; half-moon 202; herring-bone 75, 104, 201; mosaic 199; network 77; plaited band *85*, *86*, *132*, *163*, 167, 176, 180, 201; plant 48, 127, 146; rosette *85*, 130, 199f., 203; tendril 201, 203; zigzag 73, 148
Mozambique 197, 202, *207*
Mpongwe 155f.
Mtuze 210
Mucu Mushanga 174
Mulega 193
Munsa 78
Munza 193
musese *163*, 177, *187*
Musgu 79, 80, 148
musical instruments 45, 131f., *132*, 150, *162*, 194, 205
Mutesa 198
Mvai *135*, 153
Mwenze 210
mythology 26f., 99, 119, 122, 132, *134*, 141, 149, *163*

Naba 99
Nago 126
naja 155
Nalu 104
Napata Meroë (G), 15, 47, 51, 197
naturalism 60, *64*, *68*, *69*–71, 103, 104, 107, *115*, 120, 125, 145f., 149, 154f., *162*, 168, 189
N'Buya 173
Ndebele 74, 202
ndungu 169
neck-rest (G), *170*, 170, *185*, *189*, 190, 198, 202, *202*
neo-Sudanese (G), 49f., 83, 100, 132, *135*, 149, 166, 219f.
Ngbaka: cf. Bwaka
Ngbandi 194
Ngi *136*
Ngolo 152
Ngombe 194
Ngutu 152
Niger 15, 82f., 96 *111*, 131, 219
Nigeria 28f., 70, 76, 83f., *87*, 126-147, 220; early cultures of 126–132; northern 47, 92, 126, 146f.; southern 51, 56; southeastern *112*, *114*, 143–146; south-western *113*, 132; cf. also Benin, Ife, Yoruba etc.
Nile 12, 15, 47, 58, 83, 127, 166, 196f.
Nilotes 13, 77, 196, 219
nimba 62, 104
Njoya *133*, 151
Nkanda *160*, 171
nkisi 169
nobility 32, *133*, 168, 190
Nok 46f., 126f., *127*
nomori 105, *107*
Noqui 168
North Africa 12, 47f.
N'tomo 95
Ntum 153
Nuba 196
Nuer 78, 196
Nuni 94
Nupe 48, 76, 83, 131, 146
Nyama 28, 99
Nyamye 119, 121
Nyangbai mask *107*
Nyendael 129

Oba 90, 129
Obang 145f.
Obatala *86*, 141
Odongo 210
Odudua 26, *86*, 141
Ogboni *132*, *141*, 142f.
Ogoni 145
Ogowe *138*, 153, 154
Ogun 141
Oguola 129
Oku Ampofo 210
Old Calabar 145
Old Nigritic culture (G), 13, 45, 60, 81, 100, 132, 219f.; tribes 16, 83, 196, 219f.
Olokun 130, 141
Olorun 141
Omaboku 210
Ondumbo 154
open-work 37, 45, 51, 126
Opobo 145
oracles 23, 101, 176; cf. divination implements
Orient 15, 48, 58, 76, 81f., *132*, 146, 196, 202f., 219f.
orisha 141
Orisha-Oko 141
ornamentation 17, 47f., 71f., 75f., 103, 131, 137, 150f., *164*, 166f., 173, 176f., 180, 198f., 202
ornaments 49, *91*, 103, 121, 123, 126, 129f., 141, 147, 199
Oron clan *114*, 145

Oron-Ibibio 59, 145
Osanhim (Osanyin) 141
Osei Tutu 124
Osemwenede 131
oshe shango 110
otobo 111
Ovimbundu 189
Owo 131, 143, *143*
Owu *111*, 145
Oya 110
Oyo 141

Pabir 147
painting 73f., 209; on bark *159*, 170, 177; on fabrics *37*; on masks 95, *136*, 155f., *164*, 169, 171, 189; on sculpture 71, 155, 193; on shields 198f.; on walls 107, 132, 146f., 190, 197, 202; cf. rock painting
Palaenegrids 13, 220
Pangwe 29, 56, 59, *135*, *136*, 152, 153f., 194
pastoral peoples 13, 197, 201, 203, 219f.
patina 36, 54, 71f., 97, 172
patriarchy (G), 83, 166, 179, 192, 197, 219
Persia 15, 196, 199
Pilipili 210
Piri *58*, 147
plaiting 50, 146, *163*, 199; cf. basket-work
plangi technique (G), 51, 66, 122, 151
plush 51, 175, *163*, 177, *187*
po 118
poker-work 73, 198, 202
pole sculpture (G), 59f., 152, 166, 192, 194, 197, 199f., *203*
Pomdo 25, 107
Poro 20, 101, 106, 107
Portuguese 91, 105, 123, 129, 167, 170, 197, 201; Portuguese Guinea 103
pottery 32, 46, 78, 125, 145f., 151, 167, 170, 177, 198, 202
primitive (G), *19*, 57, 125, *110*, 148, *196*, 197
printing 51, 124
proverbs 31, 45, 124
pygmies 13, 76, 177, 219f.

ram 119, 121, *122*, 128
relief 46, 72, 79, 102, *105*, *109*, 121, *121*, 125, 129, 132, 197, 203
religion 21–29, 30, 35f., 104, 168, 204; cf. magic, vital force
repoussé technique (G), 48, 84, 199
'resist' technique 51, 151, 177
Rhodesia 72, 156, 166, 178, 189, 192, 196, 199, 202, 220
rites and cults 22f., 26f., 33f., *44*, 63, *85*, 95, 99, 101, 103, 108, *112*, *113*, 122, 145f.,

151, 173, 201; *rites de passage* (G), 31f., 177; ritual implements 29, 72, *85*, *88*, 98, 125f., 129, 167, 179, 190, 203
rock painting 15, **73**
Rome, Romans 14, **81**
round sculpture (G), 59, 166, 191, **199f.**
Rovuma R. 16, *207*, 220
Rukwa 221
Ruandi-Urundi 196

sacral kingship (G), 15, 31f., 60, 83, *91*, 123, 166, 189, 196, 220
sacrifices 22, 25, 28f., 36, 95, *110*, *114*, 121, 132, 157, 180, 197f.
Sahara 11, 12, 76, 81, 219
Sahel 11
sakrobundu 102
Sankuru 51, 174
San Salvador 167
Sao 46, 148
Sara 197
Sards 14, 48
savannah (G), 11, 81f., 119, 166, 219
Savé 86
scarification 55, 71, 75, *87*, 156, 178, 189f., 199; cf. tattooing
scorpion 124
secret societies (G), 20, 30f., 67, 93, 104, *111*, *113*, *115*, 118, 122, *136*, 153f., 176, 190f., 204
Segu 82, 94f., *37*
Sekuapu *111*
semi-Bantu 13, 143f., 149, 220
Semitic peoples 128, 196f., 220
Senegambia 103
Senufo 44, 59f., *61*, 75, 101, 119
sepulchral figures 26, 46, 107, 124f., *157*, 178, *181*, 198, 202f.; monuments 60, *157*, 198; posts 202f.
Sequeira 129
Serer 103
Shamba Bolongongo *162*, 174f.
Shango 26, *110*, 141
Shankadi 191
Shankpanna: cf. Shopono
Shari 148
shene-malula mask *164*, 177
Shien 108
Shilluk 196, 198
Shir 197f.
Shirazi 196, 199
Shopono 141
Sierra Leone 59, 105
Sigi 100
silk 51, 125
silver 45, 49, 125, *126*, *198*, 199
Simo 63, 104f.

237

slavery 81, 124f., 180, *182*
smith 23, 32f., 94, 146, 172, 175
snake 24, 71, 76, 130, *133*, *139*, 156, 169
soapstone: cf. steatite
Sobo 144
sociology 30-34, 79, 117, 124
Somali 12
Songhai 82
Songo, Sam 210
Soninke 51
sorcerers 24, *61*, *136*
South Africa 14, 16, 221; South-east Africa 45, 48, 59, 74, 77, 201f.; South-west Africa *19*
souvenirs, export of 15, 46, 102, 126, 170, 204
Spanish Guinea 153, 220; Spanish-Moorish style 49
spider 149, 151
spirits 20, 28f., 36, *42*, *66*, 95, 99, *112*, 132, *137*, 145, 154, *160*, 169
Stanleypool 165
steatite 46, 105, 107, *167*, 168, *201*
stencil technique 51, 151, 177, 198
stone sculpture 39, 46, 107, 128, 131, 168, 198, 201; stone axes 14, 47, 107; stone buildings 199, 203; Stone Age (G), 14
Suaheli: cf. Swahili
Sudan 13f., 32f., 50, 74f., 81, 94, 107, 153, 219f.; central 19, 77, 219; eastern 219; south-eastern 196f.; western 16, 47, 50f., 59, 70, 76, 81-102, 123, 146, 197, 219; French 20, *38*, *39* 100f., 219
Suguni 96
surrealism 53f., 96, 108
Swahili Coast 199
symbols 27, 52, 73, 76, 123, 170, 198
symmetry 10, 54

Tada 131
Tanganyika 196f.; Lake 156, 191
tanning 49f.
tattooing 25, 45, 165, 168, *181*, 194, 199
tellem 97f., 105
tembe (G), 79, 198
Tempels, Placide 21f., 117
terracotta 46, *89*, 125f., 127f., 148
textiles 37, 51, *66*, 124, 151, 165, 175, 177, *187*, 203, 206; cf. clothing
Tikar 48, 151f.
tobes 51, 76, 147
Togo, Togoland 49, 78, 84, 125, 132
Toma 20, 59, 107
totemism 27, 73
trade 14, 35, 50, 81, 123, 146, 153, 165, 167, 173, 196, 204
tritik 51

Tsimihety 203
Tuareg 12, 76, 81
tudansi *160*, 171
tukula (G), 25, 46, 52, *163*, 172f., 176, *187*
Turkana 198
twilling technique 50, *160*
twins 101, 141f., 192

Uame 107
Ubangi 166, 174; Ubangi-Shari 74, 148, 220
Udo 131
Uganda 15, 196f., 201
ulaga 145
Upper Sassandra 107
Upper Volta *40*, *42*, *43*, 82, 100f., 219
Urua 191
Usambara 198
utensils *19*, 72f., *85*, 96, 118, 121, 126, 147, 150, 154, *163*, 165, 167, 170, 175f., 190, 193f., 198f.

Vai 106
vital force 21f., 26, 31, 54, 72, 99, 108, 154, 192
Voania Muba 170

Wabembe 154, 191f.
Wabondei 198
Wachagga 196
Wadai 220
Wadoe 198
Wagiryama 196, 198
Waguha: cf. Baguha
Wahima: cf. Bahima
Wakerewe 198
Walega: cf. Balega
Wambundu 165
Wamuera 199
Wangata 194
Wango *41*
Wangoni: cf. Angoni
Wanyamwezi 74, 196, *197*, 198
Wanyika 198
Wanyoro: cf. Banyoro
wars 79, 103, 117, 122, 125, *134*, 170, *182*, 206
wart hog 108
Wasaramo 196, 198
Washambala 196, 198
waste mould: cf. *cire perdue*
Wasuaheli 196, 199
Watutsi: cf. Batutsi
wax 47, 199
Wayao: cf. Yao
weaving 32f., 50f., 84, 122, 125, 146, 151, *187*

weapons 48f., 105, *109*, 125f., 151, *162*, 167, 199, 202	
Welle R.	*18*, 46, 74, 193f.
West Africa (G), 15, 32, 45, 50f., 78, 81–93, 167, 174, 197, 199, 220	
Wobe	108
Woto	47, *163*
Wuri	153
Yabassi	59, 152
Yaelima	174, 194
Yakuba	107
Yâkut al-Rumi	82
yam cult	(G), *112*, *113*
Yangere	194
Yao	46, 199
Yassi	106
Yatenga	*41*
Yaunde	153f.
Yaure	67, 122
Yoruba 34, 45, 48, 51f., 56, 58f., 70, 75, 83, *88*, *110*, 125, 132–143, 170; southern Yoruba *86*	
Zamle	122
Zambezi	202
Zimbabwe	46, 201, *201*
Zinder	79
Zlan	117